ARCHAEOLOGIC IN DIALOGUE

Archaeological Theory in Dialogue presents an innovative conversation between five scholars from different backgrounds on a range of central issues facing archaeology today.

Interspersing detailed investigations of critical theoretical issues with dialogues between the authors, the book interrogates the importance of four themes at the heart of much contemporary theoretical debate: relations, ontology, posthumanism, and Indigenous paradigms. The authors, who work in Europe and North America, explore how these themes are shaping the ways that archaeologists conduct fieldwork, conceptualize the past, and engage with the political and ethical challenges that our discipline faces in the twenty-first century.

The unique style of *Archaeological Theory in Dialogue*, switching between detailed arguments and dialogical exchange, makes it essential reading for both scholars and students of archaeological theory and those with an interest in the politics and ethics of the past.

Rachel J. Crellin is Lecturer in Archaeology at the University of Leicester. Her research interests center on archaeological theory, especially new materialist, feminist, and posthumanist approaches. She is also a specialist in the Neolithic and Bronze Age of Britain, Ireland, and the Isle of Man, and a metalwork wear-analyst. She is the author of *Change and Archaeology* (Routledge).

Craig N. Cipolla is Curator of North American Archaeology at the Royal Ontario Museum and Associate Professor of Anthropology at the University of Toronto. His research interests include archaeological theory, colonial North America, and collaborative Indigenous archaeologies. His publications include *Becoming Brothertown* and *Archaeological Theory in the New Millennium* (co-authored with Oliver J.T. Harris, Routledge).

Lindsay M. Montgomery is Assistant Professor of Anthropology at the University of Arizona. Her research focuses on Indigenous history in the North American West, with particular interest in social justice, interethnic interaction, settler colonialism, and cultural resiliency among Native peoples. She is co-author of *Objects of Survivance* and is currently finishing a book entitled *A History of Mobility* (Routledge).

Oliver J.T. Harris is Associate Professor of Archaeology at the University of Leicester. He is co-author of *The Body in History* and *Archaeological Theory in the New Millennium* (Routledge), the latter with Craig N. Cipolla. He researches new materialist, posthumanist, and Deleuzian approaches to the past. He is currently finishing a book entitled *Assembling Past Worlds* (Routledge).

Sophie V. Moore is Lecturer in Medieval Archaeology at Newcastle University. Her research focuses on the experienced past, using phenomenological approaches to material culture to investigate lived moments in the Byzantine world. She is a member of the Sagalassos Fieldwork Project in Turkey, where she uses courseware ceramics to investigate the "dark age" transformation of urban space between the sixth and thirteenth centuries CE.

ARCHAEOLOGICAL THEORY IN DIALOGUE

Situating Relationality, Ontology, Posthumanism, and Indigenous Paradigms

Rachel J. Crellin, Craig N. Cipolla, Lindsay M. Montgomery, Oliver J.T. Harris, and Sophie V. Moore

Routledge
Taylor & Francis Group
LONDON AND NEW YORK

First published 2021
by Routledge
2 Park Square, Milton Park, Abingdon, Oxon OX14 4RN

and by Routledge
52 Vanderbilt Avenue, New York, NY 10017

Routledge is an imprint of the Taylor & Francis Group, an informa business

British Library Cataloguing-in-Publication Data
A catalogue record for this book is available from the British Library

Library of Congress Cataloging-in-Publication Data
Names: Crellin, Rachel, author. | Cipolla, Craig N., 1978– author. | Montgomery, Lindsay M. (Lindsay Martel), author. | Harris, Oliver J. T., author. | Moore, Sophie V., author.
Title: Archaeological theory in dialogue : situating relationality, ontology, posthumanism, and indigenous paradigms / Rachel J. Crellin, Craig N. Cipolla, Lindsay M. Montgomery, Oliver J. T. Harris, and Sophie V. Moore.
Description: Abingdon, Oxon ; New York, NY : Routledge, 2021. | Includes bibliographical references and index.
Identifiers: LCCN 2020025943 (print) | LCCN 2020025944 (ebook) | ISBN 9780367135454 (hardback) | ISBN 9780367135478 (paperback) | ISBN 9780429027147 (ebook)
Subjects: LCSH: Archaeology—Philosophy. | Archaeology—Methodology. | Archaeology—Fieldwork.
Classification: LCC CC72 .C743 2021 (print) | LCC CC72 (ebook) | DDC 930.1—dc23
LC record available at https://lccn.loc.gov/2020025943
LC ebook record available at https://lccn.loc.gov/2020025944

ISBN: 978-0-367-13545-4 (hbk)
ISBN: 978-0-367-13547-8 (pbk)
ISBN: 978-0-429-02714-7 (ebk)

Typeset in Bembo
by Apex CoVantage, LLC

RJC: For my Grandma and Grandpa, who teach me about talking, listening, and caring

CNC: For my grandmother, Theresa Cipolla (1919–2020)

LMM: For my grandmama, Martel Wilcher Montgomery (1931–2015), who taught me to speak truth to power

OJTH: For the India gang, who love to dialogue

SVM: For the singers of Sheffield

CONTENTS

PROVOCATIONS

FIGURES

TABLES

ACKNOWLEDGMENTS

Like all books, especially one with five different authors, this volume emerges from a complex history of entangled conversations, interactions, lectures, seminars, conferences, teaching events, encounters in the field, collaborations, and, in some cases, confrontations. The process of learning and engagement is ongoing; it is one of dialogue; and we would like to thank all those people who have taken part in discussing archaeological theory over the years. Collectively, we would like to thank Ben Alberti, Amélie Allard, Susan Alt, Emily Banfield, Huw Barton, Alex Bauer, Brian Boyd, Jo Brück, Charlie Cobb, Hannah Cobb, Noa Corcoran-Tadd, John Creese, Karina Croucher, Zoe Crossland, Marta Diaz-Guardamino, Marianne Hem Eriksen, Neal Ferris, Jeff Fleisher, Chris Fowler, Sev Fowles, Tiziana Gallo, Andrew Gardner, Mark Gillings, Nathan Gubbins, Yannis Hamilakis, Kat Hayes, Justin Jennings, Ben Jervis, Andrew Jones, Art Joyce, Diana Loren, Luíseach Nic Eoin, Yvonne Marshall, Steve Mrozowski, Yvonne O'Dell, Tim Pauketat, Bob Preucel, Artur Ribeiro, Brandon Rizzuto, John Robb, Andy Roddick, Alice Samson, Steve Silliman, Tim Flohr Sørensen, Ed Swenson, Julian Thomas, Sylvia Tomášková, Christina Tsoraki, Uzma Rizvi, Ruth Van Dyke, Chris Watts, Darryl Wilkinson, and Alasdair Whittle. We are grateful to Michael Adler, David Horan, Pieta Grieves, Jody Joy, Alex Sangster, Tim Flohr Sørensen, the Museum of Archaeology and Anthropology, Cambridge, and the Royal Ontario Museum, Toronto (particularly the Earth Sciences section) for either granting permission to use their images in the book or facilitating access to others. We also thank Eva Mol for asking a question about dialogues during a panel discussion, which led to a conversation in a car, somewhere between Boston and Binghamton, that ended up, for now, in this book.

With regard to the mechanics of the book itself, we would like to thank Matt Gibbon and Katie Wakelin at Routledge for supporting the process and for their patience whilst we pulled it all together. We would also like to thank Balaji

Karuppanan for overseeing the copyediting and formatting and Kelly Ferguson for proofreading and indexing. Finally, we give a huge vote of thanks to Douglas Armstrong, who, on the eve of hosting TAG at Syracuse, let five random archaeologists occupy his lab and cook up much of this project. Doug, we all owe you a beer!

Rachel J. Crellin. The scholarship of both Jo Brück and Marie Louise-Stig Sørensen inspired my love of the Bronze Age as an undergraduate and provoked my long-term obsession with rethinking narratives and power. Huge thanks to my co-authors for both dwelling with me in discomfort and sharing with me in affirmative joy. I first learned to dialogue archaeological theory with *Team Archaeology* back in 2007, what began as a physical dialogue became an online dialogue across time and space – my thanks to them all. I am grateful for the amazing and varied colleagues and students I work with and alongside – most of whom love to chat! My family, dispersed across two islands, keep me grounded but never hold me back. Dave is my ever-shifting constant who improves my every day.

Craig N. Cipolla. My contributions to this book were inspired by countless interactions with many excellent students, mentors, colleagues, friends, and family. I offer special thanks to Jay Levy, James Quinn, and my co-authors for so many productive dialogues over the years. None of this would have been possible, however, without Kelly, Maya, Siany, and Pete – the ones who put up with me every day, even when I only want to talk theory.

Lindsay M. Montgomery. This work is indebted to the thinking and writings of many Indigenous scholars, including Vine Deloria Jr., Donald Fixico, Eva Marie Garroutte, and Dale Turner. I would also like to thank my mentors Severin Fowles and Michael Wilcox for their guidance in thinking through the theoretical and political aspects of working with and for Indigenous communities. Finally, this work was inspired by my graduate students, Ashleigh Thompson, Caitlyn Shoulder, and Mariah Claw, whose research as Native American women and scholars has pushed my own thinking in new directions.

Oliver J.T. Harris. Much of my writing here stems from the conversations I have every day, and I am fortunate to work in a place where people are so supportive and encouraging when it comes to archaeological theory. Huge thanks therefore to all the staff and students, past and present, at the School of Archaeology and Ancient History, University of Leicester. I should also thank Yvonne O'Dell specifically for kindly offering comments on Chapter 2. Ellie, Maggie, Teddy, and Cynthia have also played an important part in maintaining my sanity in a world that increasingly threatens to prove overwhelming.

It has been a huge privilege to work on this book with my co-authors, I have learned so much from them and continue to do so. A Philip Leverhulme Prize (PLP-2016-109) also funded a period of leave during which parts of the text were written.

Sophie V. Moore. There have been three different institutions and many conversations beyond them during the writing of this book, and I am grateful to them all. The concept for Chapter 6 was very much aided by the Archaeology and Social Justice working group and Ontology Club at Brown University, and came together during my Fall 2017 undergraduate class on Byzantine Art and Archaeology. While working through ideas before they were ready for dialogue, I benefited hugely from picket line conversations with the Come Strike with Me solidarity team at Newcastle University, especially with Ben Elliott whose distaste for Heidegger was helpful. Finally, I am forever indebted to Jerrod Seifert and his couch.

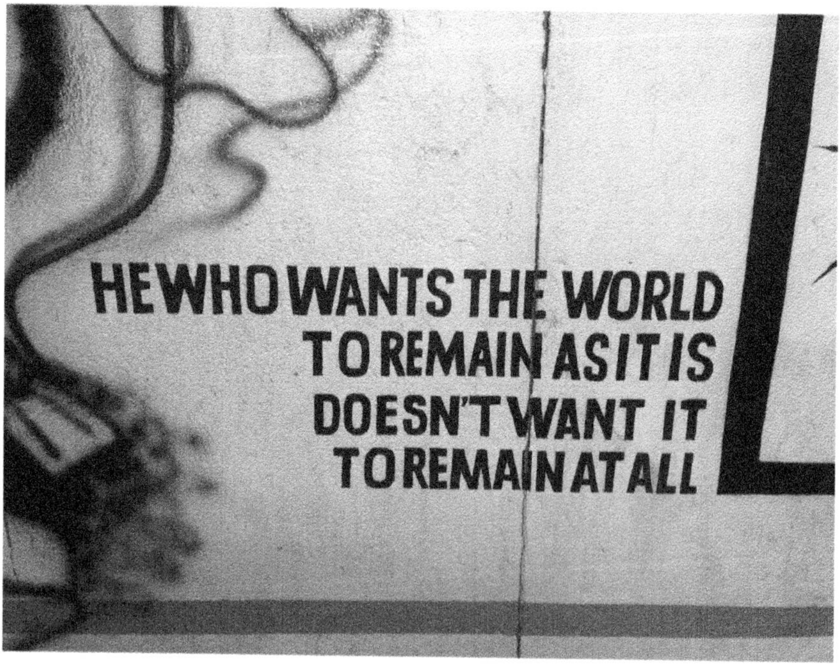
HE WHO WANTS THE WORLD
TO REMAIN AS IT IS
DOESN'T WANT IT
TO REMAIN AT ALL

1

INTRODUCTION

Locating the book

Locating theory

Where does theory happen? Does it happen in the Royal Ontario Museum as you handle a pipe shaped by a Wendat person 400 years ago? Does it happen as you drive between two cities to present seminars about a book? Does it happen as you trowel on a site in Turkey, or when you trace a piece of Comanche rock art in New Mexico? Does it matter where theory happens? And if so, what do these different locations mean for the theories that emerge from them?

Much of this book flows from discussion and conversation that took place over two days in room 415a of Lyman Hall at Syracuse University, New York. But these dialogues have a much deeper and more complicated history than that. They derive from countless previous conversations that took place in a variety of places, at conferences, in person, via email, and by Skype. These locations do, it turns out, matter.

This book seeks to interrogate contemporary archaeological theory but to do so through dialogue. If place matters, so does the act of conversation. So much of how we work through theory takes place in dialogue. You learn through conversation, and discussion opens you up to new possibilities and challenges. Reading theory is dense and difficult; the dynamics of talking allow you to contextualize it and bring out similarities and differences between alternative positions. Dialogue also allows us to engage abstract ideas with concrete examples, often making concepts easier to grasp. In this sense, to engage in theory is also to engage in a form of relationship-building, bringing different people, ideas, and things into conversation.

Discussing theory happens face-to-face, writing happens in many places. We began this project by writing the five single-authored chapters (Chapters 2, 4, 6, 8, and 10). We then came together to discuss them and to plan out our dialogues. But theory changes as you move and shifts as you converse; it is always in process.

The single-authored chapters changed in the light of our conversations and so our dialogues have shifted again.

Our conversation begins with materialized positions that open us up to each other. Our stance is that dialogues don't end – this conversation will always remain open. In this sense, the "conclusion" sections to each dialogue chapter are really summaries of our current thinking and positions rather than a definitive or programmatic statement. This is not a solution; this is not teleology. The final published product of these discussions will only be a snapshot of this larger and ever-evolving dialogue and therefore should not be taken as the final word on the topics discussed in each chapter.

Our aim in this book is to open up theory to dialogue, to capture something of its ongoing and shifting becoming. This means several things. First of all, it means risk. By being open, by accepting that our own learning is unfinished, we have to face up to what we *don't* know and be comfortable with disagreement. Our aim in this book is not to solve problems or present resolutions, rather it is to be open about the process of doing theory itself, the issues it poses for us, the way it can make us feel uncomfortable. Here we have to acknowledge the absence of authority, both between us as multiple authors and also between us, our readers, and our critics. Too often theory is written as a lone voice revealing mastery of the discipline; for us theory is much more complicated than this. It and we are multiple, unfinished, messy, and sometimes confused.

Opening ourselves up to different places, to different voices, and to different backgrounds is part of bringing different people together. As archaeologists we work in Europe and North America, on periods from many thousands of years ago to the last few centuries. Some of us work with Indigenous Peoples and some of us do not. Some of us rely upon text, some of us do not. These differences matter in some ways, in others, they do not. Different people, different theories, different places, different times, different questions: difference matters – but how? Here are some of the ways that we are different.

RACHEL: I am an archaeologist who studies the Neolithic and the Bronze Age of Britain, Ireland, and the Isle of Man: I also specialize in the study of metalwork. I study those periods because I am absolutely fascinated by how very different they are from the world I live in.

I grew up on the Isle of Man, a small island in the middle of the Irish Sea between England, Ireland, Scotland, and Wales. The island is littered with the presence of the past from Viking boat burials to Neolithic stone circles: I knew I wanted to be an archaeologist from a young age. I moved to the UK for an academic job, but part of me always wants to go back home. I now direct fieldwork on the island, allowing me to spend at least a month there every year. The Isle of Man is a between place: it sits within the British Islands[1] but not the UK; we speak English but have our own native Gaelic language.

I am a feminist, though I don't think I always have been. My parents jointly ran a small bed and breakfast hotel and split the work between them evenly, my Mum had a 51% stake in the business and my Dad 49%. My parents and grandparents did not go to university. As a child, "girl" never seemed less than "boy." I was privileged enough and lucky enough that the world seemed pretty fair. Nowadays, the naivety of that position is very clear. One of the things I think the most about is how I can use the work I do to try and create worlds very different from our own and worlds that I want to be a part of. Theoretically, I situate myself as a posthumanist and a new materialist.

CRAIG: I'm an American (born and trained) museum curator and anthropology professor living in Toronto, Canada. My main interests include theory, the archaeology of colonialism, collaborative Indigenous research, and historical archaeology. I work in New England and the Great Lakes – two areas for which *I am foreign*, i.e., I am a settler colonist descended from a mixture of Italian and various other unidentified European groups. In any case, I come from places and groups different from the landscapes and communities in which I work. This is important to remember and something I always make sure to stress to my students and colleagues.

I am a first-generation academic who has special interest in increasing the breadth of our discipline by helping to pave the way for fellow first-generation academics, heritage managers, and/or archaeologists. I devote my scholarship and teaching to the broader project of decolonizing archaeology and anthropology, though I see this project as never ending. For me decolonization relates directly to attempts to reduce Eurocentrism and to help diversify the community of practitioners. I recognize that I cannot do these things on my own; it is a collaborative project through and through. But, perhaps unlike some of my colleagues who are devoted to similar projects of decolonization, I place great emphasis on theory (cf. Smith 2012; Cipolla in review a) in such projects as it helps me to think through and understand the world in which I work. Other aspects of my work and my experiences as an archaeologist are developed further throughout the book, so I won't specify any further at this stage.

LINDSAY: I was raised in the suburbs of Washington, DC, in a middle-class mixed-race family. I am descended from a long line of educators and storytellers and was told from a young age that history mattered and that I should do work that made the world a better place. I am now an assistant professor in the School of Anthropology at the University of Arizona, where I write and teach about Indigenous history, colonialism, resistance, and interethnic interaction. My current fieldwork is part of a multi-institutional collaborative project with Picuris Pueblo in northern New Mexico, which focuses on documenting archaeological evidence of agricultural production and interethnic exchange at the Pueblo from the thirteenth century onward. Unlike some of my colleagues, I do not necessarily gravitate toward theory. My primary interest in social theory is in its utility as a language of empowerment: a lexicon with which to speak to the academy about things outside of academia.

Although my graduate degree is in archaeology, I position my work at the peripheries of a wider range of disciplines and methods, including ethnography, history, American Indian studies, and law. I often think of myself as a cultural Historian rather than an Archaeologist or Anthropologist per se because I am interested in bringing together a variety of archival, oral, and material sources to understand the lives of Indigenous people in both the past and present. My approach to research has been shaped by the work of various women of color, from the lessons I learned sitting at my grandmama Martel's dining room table, to the creative writing of novelists like Toni Morrison, to academic texts by Ella Deloria, Viola Cordova, Theresa Singleton, Sonya Atalay, and many others. These female voices have inspired my long-standing interest in cultural history and the role of brown and black people in creating and preserving such histories. More than that, they have inspired my abiding investment in activist scholarship, which uses academia as a platform for creating change in the world. Accordingly, I view myself as an advocate and an ally for Tribal Nations working toward social justice and decolonization in the present.

OLLIE: As an archaeologist, I work on a range of different issues. My main passion is archaeological theory; I love enquiring into how we think about archaeology and how we understand the past. Within that, in recent years I have become especially interested in new materialism, and I am often accused (mainly by my co-authors of this book) of an unhealthy passion for the philosophy of Gilles Deleuze. Beyond theory, my work focuses principally on Britain in the Neolithic, but I have written about European pasts from the Paleolithic to the present, and even dabbled in a little contemporary archaeology. I direct fieldwork on the west coast of Scotland and excavate sites from all periods of the human past. This means working with local people, visitors, and our diverse student body in a host of different contexts.

Writing about position is hard for me, because it forces me to face up to what Rosi Braidotti (2019a:478) calls my "unearned privilege." I am the very model of a "majoritarian" subject: white, middle class, able bodied, straight, with middle-class parents; I never considered *not* going to university, and when I was there, I decided to be an academic and have been helped in all kinds of ways by that privilege. For me, I have become increasingly committed to thinking about the past through a Deleuzian lens because of the way this challenges the assumptions that sustain my privilege. A Deleuzian approach, especially one influenced by feminism, is committed to unpicking the claims to a universal humanity. It asks us: "What can a body do?" When you start asking that question about the past, you start asking it of yourself and asking it of others around you too. The answers force you to check your privilege.

SOPHIE: My work sits between disciplines; I am primarily an archaeologist, but I am also a Byzantinist. I am currently a temporary lecturer in Medieval Archaeology at Newcastle University, my sixth fixed-term role held across three continents since finishing my Ph.D. in 2013. Byzantine Studies is a messily constructed discipline focused on the Eastern Mediterranean between approximately 500 and 1500 CE, encompassing textual, art historical, and archaeological methodologies. In many ways on the fringe of Classics, Byzantine Studies has largely focused on elite culture, an aspect of the discipline that my work disrupts through working on questions of everyday life in rural Anatolia.

I was born in Britain, to a Northern Irish father and a Yorkshire mother, both of whom came from working-class backgrounds and went on to get university degrees. We're all atheist (I'm either second- or third-generation atheist, depending upon which grandparent you trace lineage through). As I got further into my undergraduate degree in archaeology, however, I came to realize that we are very protestant atheists. From an early age, I was fascinated (as I think lots of children are) by who else I might have been if I had been born in another time or place. Part of thinking through this question at university meant reckoning with the almost evangelical atheism of my upbringing. Early on in my archaeological education, my driving question therefore became whether I could get to a point where I could accept, really accept, that other people have a different understanding of the world than me. This became my entry point to archaeological theory, and particularly into thinking about both phenomenological approaches to the past and ontologies in terms of faith, belief, and knowledge.

Relationality, ontology, posthumanism, and Indigenous paradigms

Over the last few decades, relationality, ontology, posthumanism, and Indigenous paradigms have emerged as serious topics of interest and debate in archaeological circles (e.g., Alberti 2016a; Fowles 2013; Fredengren 2013; Harris and Cipolla 2017; Thomas 1996; Witmore 2007). The origins of – or reasons for – these shifts are multiple. Some came from within theoretical debate and critique, but others emerged from a general dissatisfaction with the status of our discipline in the world. Internally, thinkers like Bjørnar Olsen (2003) critiqued post-processual archaeology's textual metaphor (e.g., Hodder 1986) and urged archaeologists to "re-member" things. According to him, the textual turn had deleterious effects in our discipline; in its emphases on ideas, social relations, and culture in general, the actual stuff of archaeology was swept to the background. Archaeological materials became secondary to the past symbolic values that they might have carried. Concomitantly, archaeological interests of the time favored cultural construction and epistemology over realism and ontology.

External to these theoretical discussions, and preceding them by decades, was a growing scrutiny over archaeology's colonial nature. This included critiques from Indigenous activists and academics like Vine Deloria Jr. (e.g., 1997, 2014). Such challenges highlighted the homogeneity of our field at the time – i.e., archaeology was most often practiced by white, western,[2] middle-class males. Yet these challenges also drew attention to the culturally insensitive (and imperialistic) ways that archaeologists treated ancestors – human remains – and generally handled the heritage of underrepresented and colonized groups. The hubris of archaeologists' claims to know and to represent very different pasts from their own was *and is* a major point of contention. Echoed in post-processual approaches, such as Joan Gero and Margaret Conkey's (1991) groundbreaking writings on gender, these critiques laid bare the disparities, contradictions, and asymmetries of archaeological research, showing that archaeology was far from a neutral scientific endeavor. Among the responses to these critiques were new ways of practicing archaeology, including Indigenous, collaborative, and community-based frameworks along with a general emphasis on increasing the diversity of practitioners. Implicit in this work is a growing scrutiny over the intellectual history of archaeology and the arbitrariness of the discipline's Western assumptions – a trend that is partly mirrored in theoretical discussions featured throughout this book.

For instance, a majority of the theoretical struggles of late challenge the Enlightenment-inherited defaults that many archaeologists continue to rely upon (cf. Thomas 2004). This is most evident in the discipline's struggle to come to grips with dualistic ways of seeing – and being in – the world. By emphasizing symbolic meaning over almost everything else, post-processual critiques operated within a binary framework that divided the world into ideas and materials, culture and nature, humanity and the world around it. The last few decades of archaeological thought explored the arbitrariness of these dualistic modes of thought, discussing how they obscure our understandings of the world, including our main subject of inquiry, *the past*. Thinkers like Timothy Webmoor and Christopher Witmore (2008) argued that the dominant framework of social archaeology was constructed on arbitrary and false divisions. Instead, they suggested that archaeologists should attend to the complex amalgamation of human–non-human relations that surround us. For these thinkers, the dominant dialectical models of post-processual leaning archaeologists did more harm than good. Of course, for these thinkers, the models that post-processualism critiqued were no better. This is because, broadly speaking, both processual and post-processual critiques adhered to the same dualistic way of seeing the world: one simply favored nature and materials, the other, culture and symbols (Harris and Cipolla 2017). Similarly, if we think through the most traditional of archaeological "paradigms," culture history, it too operates through the same dualistic lens, cleaving the world into binaries and favoring one side over the other.

So how have archaeologists sought to move away from these dualistic frames and embrace the complex amalgams that Webmoor and Witmore urged us to look for? One of the primary routes has been to emphasize the world of relations – that is, how people, things, architecture, and landscapes are better understood by focusing on what connects them, rather than thinking of them as individual and bounded entities. Relations form one of the critical topics we investigate in this book (see especially Chapter 2). Within European archaeology, this interest in relations grew out of engagements with phenomenology, which emphasized how things could be understood as gatherings of relations (Thomas 1996). Alongside this, the burgeoning concern with personhood did the same for human beings (e.g., Fowler 2004). The influence of ethnographic accounts of Indigenous understandings of personhood convinced many archaeologists that dominant archaeological modes of writing about human pasts universalized a specific, modern, Western form of the individual. Instead archaeologists explored how personhood could be relational in different ways in the past (Brück 2006, 2009, 2019; Chapman 2000; Gillespie 2001). Two other critical influences further cemented this turn in archaeology. The first was Actor-Network Theory (ANT), which developed a relational approach to how agency worked (e.g., Latour 2005a; see also Chapter 6). Rather than seeing agency as a possession of a human being, or an object for that matter, ANT sought to explain how agency emerged relationally (cf. Robb 2010). So, in Bruno Latour's (1999) famous example, the agency of a person and a gun is different from the agency that either the gun or the person has alone. ANT, and especially the work of Latour, formed a critical inspiration for symmetrical archaeology, one of the first calls to arms that explicitly sought to move on from post-processualism (see Chapter 6). The final key element of the move to relations was the importance of Indigenous paradigms, which we outline in more detail later. While concepts of personhood from non-western contexts proved stimulating in European archaeology, in North America the emphasis that some Indigenous paradigms place upon relations inspired archaeologists to rethink human, non-human, and more-than-human archaeologies (e.g., Pauketat 2012; Pauketat and Alt 2018). In their different guises, relations have become central for many new forms of archaeological theory in the twenty-first century.

If a turn to relations opened up new ways of thinking for archaeology, it was not long before the other implications of this move came to the fore. If archaeologists were to genuinely move away from the binary oppositions that had characterized the discipline until this point, in all its various guises, then this meant a more radical shift in how we conceptualized the past. As authors from the middle of the 2000s pointed out, archaeologists had historically shared a single set of understandings about how the world worked, a single ontology, which was now being fundamentally challenged. If the world is relational, for example, rather than being made up of bounded entities, if Indigenous thought needs to be taken seriously, and not used to just illustrate interpretations, if things can be people too, or have agency, then this requires an alternative approach to ontology – to what actually exists. Thus, archaeologists have become increasingly interested in finding different ways of approaching the world, the past, and their own role within it (e.g., Fowler 2013; Lucas 2012; Shanks 2007). If ontology is a new focus for the discipline, archaeology needs more consensus on how to engage with this concept; there has been little unified agreement about how to approach this topic or indeed what it means to do ontological archaeology (Alberti 2016a; see also Chapter 10). While some archaeologists have turned to philosophers like Deleuze for an alternative approach (see Chapters 2 and 8), others see such a move as just another attempt to generate an alternative universal theory and have sought out local approaches to ontology instead (Alberti 2016a; Alberti and Marshall 2009). These latter approaches tend to focus on specific moments of ontological difference, that is, instances of radical difference when worlds emerge that challenge how archaeologists understand them. A critical term here is metaontology, a term used by Alberti to characterize approaches that seek to replace one world (say a Cartesian one filled with dualisms) with another (say a Deleuzian one filled with flows, rhizomes, and relations). In this book, we use the term metaontology to capture how it is possible both to work within particular worlds (ontologies) and to explicitly reflect on how those worlds work (metaontology). Critical within this, again, is the status of Indigenous paradigms, and how they are employed in archaeology. Are they a form of analogy? A form of theory? Something that resists "domestication" and translation into these colonial categories (see Chapter 5)? How, indeed, have western philosophies already employed Indigenous paradigms in ways that they have not always – or ever? – fully acknowledged (Todd 2016)? The term "ontology" remains one of the most contentious and debated terms in the current theoretical lexicon.

Our third key term is posthumanism, another word that is understood in a range of different ways (Cipolla in review b; Crellin and Harris in review). Posthumanism, at its heart, is a fundamentally ontological orientation. Whilst there are many different ways of adopting posthumanism, the central tenet that these approaches share is that the image of the individual human subject, as it has been understood under the banner of humanism, is deeply problematic. Building on the critiques of "Man" offered by Foucault (e.g., 2002), posthumanist approaches argue that the figure of the human needs to be radically rethought as historically emergent, rather than universal, as *immanent*, instead of transcendent. The *human* of humanism is always implicitly white, male, heterosexual, middle class, and able bodied; all other humans are classed as different from this, and different in a way that marks them as less-than (Braidotti 2013; Ferrando 2019). Posthumanist thinking often draws on postcolonial critiques, feminism, and queer theory as it seeks to move away from "Man" and toward the "missing peoples" (Braidotti 2019b:49) who have not been the focus of past enquiry. Posthumanist thinkers like Rosi Braidotti (2013, 2019b) – themselves in turn often drawing on readings of thinkers like Baruch Spinoza and Deleuze – seek to reconfigure what it means to be human through a posthumanist lens (for a recent archaeological example of the application of these ideas, see Bickle 2020).

Within archaeology, the term posthumanism is often used to cover a variety of approaches, including those that tend to emphasize the potential of investigating a world without humans (e.g., Pétursdóttir and Olsen 2018). Often inspired by object-oriented ontology (OOO), which emphasizes how things have a withdrawn and unknowable essence (Harman 2011), these symmetrical approaches take a different tack to the kinds of posthumanism discussed primarily in this book. Where OOO itself has often discussed topics involving humans as key components – for example, the Dutch East India company (Harman 2016a) or the American Civil War (Harman 2018) – this is not always the case with the archaeological approaches they have inspired. Indeed, we might better think of these archaeological accounts as *ahumanist* because they often avoid the human altogether. Ahumanism, however, is a theoretical approach in its own right, which need not overlap with OOO. Ahumanist approaches developed from the work of the philosopher Patricia MacCormack (2012, 2014, 2020). MacCormack's work builds on posthumanism; both posthumanism and ahumanism critique anthropocentrism and the damage that humans have done to the world and each other, but ahumanism goes further to take the rather extreme position of actively advocating for human extinction (MacCormack 2020).[3]

The conflation of these different approaches has often meant posthumanist accounts have been accused of being unable, or unwilling, to address political questions (e.g., Van Dyke 2015). When applied to feminist versions of posthumanism, such attacks seem very wide of the mark (cf. Cipolla 2018). Such misunderstandings often emerge from the shared commitment across different versions of posthumanism to a "flat ontology" (Cipolla in review b; see also Barrett 2014, 2016). A flat ontology holds that the analyst cannot declare – in advance of the analysis – whether people, animals, things, landscapes, or whatever is playing a more or less important role. What that does *not* mean, for posthuman feminists, is that the process of analysis cannot reveal this. Thus, here the political outcomes, and the ethical impact, of the analysis are not decided in advance, but they follow nonetheless. A more critical issue, still to be truly teased out, is the relationship once again between Indigenous thought and posthuman feminism. The latter is committed to a decolonial stance, but how does this relate to its fundamental ontological starting points? How does posthumanism interact with Indigenous perspectives, which might celebrate hierarchy, or reject a flat ontology (cf. Wilkinson 2017a)? Furthermore, how do differences across Indigenous perspectives challenge the entire intellectual project of creating universal theory (see Chapter 11)?

As these discussions show, each of the key themes considered thus far – relations, ontology, and posthumanism – is in close conversation with our fourth topic, Indigenous paradigms. Over the course of this book, we touch upon a wide range of issues relating to Indigenous peoples, including what constitutes an Indigenous ontology, the Indigenization of theory, and the politics of archaeological praxis in settler colonial contexts. We struggled to come up with a shorthand for describing these various topics, but have settled on the term "Indigenous paradigms." To be explicit, for us, the term *Indigenous* refers to peoples living in the Americas, Africa, Australia, New Zealand, and other regions of the Pacific who have historical connections with preinvasion and precolonial societies through self-identification and/or legal recognition (Secretariat of the Permanent Forum on Indigenous Peoples 2004:2). This is not to say that Indigenous paradigms cannot apply to other descendant communities, only that we use this term with a particularly "settler colonial" bent in order to draw a stark distinction between "western" (non-colonized) societies and "Indigenous" (colonized) ones.

A key part of the debates and discussions in this book is how Indigenous paradigms connect, or do not connect, with the other concepts explored throughout. We use the notion of a "paradigm," instead of philosophy or theory, to encompass a broad range of discussions surrounding the incorporation of Indigenous peoples, knowledge, and histories into anthropology, archaeology, and the academy more broadly. This movement has largely been led by Indigenous scholars as part of a broader sociopolitical effort toward actualizing Indigenous sovereignty and self-determination in the face of ongoing disenfranchisement and erasure (Brown and Strega 2005; Denzin et al. 2008; Gill 2002; Henderson 2000; Smith 2012; Waziyatawin and Yellow Bird 2005; Wilson 2008). Within archaeology, more specifically, these efforts are led by "Indigenous archaeologists" who have concentrated their efforts on developing collaborative methodologies that diversify the discipline through Indigenous-led research initiatives, Tribal archaeology programs, and the incorporation of Indigenous peoples into the interpretation and care of material remains and landscapes. Much of this work has been inspired by (if not directly in dialogue with) the writings of Cree scholar Shawn Wilson who describes an Indigenous paradigm as having four essential aspects: ontology, epistemology, methodology, and axiology (2001:175). Wilson's model of knowledge and research encapsulates many of the ideas raised by the authors of this book (see Chapters 4 and 10).

Relations, ontology, posthumanism, and Indigenous paradigms are contested and conflicting terms that open up a range of different ways into archaeological theory, and thus to the differing pasts that archaeologists help to create. Teasing out the impact of these approaches, their relationships with each other, with us, with where we write, and what we write about, are critical aims of this book.

How this book works

We owe a debt to the many archaeologists before us who experimented with dialogue as a writing tool or who attempted to represent the different ways in which opinions might clash. Journals such as *Archaeological Dialogues* and *Current Anthropology* make excellent use of this general format. For some readers, our use of dialogue might harken back to the infamous typological debate between James Ford (1954) and Albert Spaulding (1953, 1954) in the pages of *American Antiquity*. Others might remember Kent Flannery's (1982) article, "The Golden Marshalltown: A Parable for the Archaeology of the 1980s," in which he presented a narrative of several fictive archaeologists – each representing a theoretical paradigm – interacting with one another on an airplane; Flannery used this format to help expose what he saw as the respective strengths and weaknesses of culture history, processual, and post-processual archaeologies. Similarly, Ian Hodder's and Robert Preucel's (1996) dialogue at the end of *Contemporary Archaeology in Theory* presented a discussion between six fictive voices (perspectives "a–f") to help explore what the editors saw as the key theoretical issues and tensions at play in western archaeology in the mid-1990s. Rosemary Joyce's (2002) *The Languages of Archaeology* included dialogues between her and other actual archaeologists in order to lay bare different orientations to archaeological interpretation and writing. More recently, Ian Hodder and Gavin Lucas (2017) used dialogue to help explore their respective understandings of human–thing relations. Like us, Hodder and Lucas present relatively short responses to one another to help the reader consider multiple points of view and to explore dissonances and overlaps between different orientations.

With many of these dialogically structured publications, readers are left to decide for themselves or, at the very least, are made aware of how different positions might parallel one another and/or clash. We find the unresolved tensions in this form of writing to be highly productive when it comes to contemporary archaeological theory. One could make the argument that a majority of archaeological thought comes in the form of monolithic single-authored arguments designed to oppose one another and to expose stark differences between theory A and theory B. For instance, diffusion and description were limiting, so Lewis Binford proposed something new to replace them; likewise, Hodder and colleagues were tired of structural functionalism and environmental determinism, so they wrote new post-processual ways of seeing to replace those supposed outmoded genres of archaeological theory. This conventional model of archaeological discourse usually results in something resembling manifestos. This is clearly evident in the fairly recent rise of symmetrical archaeologies (for which we have an actual manifesto, or at least excerpts from one, i.e., Witmore 2007) and the way in which they disregard previous forms of archaeological thought for what seems to be a completely new one. It is worth noting that this form of paradigm-shifting argument is, of course, bolstered by the very structure of academia in which one is more likely to be rewarded for big, stark changes that rattle the foundations of a discipline rather than subtle shifts that productively build on what came before.

For us, this is not how archaeological theory actually works. First of all, even those "paradigm" shattering arguments from thinkers like Binford were much more dialogic than portrayed (cf. Crellin 2020; Trigger 2006). Second, we see all archaeological "paradigms" as building on one another rather than cancelling out what came before (Harris and Cipolla 2017). Third, and perhaps most important, these conventional dualistic modes of theoretical discourse don't seem to work in the 2020s, when our discipline is undergoing major changes related to some of the critiques outlined in the previous section. In the context of Brexit and the Trump presidency, we have seen a proliferation of strictly opposed views and how they lead not to dialogue but instead produce intransigence and division. Instead of looking at how new ideas negate old ones, we seek to address how new ideas refract across a small spectrum of archaeologists from different backgrounds, with different constraints, and with different interests.

To explore these issues, the book moves between a series of single-authored chapters, interspersed with dialogues. The single-authored chapters act as extended arguments that explore issues that we, individually, feel are particularly important. In Chapter 2, Ollie asks: "What do we mean by relational anyway?" This opens up a comparison of the different ways archaeologists approach relations along with their surprising unwillingness to define what they mean when they use this term. Arguing that we need to embrace the affective and intensive elements of relations, Ollie offers a new descriptive vocabulary for thinking about relations. By contrast, in Chapter 4, Lindsay explores a different set of relations, those between archaeology and Indigenous paradigms. What is the relationship between these things? How have recent calls to explore "object agency," for example, placed certain kinds of political connections at the risk of being forgotten while others are foregrounded?

In Chapter 6, Sophie investigates the place of experience and phenomenology within these new approaches. By focusing on the immaterial world of Byzantine song, which emerges in thoroughly material settings, Sophie seeks to explore the complexities of agency, belief, and experience in a world that takes non-humans seriously. Chapter 8 moves from experience to power and posthumanism, as Rachel explores how we can reapproach power from within relational and "post-anthropocentric" approaches, as she terms it. For Rachel, rethinking power in this light allows new ways of writing about the past to emerge, which confront political issues without depending on a universal form of transcendent humanism. Finally, in Chapter 10, the last of the individual chapters, Craig explores tensions around the critical term "ontology." He examines how different uses of the term ontology propose different kinds of pasts, and reconsiders how these work in relation to Indigenous paradigms, including collaborative archaeologies involving diverse communities of practitioners. How does alterity function in these contexts? What does it mean to reach for radically different pasts?

Following each of these chapters is a dialogue chapter. Therein we explore the different ideas that each author presents and tease out different connections between various parts of the book. It is in these dialogues where uncertainties and tensions come to light for exploration. Each dialogue chapter tries to capture something of the live debate of archaeological theory, the way it shifts, and none of these should be seen as settled – we are still having some of these debates now! These sections of the book also allow us to pose questions to draw out further details of elements that might be unclear in any one particular chapter or argument. While we could have simply gone back and edited our individual chapters to clarify certain points, the aim in this book is not to hide how we learn and to develop our arguments in conversation with one another; we want to celebrate how our dialogues help to refine our ideas.

The book as a whole thus has a complex model of authorship. This chapter and large parts of the conclusion are mainly co-authored in a traditional sense, with individual voices emerging occasionally. The authorship of the individual chapters is clear. The dialogues are more complex; they largely capture the points each of us has made, but we have all edited and polished these elements too. None of these dialogues are simply recorded conversations. Some were written sequentially in a Google document, others were written together over a computer, others started life as emails flying back and forth across the Atlantic. As a whole, we hope this book is seen holistically. Chapters, especially the dialogues, refer back and forth to other arguments. It is not a monograph in the traditional sense, nor is it an edited volume; we are all co-authors, *even of the parts we did not write ourselves.* Thus, the order of the authors of the book as a whole is arbitrary, and does not relate to comparative contribution, status, or the conceptual origins of the book.

One final remark: this book covers a range of perspectives and theoretical approaches, from Indigenous paradigms to new materialism, via turns to ontology, to phenomenology, and ANT. It is not, however, universal or comprehensive. There is no engagement here with evolutionary theory, no articles written by strong advocates of symmetrical archaeology or object-oriented ontology, and none written by archaeologists who reject all of these recent turns in archaeological thought. There are a few reasons for this. First, one book can only cover so much material and relations, ontology, posthumanism, and Indigenous paradigms seem like enough for now. Second, we are interested in debates and dialogues here that get beyond simple first principles and provoke real engagement in the nuance and detail of debate. This book is about exploring what happens when you try reconciling the distinctions and differences that lie in the hidden fractures within and between related theoretical approaches.

Notes

1 British Islands is the legal term for the United Kingdom, Channel Islands, and Isle of Man. British Isles is commonly used to refer to Britain, Ireland, and the surrounding islands; it is often presented as a geographically "neutral" term; however, the use of the phrase "British" implies ownership and empire and is therefore clearly inappropriate when talking about the Republic of Ireland in particular. As a result, I avoid the term British Isles and prefer to talk about Britain and Ireland.

2 A note on capitalizations. Throughout this book, we variously switch between capitalizing the term "western," as well as the people of Indigenous "people." When capitalizing Western, we refer to hegemonic positions within the west, e.g., the "Western" cannon, or dominant traditions of Western thoughts. When noncapitalized, the western is purely descriptive and non-hegemonic. For more on the term western, see discussions in Chapter 12. Similarly, "Indigenous People" is capitalized when referring to a specific group of people, and "Indigenous people" when referring to a more general term. Indigenous, with one quite deliberate exception in Chapter 12, is capitalized throughout.

3 Each of these lines of thinking and critique is also different from "transhumanism." This branch of thinking focuses upon a future-oriented utopian vision of a world where technology drives human progress. Transhumanist philosophy explores a world where we can move beyond "the physical, intellectual and sensory limits of the individual" through technology and is firmly rooted in Enlightenment thinking (Caraher 2019:372; cf. Ferrando 2019).

2

WHAT DO WE MEAN BY RELATIONAL ANYWAY?

Oliver J.T. Harris

Introduction

For many years now I have conceptualized the work I do as an example of relational archaeology. This means that rather than thinking about the world as full of bounded entities, I, along with many archaeologists, focus on how people, places, and things emerge through their connections to one another. Yet a critical issue here is that archaeologists are not always clear about what they mean by the term relation. Christopher Watts (2013a:1) offers one definition of relationality as "a suite of approaches aimed at conflating the abstract and immutable dualities of modernist ontologies." Ok, but once this conflation has been completed, and the move to identify relations has begun, we are still left with a whole set of questions. What actually are relations? Are all relations equal? If not, how do we begin to divide them up, to qualify them and describe them? Do the relations we are describing refer to what the people in the past thought about the world, or to a more basic underlying metaphysical commitment on behalf of the archaeologist: that the world is relational?

As Astrid van Oyen (2016:357) has argued, if we leave these questions unanswered, we run the risk of trivializing the importance of this relational turn and reducing its power to merely being satisfied with the simple recognition of relations. Clearly, not all relations are equal. The manner in which an archaeologist relates to a pot is potentially very different from how a pot relates to its contents. The relationships between a set of objects deposited in a grave may differ to those between materials mixed together in a midden. The relations between parents and children are different to those between a person and the tick currently feeding on their blood. As Erica Hill (2018:42) has put it: "simply characterizing Indigenous ontology as 'relational' tells us very little about the experience – the dwelling-in-the-world – of specific persons." Similarly, Darryl Wilkinson (2013:419) has shown that if the world is relational, at a fundamental level, then describing specific elements of that world as relational tells us nothing significant about them.

I aim to write relational accounts of the past, but it has become clear to me that to do so I am going to need to develop a much more detailed and specific way of talking about relations. The aim of this chapter is to start that process. I begin by identifying three broad approaches to relations in archaeology, drawing on distinctions identified by Van Oyen (2016:357). The first views relations as critical to how people in the past conceptualized their worlds. I will term these approaches "relations as epistemology," and they have much in common with what Craig calls "worldviews" in Chapter 10. The second approach focuses on "relations as methodology," that is how archaeologists employ relations as tools to characterize networks. Finally, there are those approaches that understand relations as the fundamental building blocks of the world. These will be united under the banner "relations as metaphysics."[1] These different approaches are not necessarily opposed or incompatible, and each, I will suggest, offers us useful tools.

Having briefly examined these approaches, the second part of this chapter will outline the next steps for a relational archaeology. First, we require a deeper consideration of what a relation actually is and the status relations have within our interpretations. Second, we are beholden to develop a new vocabulary for describing these relations. This will allow both an approach and a vocabulary for considering relations in detail. I will conclude with a brief example of this in practice. To be clear, my aim is not to provide a typology of relations, a point we return to in the dialogue that follows this chapter. Rather, I aim to outline some of the concepts that may prove useful in offering a richer description of the relations that operate in both past and present.

Relations in archaeology

The interest in relations in archaeology can be traced back to at least the start of post-processualism (Harris and Cipolla 2017). From the mid-1990s, a raft of concerns began to focus on relations in increasingly explicit ways. These included new conceptions of identity coming from feminist and anthropologically informed understandings (e.g., Fowler 2000) alongside a growing interest in network analysis (for a full history, see Brughmans 2013) and more philosophical concerns emerging from phenomenology (e.g., Thomas 1996). As already noted, these different concerns can be grouped into three different approaches to relations, although the boundaries between these groups – as with all boundaries – are slippery and ill-defined. Nonetheless, they serve as a useful heuristic to structure our review of relations in archaeology.

Relations as epistemology

One of the fundamental sources for thinking about relations in archaeology emerged through an encounter with the writings of anthropologists, and especially the work of Marilyn Strathern (1988, 1992). Strathern's ethnographic work outlined how for Melanesian people the world did not begin with neatly bounded individuals, but rather with relationships. The primacy of relationships in Melanesia meant that very different understandings of identity, agency, and community emerged. In archaeology, her work was taken up by scholars interested in the concept of personhood (e.g., Chapman 2000; Fowler 2001, 2004; Gillespie 2001). To give one example, Chris Fowler (2000, 2001, 2004, 2008) drew on Strathern, and other anthropological accounts, to argue that different sets of relationships could be identified that led to differing forms of personhood. Although these accounts of personhood have been critiqued for lending the European past a "Melanesian flavour" (Jones 2005:195), or relying on an ahistorical concept of fragmentation (Brittain and Harris 2010), the underlying argument – that personhood is fundamentally relational – has been widely accepted (e.g., Harrison-Buck and Hendon 2018a; Watts 2013b). More recently, Fowler (2016) has offered an extended development of his arguments on relational personhood. Reflecting on various critiques, he develops his analysis of personhood to identify a range of tensions out of which personhood can emerge, which he calls "axes of relationality."

Anthropology continues to offer archaeologists a welcome resource for thinking through relations, both in connection to personhood and more widely (Zedeño 2013). One of the key elements that has emerged from this is the notion that personhood need not be restricted to human beings (e.g., Hill 2018; Howey 2018). These approaches emphasize how people in the past conceptualized and understood identity and agency in a relational manner. Harrison-Buck and Hendon, for example, introduce their volume on relational identities by stating that such a relational approach "involves a *conscious awareness* in the world of one's positioning and activity in the world as a reciprocal and relational being" (2018b:10, my emphasis). The stress placed on "conscious awareness" indicates that relationality here depends upon human engagement, and is not a statement about how the world works regardless of what people think about it. It is for this reason I have termed these approaches *relations as epistemology*.[2] Without question, they offer us a series of useful tools for thinking about relations. They rely heavily on ethnographic data, which can be highly appropriate where direct historical connections exist. This means, however, that the relations described are curtailed to those of which people are aware. They do not, therefore, amount to a complete account of how relations shape worlds past and present. As Fowler's (2013) own work elsewhere shows, other elements are required if we are to fully address the role of relations in archaeology.

Relations as methodology

A second set of approaches have focused on relations as a methodological tool for thinking about the past. Less concerned with past people's understanding of relations, they argue we can trace and detect particular connections in the material. This can be done through both formal network analysis and more theoretical work, including Carl Knappett's (2005, 2011) link between networks and Peircean semiotics and Hodder's (2012, 2016) concept of entanglement.

Network analysis offers archaeologists the means to examine the relations between different archaeological entities, be they specific features, people, sites, or regions (for reviews, see Brughmans 2010, 2013; Mills 2017). They examine nodes and the relations that connect them, their form, density, and frequency, and provide archaeologists with a methodology for describing certain elements, especially economic relations of production and consumption.

Whilst relations can be quantified through these kinds of analysis, given values such as strong and weak, and take a variety of forms, they often still remain underexamined theoretically and are secondary to the nodes they connect (Brughmans 2013; Collar et al. 2015). This is not to say that relations do not matter in these approaches, as Collar et al. (2015:4–5) rightly stress they clearly do, but nonetheless they matter *because* of the effect they have on the nodes – they do not have an independent existence. In contrast to relational concepts of personhood, where relations are what constitute people and are primary, nodes come first in this mode of analysis, relationships afterward. This clearly differentiates it from the approaches we will examine later as well.

Knappett, however, brings together formal network analysis with a range of philosophical approaches, particularly the complex semiosis of Charles Sanders Peirce in order to provide concrete studies of how we can approach relations. This is not the place to offer a detailed summary of Peirce's ideas (for more detail, see Cipolla 2013a; Crossland 2018; Crossland and Bauer 2017; Harris and Cipolla 2017:Chapter 7; Preucel 2006).[3] Broadly speaking, however, Peirce developed an analysis of how meaning emerges in the world quite different from the standard analysis of semiotics made popular by Ferdinand de Saussure. Rather than working on a simple dualistic opposition between signifier and signified, Peirce introduced a third term – the interpretant – making all sign relations triadic (Preucel 2012:117). Many archaeologists using Peirce's work have drawn extensively on three particular sign types Peirce developed: icons – where two things have a likeness, often visual, such as a portrait and its subject; indexes – where one thing is caused by another, such as where the presence of smoke is an index of the fire; and symbols – where the links between a sign and what it indicates are conventional, as is the case with many of the linguistic signs we use every day (cf. Knappett 2005).

Knappett's work, and the concepts developed by Peirce in particular, clearly offers archaeologists a useful set of terms for particular kinds of relationship. Indeed, no doubt further analysis of Peirce's work would render yet more (see also Knappett 2012). However, the relations still follow on here from the different objects under study, meaning relations are still secondary to the terms they link, rather than full actors. That means this approach differs from the others we will see that have dealt with relations in metaphysical terms.

A final example of how relations are used methodologically comes from the work of Ian Hodder (2012, 2016), who like Knappett aims to relate social connections to the broader worlds of formal network analysis (see also Hodder and Mol 2016). Hodder (2012) seeks to explore how humans and things become entangled with each other, and how we can characterize their relationships in a number of ways, including elements that are "strong, weak, integrated, redundant, concentrated, dispersed and so on" (Hodder 2012:107). For Hodder, like Knappett however, it is clear that these relations follow on from the emergence of things and people, rather than taking on their own importance as metaphysical elements of the world. So, for example, Hodder (2012:93) argues that we need to maintain a fundamental opposition between people and things. Our last set of approaches challenges this division.

Relations as metaphysics

The metaphysical concern with relations can be traced back to the mid-1990s, in fact to some of the same texts that introduced archaeology to anthropologists like Strathern (e.g., Thomas 1996). Critical here was an increasing suspicion of the ways in which archaeological thought was structured around binary oppositions or dualisms such as mind and body, culture and nature, representational and real, and so on (Harris 2018a; Harris and Cipolla 2017; Thomas 1996, 2004). This way of approaching the world can be referred to as Cartesian, after the French philosopher René Descartes, which takes the basic substances of the universe to exist ahistorically, and prior to coming into contact with one another – prior to relations in other words.

Cartesian approaches have been critiqued from a range of theoretical positions in archaeology, each tending to draw explicitly on the notion of relations, including phenomenology, materiality, and object agency (see Harris and Cipolla 2017:Chapter 6). Another key approach that has led archaeologists to a metaphysical engagement came from readings of Actor-Network Theory (ANT) and of Bruno Latour (1993, 1999, 2005a, inter alia) in particular (e.g., Jones 2001; Domańska 2006; Whitridge 2004a), which has most famously inspired symmetrical archaeology (Olsen 2003, 2007; Olsen et al. 2012; Shanks 2007; Webmoor 2007; Webmoor and Witmore 2008). Symmetrical archaeology argued that the world was fundamentally relational. "Archaeology begins with mixtures," Witmore's (2007:549) manifesto for the movement declares. "Things Are Us!" is the title of another paper (Webmoor and Witmore 2008). For Latour (1999), what defines an entity is the extent to which it connects with the world around it, how it effects, or does not, other things linked to it within a network. This ability to affect the world, or agency as it is sometimes called, emerges from the particular arrangements of people and things within networks and is thus a quality of relationships. Drawing on this, symmetrical archaeologists sought explicitly to construct a relational approach.[4] The world here is relational not because people believe it to be the case, but because relations form a critical dimension of reality (cf. Fowler and Harris 2015).

Symmetrical archaeology set the scene for others to emphasize the metaphysical and ontological importance of relations. Central has been new materialism, which argues that matter is vibrant, agentive, and emergent through relations (Barad 2007; Bennett 2010; Conneller 2011; Fowler 2013; Ingold 2007; Jones 2012; Marshall and Alberti 2014), and the related concepts of assemblage thinking (Jervis 2018; Jones and Hamilakis 2017). The latter treats the world as fundamentally relational, and the different components that make up the world, whether humans, animals, people, things, communities, materials, waterfalls, or water molecules, as amalgamations and arrangements of different elements that cohere together through specific historical processes. This draws variously on the work of Gilles Deleuze and Félix Guattari (2004) and often upon the version of their thought developed by Manuel DeLanda (2006). Assemblages are always in the process of gathering relations together or breaking them apart (Deleuze and Guattari 2004:556) (for an archaeological discussion, see Harris 2014, 2017). These processes, along with others from Deleuze and Guattari that I will go on to discuss, offer another important addition to our conceptual toolbox.

New materialism differs from symmetrical archaeology in a number of critical ways. First, the relations within the former are always in the process of becoming. This means that the static networks of ANT are replaced by a constant ebbing and flowing of relations (Crellin 2020). This is important because it helps us see why, in comparison to symmetrical archaeology, new materialism tends to be more interested in explaining what happened in the past. For symmetrical archaeology, new networks appear whenever a relation shifts; this means that only the current arrangement of materials are of interest (Crellin 2020; Garcia-Rovira 2015; Harman 2009). For new materialist approaches, all assemblages are the product of specific historical processes that have to be traced and explained (DeLanda 2006). This means that new materialism leads you inevitably toward an explanation that looks at the past as well as the present. New materialist approaches, therefore, like epistemological engagements, are interested in how people understood and engaged with the world; however, the claim to relationality in this case does not depend upon past people's understanding.

A good example of this kind of analysis comes from the work of Timothy Pauketat and Susan Alt (2018). They examine the role of landscape, people, and materials in the emergence of Cahokia and the Mississippian way of life. From a new materialist position, the authors explore how the material properties of a variety of media, from maize to shell to sweat to mud, related people, things, and places in particular ways. They argue that particular historical process worked through the relational characteristics of this specific location to produce the gatherings that formed the Mississippian world. Elsewhere, Alt (2019) has developed a sophisticated analysis of how the relational properties of the karstic geology of the landscape around Cahokia also played a critical role in bringing together the specific gatherings of people and things that characterized this time and place.[5]

Reconceptualizing relations

Each of the three approaches has important things to offer. Treating relations as central to how people understand the world allows us to conceptualize how past societies operated with a very different set of preconceptions. Treating relations as a methodology allows us to map connections in new ways, although network analysis will not form part of what follows. Starting with a metaphysical approach to relations allows new kinds of questions to be asked about the role of non-humans in the past and present. However, there is still more work to be done. Outside of specific examples, archaeological effort has gone predominantly into thinking about what kinds of things were related to each other in the past, or into the outcome of taking a relational approach toward archaeological interpretation, and little into *what relations actually are*. To move forward, I argue we need to pause for a moment, and reconstruct our approach from the ground up. The first step, one that archaeologists have largely skipped over, is to ask about the specific status of relations themselves: what place do relations take in our metaphysics, and how do they themselves connect to other archaeological entities (objects, sites, contexts, and so on)? The second step will be to develop this to provide a new way of describing relations, incorporating some of the useful terminology already encountered. Finally, I will look at how these groups of relations can be examined in connection to a specific example. This threefold process will set out an approach that refocuses archaeology toward a specifically situated engagement with relations.

Part 1: on the status of relations

Let us return to the paper authored by Pauketat and Alt (2018). They offer one of the few clear definitions of what a relation is in archaeology[6]:

> Relations are those physical properties, experiential qualities, and other flows or movements of substances, materials, and phenomena that become attached to, entangled, or associated with others and, in the process, define not only people but other organisms, things, places and the like.
>
> *(Pauketat and Alt 2018:73)*

This is an excellent starting point. Pauketat and Alt identify relations as properties and qualities. A physical property like hardness is a relation because it requires connecting a substance that is being pressed on the one hand and resisting that pressure, with something doing the pressing, on the other. As we will see later, the same argument can be made for experiential qualities. More than this though, Pauketat and Alt note that not only do such relations become attached to, or associated with, other things, they come to define them. This is critical, because it indicates that relations, in part, do not simply connect preexisting entities but are rather central to their emergence (Barad 2007). As Tim Ingold (2011:69–70), writing from a broadly new materialist perspective, emphasizes, relations here are lines along which life is lived, always in motion, or in becoming.

We can develop this to make three metaphysical claims about relations. To do so, I suggest we need to work within the new materialist tradition where it directly discusses relations (e.g., Deleuze 1990, 1991a; Massumi 2002, 2015;

Spinoza 1996). New materialism offers us the best potential here, both because of its commitment to a relational starting point, as we saw previously, and because of its emphasis on historical process, movement, and becoming.

Our first metaphysical claim is that relations are relations of affect. What does this mean, and why is it an important claim? Affect is a complex term. In some parts of the literature, it is compared to the physical experience of emotion or to a precultural, biological, part of being human (e.g., Tomkins 1982; cf. von Scheve 2018). The tradition I want to draw on here takes a quite different view. Affect, from this perspective, is the manner in which bodies press into one another, changing the capacities of other bodies to act, and in so doing changing themselves. Affect is the capacity to affect and be affected (Clough 2009; Deleuze 1988, 1990; Massumi 2002, 2015; Spinoza 1996). With the notable exceptions of Yannis Hamilakis (2013, 2017) and Andrew Jones (2018a:24–30), there has been little engagement with these approaches in archaeology. Bodies, here, are not simply human bodies but bodies of all kinds, both organic and inorganic. Deleuze and Guattari (2004:283) famously cite Jakob Von Uexküll's analysis of a tick to consider how this insect lives its life through three intertwining sets of affective relations: a sensitivity to light, smell, and heat (cf. Watts 2013a:10). The way in which a cat rushes across a wooden floor and scratches the paint is an example of affect. The way in which acidic soils slowly eat away the flesh of a buried loved one is an example of affect. So too is the way in which a sudden crash from the kitchen causes you to jump or gasp. All of these are bodies in relation, bodies moving through the world with different speeds and slownesses (Deleuze and Guattari 2004:287). Affects are "lines of force" (Thrift 2008:175). Critically, the emphasis that affect is the capacity to affect *and* to be affected reminds us that relations are always two-way (cf. Bird David 2018:29). One body cannot affect another without being affected in turn. The cat wears away its claws as they wear away the paint; the acidic chemicals are transformed too in their reaction with the dead person's flesh. Relations of affect are always recursive.

Within this, we can differentiate between two forms of relations that a body has. On the one hand, there are relations being activated at any one time: your body is currently being affected by oxygen as it becomes part of your bloodstream; this body of text affects you as it produces a slight air of confusion. On the other hand, bodies have a whole range of potential affective relations that are not formally present at any one moment: the capacity you have to breathe out and alter the body of air around you, for example, the moment of clarity that descends as you gain a better understanding of affective relations, or the sudden stab of pain you might feel as you stretch your legs out and bang your toe on the desk.[7] Deleuze (1988:17) remarks, drawing on Spinoza, that nobody knows what a body can do. The potential for new affective relations reveals that bodies, of all sorts, have a host of capacities that are unrealized at any one time. This creates the potential for change, but also a realization that all bodies, and the affective relations that position them in the world, are not the product of transcendent identities (for example, what it means to be human), but are rather always historically emergent, because new bodies come into existence as new relations are formed.

This emphasis upon affect is essential for several reasons. First, it allows us to understand what links physical properties and experiential qualities. Both of these are affective, in that they are about the capacities of different bodies to affect and be affected. Archaeologists have tended to link affect to sensory or emotional elements of the world; we are now in a position to expand on this to make it a fundamental ontological quality of how bodies interact with one another and how we can investigate their capabilities. Second, this linkage allows us to see how there is nothing within this approach that prevents us from talking about human experiences of meaning, memory, emotion, power, or politics. These too are affective relations, as Jones (2018b:186) points out in relation to meaning. Approaches from a range of posthumanist positions (including ANT, symmetrical archaeology, and new materialism) have been accused of ignoring power (see Chapter 8). I would argue that affect allows us to both decenter humans from our narratives and add to our ability to describe and analyze politics in the past and present (cf. Massumi 2015). We return to the relationship between affect and power in the dialogue in Chapter 9.

The other two proposals flow from this, and can be dealt with more swiftly. *The second metaphysical claim is that relations are relations of difference.* What does this mean, and why is it an important claim? One way of thinking of relations is simply as a form of connection, that two things are linked or hold something in common. However, once we recognize the centrality of affect, we have to acknowledge that relations are things that *make a difference*, they produce a change in the bodies they connect, and increase or decrease a body's capacity for action (Deleuze 1988, 1990; Spinoza 1996). Bodies emerge through relationships, because relationships have the capacity to differentiate bodies. When a modern sculptor works with a piece of wood to produce a piece of art, or a Neolithic person works with a piece of stone to make an axe, the relationship between person, material, and other objects they may be using acts to differentiate the sculpture or the stone axe from the material. These relations produce new bodies through the fact that they make a difference. The centrality of difference also links this Deleuzian approach to relations to the wider world of the ontological critique in archaeology and anthropology. As Benjamin Alberti and Yvonne Marshall (2009:347) have argued, relations of difference are at the heart of Eduardo Viveiros de Castro's concepts of Amazonian perspectivism.[8] Rachel and I have argued elsewhere that it is this embrace of difference that is key to allowing our understandings of the past to provoke a more challenging set of questions (Harris and Crellin 2018). By embracing the idea that relations are fundamentally differential, we can also incorporate the critical concept that what counts as a relation may itself vary (Viveiros de Castro 2013:481). This means that our exploration of relations must always be based in the immanent historical contexts that we are investigating (Marshall and Alberti 2014).

The final metaphysical claim is that relations do not simply emerge from the objects we study, nor do they somehow preexist them, rather objects and relations emerge together in a continual process of becoming (FT 2018). There has been much ink spilled over whether relations are prior to their terms, or follow on from them, with Ingold

(2011:91), for example, claiming the single most defining contrast between himself and Latour is that in his case relations are primary, whilst for Latour objects take the lead and relations follow (cf. Fowler and Harris 2015). The philosopher Graham Harman (2011) has argued that all approaches, other than his own object-oriented ontology, are guilty of either undermining objects by reducing them to their relations or overmining them, by saying that they are only real to the extent they affect other entities (cf. Fowler and Harris 2015; see also Chapter 10). The claim I make here side steps this distinction because relations emerge alongside the things they relate (Viveiros de Castro 2013) or to put it in Deleuze's words "*relations are always external to their terms*" (Deleuze 1991a:66, my emphasis), and therefore "relations *can* change without the terms changing" (Deleuze and Parnet 2002:55, my emphasis). Relations here do not belong to things, they are not contained by things, they are, as Seigworth and Gregg (2010:2) emphasize, fundamentally in between.

Why does this matter? First, it allows us to deal with the reality of objects without denying that they are always in the process of change and becoming. Because relations can change without the terms changing (note *can*, not must or will), we can recognize how, as Rachel teaches us, the number 1 bus winding its way through a small town on the Isle of Man can continue to be the number 1 bus even as passengers get on and off (Crellin 2017:113–14). The bus is *always* changing, as rubber is left on the road, as petrol is burned in the engine, as the cambelt frays. It nonetheless remains the number 1 bus despite the relations changing. This allows us to approach the specific qualities of a thing[9] without having to deny that it is fully relational all the way down. If we do not embrace this continuity, we are faced with either suggesting that things have a non-relational essence (Harman's argument), which makes explaining historical change very difficult, as we see in the dialogue in the next chapter, or that each time a relation shifts something completely new comes into existence (see Crellin 2020). The former requires at least a partial rejection of relations, the latter reduces the world to an unending swirl where any form of order is simply an external imposition.

Part 2: describing relations

Thus, we can now approach relations as differentially affective and external to their terms, and move forward into describing the relations themselves (for a summary, see Table 2.1). The emphasis on affect demonstrates that we need to think about the power of relations, their ability to seize hold of things, and to demand attention and engagement. A useful way of thinking about this is to characterize relations as *intensive* as well as *extensive* (Deleuze 2004). The extensive dimensions of relations dominate the formal network analyses we saw earlier. They include how far apart two things are, or the number of links between two entities. They measure empirical properties and proportions of things in other words (DeLanda 2002). These aspects are important, and represent one part of relations we need

TABLE 2.1 Different terms for thinking through relations.

	Relations are:
Affective	They are forces that recursively press from one body (whether human or non-human) into another, shaping what it is a body can do
Differential	Relations make a difference, and they emerge through difference
External to their terms	They cannot be reduced to the terms they relate, they are always in between
	Relations can have dimensions that are:
Intensive	The force of relations is indivisible, and drives processes that shape the world
Extensive	Relations have spatial and temporal components
	Relations form assemblages, this involves processes of:
Territorialization	The process by which the components and substances of an assemblage become combined together
Deterritorialization	The process by which components of an assemblage become detached
Reterritorialization	Almost always when something becomes separated from one assemblage, it becomes part of another. This is the process of reterritorialization
Coding	The process by which the components of an assemblage are organized in particular forms
Decoding	The process by which parts of an assemblage lose their form and organization
Stratification	The tendency toward stasis in an assemblage, leading to the production of strata
Destratification	The tendency through which strata break down and change more rapidly
	Terms for describing particular qualities of relationships include:
Index	A relationship between two things that are physically connected
Icon	A relationship of resemblance, usually visual
Symbol	A relationship that emerges through a specific history and can appear arbitrary

to examine. Intensive dimensions of relations are even more critical, however, as these drive processes of change and differentiation. Intensity describes relations of force, how a punch slams into a body, or how a phone call makes a heart leap. They also capture the intensities inherent in storms and earthquakes, the flows of energy that generate geological and climatic events (DeLanda 2002). Intensive differences drive change but cannot be divided. If you heat a room to 50°C and then divide that room into two, you do not have two rooms at 25°C, you have two rooms at 50°C (DeLanda 2002). If you have two separate rooms at different temperatures, however, and open a door between them, the intensive differences in temperature will drive a change in the warmth of both rooms as the relations shift. The ways in which relations last and endure, about which Chris Fowler (2013) has written so evocatively, works precisely through this intensity. Intensity allows relations to persist through time and not exist solely in one moment; it lends relations their productive force, through the way in which differences in intensity drive change in the world. All movement is driven in this way, "one travels by intensity" (Deleuze and Guattari 2004:60). Here we can draw on the manner in which Hodder's (2012) ideas of strong and weak connections develop intensively, and the manner in which dependencies between humans and things develops precisely through the intensity of their relations.

Relations bring things together, therefore, in ways that allow for intensive connection and extensive comparison, but there are other ways to describe these links. As Deleuze and Guattari (2004:157, 586) noted, it is here that the ideas of Peirce have much to offer us. Three of Peirce's terms that have already been introduced can allow us to add to our vocabulary for describing relations: index, icon, and symbol. The former can be thought of as a form of relation where two things are related through their direct connection; the smoke and the fire as we saw earlier, or the weathervane and the wind, to give another common example. In Deleuze and Guattari's (2004:157) terms, these are "territorialized" signs, meaning they are a relation that cannot be separated, they are always together. Territorialization, for Deleuze and Guattari (2004:45, 555), is the process through which things are assembled together, so something that is territorialized with something else is bound to it in a particular way. Smoke in your office is not a sign of a fire a 100 miles away, a weathervane pointing east in Leicester doesn't mean the wind is blowing that way in Toronto, the relations are present here and now. Icons, for Deleuze and Guattari (2004:157), are signs of "reterritorialization" where something from somewhere else is revealed in a new place or location, usually through a visual connection. The photos on your desk of much missed love ones reterritorialize them in front of you through this act of iconic relation. Finally, symbols, for Deleuze and Guattari (2004), are deterritorialized signs, the link here is in the history that forms the convention of relations themselves. So there is no necessary tie between the word wasp and the black and yellow insect flying around, the relation is sustained through the conventions of language (in itself a complex set of relations).[10] The work of Peirce within archaeology has sometimes been positioned in opposition to engagements with new materialism. By repositioning Deleuze and Guattari's own engagement with Peirce, however, we can begin to reintegrate these different accounts and use them as tools for thinking about and describing relations. Recent work exploring the material qualities of Peirce's signs (e.g., Crossland 2018; Crossland and Bauer 2017) only enhances the potential for this.

Relations, however, never exist in isolation, rather they are part of complex sets, which, as we have seen, Deleuze and Guattari refer to as assemblages. When we talk about relations in archaeology, we are almost never talking about a single relation by itself, instead whether we are exploring the makeup of an ancient monument, sets of grave goods, or accumulated material in a pit, we are drawing on multiple different relations at the same time. Here we can incorporate the suggestions made by Van Oyen (2016). Although Van Oyen argues that archaeologists need to examine relations in more detail, her own solution is to propose archaeologists look at what she terms relational constellations, gatherings of relations or, if you will, assemblages. She examines three different forms of pottery production in the Roman Empire, and argues that their different characteristics allow her to define three different kinds of relational constellation: fluid, categorical, and rooted (Van Oyen 2016:362–71). These terms effectively describe different degrees to which assemblages bind together or become territorialized. Just as Peirce's terms offered us a tool for describing individual relations within an assemblage, so Van Oyen allows us to describe the assemblages themselves in useful ways.

The broader language of assemblage thinking used by Deleuze and Guattari again proves useful here (Jervis 2018; Jones and Hamilakis 2017). Assemblages for Deleuze (2007:177) are diverse "hodgepodges" of heterogeneous elements, brought together through specific historical processes. The emphasis is always on the relations between the different elements of the assemblage. These relations are brought together or territorialized in very specific ways. We can imagine an assemblage of a Bronze Age burial being territorialized as people brought grave goods to the site and placed them around the body of the dead (Harris 2016b). Relations can become deterritorialized from assemblages too, as flesh rots and decays in the ground, as metal corrodes, so the relational makeup of the assemblage shifts and changes. Here we are less concerned with the precise nature of individual relations, but rather thinking of the ways in which they shift together through historical and environmental processes. When relations become entangled to such a degree that they endure for significant periods of time, we can refer to them as stratified (Deleuze and Guattari 2004:45). Here the intensive energies of relations, in the sense defined previously, become bounded and located within strata that are enduring (Jervis 2018:41). As an example, think of how gender relations in Europe have involved the production and imposition of binary categories, and then the ranking and ordering of those categories hierarchically. The product of a specific, if long-term, history (Robb and Harris 2018), gender relations have become stratified, linked to ideas of "nature" and "biology," and are only now becoming unstable, destratified, and deterritorialized. Gender relations are also a good example of the process of coding and decoding that Deleuze and Guattari (2004:59) also use to discuss assemblages and relations. Coding is the sorting and organizing of particular kinds of relations, and in social terms can involve the construction of rules, regulations, and other forms of relation that link certain spaces, practices, and ideas together (Jervis 2018:38–9). Notions of binary gender are thus coded into spaces such as bathrooms, prisons, shelters, and so on, which are then challenged by ideas that would seek to decode and destratify these oppositions.

One final critical point emerges from this discussion – relations operate at multiple scales (Harris 2017). Gender is an excellent example of this once again:

it is an outcome of relations at the personal level, drawing on patterns of dress, language, and bodily comportment; it rests on specific social scales that shift around fashion, work, household responsibilities, and familial expectations; it also rests on long-term histories. Material things, including bodies, objects, architectural spaces, and more, are at play at every level of this. These different scales are not just organized hierarchically; they interweave and fold together, so that individual moments of gendered practice can both sustain and challenge longer-term histories and vice versa.

Part 3: relations at work

The preceding discussion offers us a new metaphysical basis for discussing relations as relations of affect and difference that are always in between. It has also offered us a new way of thinking about relations as both intensive and extensive, as becoming tied together in different ways (through territorialization, stratification, and coding), and as operating at multiple scales. It has also allowed us to think about how specific kinds of relations like icons, indexes, and symbols work within a new materialist approach to the past. In this final part of the chapter, I want to sketch out how this might let us describe a site and a historical moment in new ways; to do so I will look briefly at a specific assemblage, that of the Viking boat burial from Swordle Bay, Western Scotland, excavated in 2011 by the Ardnamurchan Transitions Project (Harris et al. 2017). Measuring 5.2 m × 1.7 m, the burial consisted

FIGURE 2.1 Pre-excavation photograph of the Swordle Bay boat burial.

Source: Photograph by Oliver Harris.

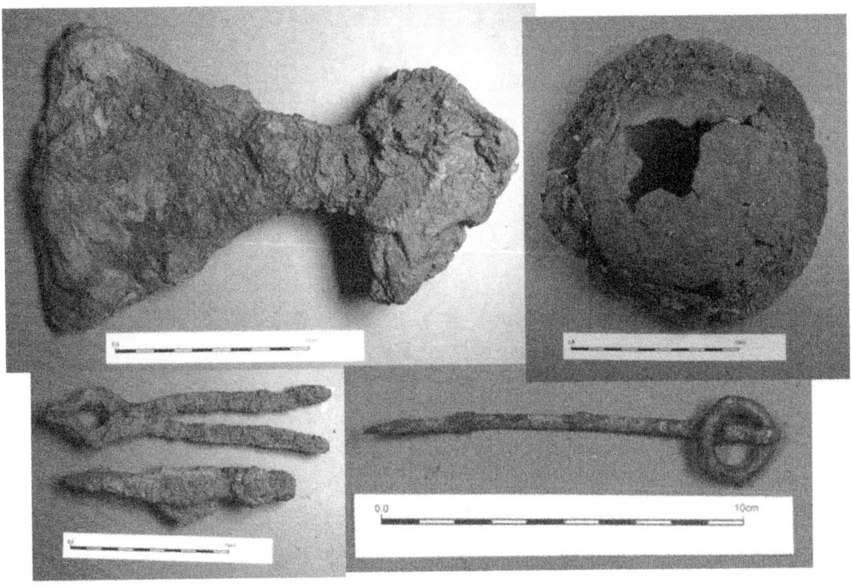

FIGURE 2.2 Some of the finds recovered from the grave (clockwise from top left): broad-bladed axe, shield boss, ringed pin, and the hammer and tongs.

Source: Photographs: Pieta Greaves/AOC Archaeology, reproduced with permission.

FIGURE 2.3 The sword in situ (top); the mineralized textile remains (below right); detail of the decoration after conservation (below left).

Source: Lower photographs: Pieta Greaves/AOC Archaeology, reproduced with permission. Upper photograph by Oliver Harris

of the deposition of a clinker-built boat into a natural shingle mound. Within the boat, the body of a Viking was laid, along with a range of grave goods, including a sword, an axe, a ladle containing a hammer and tongs, a whetstone, a drinking horn, a sickle, and a ringed pin. The burial was then backfilled with large stones, likely taken from a nearby Neolithic burial cairn, with a shield and spear, the latter deliberately broken, deposited as the stones were being added.

How might our new vocabulary help us to understand this site? What affective relations can we map here? What kinds of bodies pressing into one another, changing each other's capacities, are present? The body of the deceased is one obvious example. When the boat burial was assembled, the body would have been a critical part of this, the act of separating it from the community changing the relations amongst the living as well as the dead, something archaeologists have long recognized (Parker Pearson 1999). Fundamentally, this act of deposition was a funeral, and this would have brought with it powerful emotions and memories, specific forms of affect emergent in the relations between living and dead, people and place. Non-human bodies played their role too in the generation of meaning. On the one hand, complex and important objects like the sword had their own biographies and life stories, affective and symbolic relations with the living now curtailed. The same applies to the sickle and the boat. These too were territorialized within the grave, coding the person buried here with different kinds of identity: warrior, farmer, sailor. These different identities are more-than-representational, they are materially cited and indexed (cf. Harris 2018b). Zoë Crossland (2018) has set out how fingerprints operate as indexical signs in forensic and criminal investigation. Here non-humans operate as indexical relations of practices and performances that took place elsewhere; so too the stones that filled the grave. Taken from the nearby Neolithic chambered tomb of Cladh Aindreis, these territorialized stones passed into a new place, taking ownership of it in a new way. The movement of the stone came to index how place itself was reconfigured under Viking control, given new meanings, and understood differently. Given the wider histories of Viking interference in older monuments (Williams 2014), there seems little doubt that these relations were being consciously reflected on.

But the burial also created new affects. The rusting of the sword, emergent in the affective relations between soil, water, and iron acted to preserve the fabric the sword had been wrapped in prior to deposition. The change in capacity of one body (the sword) altered the capacity of another (the fabric). This change was driven by the differences that existed between the soil and the sword, the metal and the fabric. These set up intensive energy gradients with differential outcomes for different parts of the assemblage. This process of differentiation is not simply limited to relations between non-humans. The act of making the Viking boat burial strongly differentiated this place from the world around it, this landscape was marked as different. New names came to be attached to this place, "Swordle" is a Norse word meaning grassy valley; new meanings emerged, new memories formed, and new stories told. The act of burying this body helped to code the rest of the landscape in new ways. Indeed, even as the memory of the grave faded and deterritorialized, the relation between burial and place was stratified in the new name of the landscape; an intensive relation replaced with an extensive one. Other extensive relations can be mapped much like their intensive counterparts, and the grave reaches out to Norway, the likely birthplace of both the deceased, judging from the isotope evidence, and much of the material contained in the grave, and Ireland where the ringed pin likely originated (Harris et al. 2017).

Whilst these affective relations were made present in the world through deposition, others remained only potential, including the capacity for these objects to be deployed to help understand the Viking history of Ardnamurchan. These relations emerged once the burial had been excavated and new bodies, those of archaeologists, conservators, and students, entered the assemblage (cf. Fowler 2013). New bodies mean new affects and new relations, new things for these bodies to do. None of these relations are in the elements of the boat grave any more than they were in the bodies of mourners in the tenth century AD or the bodies of archaeologists in 2011, they were always in the interstices between the bodies, always in between and external to their terms. The assemblage shifts, the relations change, but a continuity of becoming can be revealed.

The Viking boat burial also allows us to reflect on the scales of relations and assemblages under study. Some relations here are intimate and specific: the moments of mourning, the breaking of the spear before it went in the ground, hands carrying rocks down the gentle slope from the chambered tomb, or dragging the boat up from the sea. But there are larger-scale connections too: from the extensive relations in space that reach out across the sea and across the Viking diaspora to the long-term relations inherent in Swordle Bay and how that draws on the properties of soil and water, the capacity of this land to grow crops, and the histories stratified into its geological forms and archaeological evidence (cf. Harris 2016a). Relations here are intensively immediate but also enduring, drawing on the power of differentiation over the long term and enfolding and producing archaeological bodies in their flow, flux, and becoming.

Thus, we can certainly describe the Viking boat burial relationally; we can say identities are relational, place is relational, and Viking worlds are relational. Once we open up new ways of thinking about, reflecting on, and describing relations, however, many more kinds of understanding and ways of writing history become possible. Rather than relying on relational as a catch-all, we can begin to map the affective, intensive, extensive, and meaningful connections that are present in an assemblage, but also reach out beyond it and connect it to worlds past and present.

Conclusion

Relations have become one of the critical elements of archaeological thought. Since the mid-1990s in particular, they have emerged as central to how we engage with material culture, identity, landscapes, and even the philosophical basis of archaeology itself. Many archaeologists now orientate themselves from a relational starting point, with others using relations as a methodology or means of understanding alternative worldviews. Given this diversity, it is perhaps surprising, therefore, that relations themselves have remained under-described. This has allowed them in turn to play multiple different roles and to work as a black box, which can stand in for explanation and interpretation. In contrast to this, in this chapter, I have argued that we have the tools at our disposal to describe and characterize relations in a lot more detail. Working from a Deleuzian perspective, I suggest we have much to gain by thinking of relations as affective, differential, and external. In turn, we can characterize them as intensive and extensive, as territorialized, stratified, and coded within assemblages, and think about their connections through ideas like icons, indexes, and symbols. These different tools provide a firm starting point to offer relational engagements with the past in a manner that allows us to go beyond the critical first step of recognizing that the past is relational. This centrality of relations is an argument for going further than we have before; we have been using relations in archaeology to define terms like personhood, or to link places through networks. If relations exceed and shoot out from their terms, however, then they are not reducible to them and are critical entities worthy of description (Bains 2006). Thus, our relational approaches are not solely about how relations form persons or things, they are about what relations are in their own right and how they exist in parallel with, not prior to or after, the emergence of the worlds we study. As Deleuze and Guattari (1994:130) would say, this is the truth of relations.

Notes

1 An intuitive reader may well have expected this category to be termed relations as ontology. I have avoided this for reasons that will be set out later in the chapter.

2 The tensions between epistemology and ontology can be confusing. However, the emphasis on people's understanding means that epistemology makes for an appropriate label, although one could also use the term "social ontology," following Alberti (2016a:169). It is because some of the approaches explored in this first section call their approach ontological that I term the third approach relations as metaphysics to avoid any undue confusion. Further discussion of these issues takes place in Chapter 10.

3 It is absolutely the case that Peirce's work, and the work of some of the archaeologists that have drawn on him (e.g., Cipolla 2013a; Crossland 2018; Watts 2008), could appear in the following section on relations as metaphysics – indeed, we will include Peirce's terms in our descriptive vocabulary that follows, and Peirce was influential on Gilles Deleuze. However, Peirce does not fully embrace the potential relationality and vibrancy of non-living matter (Harris and Cipolla 2017:126), and so his work is introduced in this section. It does, nonetheless, have metaphysical implications.

4 More recently, some symmetrical archaeologists have steered away from relational accounts toward more object-oriented studies (e.g., Olsen 2010; Olsen and Witmore 2015), arguing that we need to appreciate the non-relational essences of objects. This is a significant shift in symmetrical archaeology that has led myself and Craig to describe it as a second wave (Harris and Cipolla 2017:Chapter 10). We will discuss object-oriented ontology further in the dialogue in the next chapter.

5 Pauketat and Alt's argument shows how ethnographic information can be used to blur boundaries between "relations as epistemology" and "relations as metaphysics." Pauketat's

(2012) concept of bundling is an example of a conception of relations that is both at the same time.

6 See also Matt Edgeworth's (2011) work on rivers.

7 Relations are thus both what Deleuze would call actual (present in the world) and virtual (real but not actual). "The virtual is not opposed to the real, but to the actual," he famously says (Deleuze 2004:260; cf. Harris 2017, 2018a). In *A Thousand Plateaus*, Deleuze and Guattari (2004:287) distinguish between the two as latitude and longitude, two dimensions by which to define bodies, and elsewhere Deleuze (1988:49) retains the Spinozan distinction between them as affect (virtual and intensive) and affection (actual and extensive). We discuss the concepts of virtual and actual in Chapter 3.

8 Further work would need to be done to explore the precise connections here. Viveiros de Castro (2010, 2013) does not hide his debt to Deleuze.

9 Its haecceity, or thisness, in the terms of both Deleuze and Guattari (2004:279) and Peirce.

10 We could also add that both Peirce and Deleuze and Guattari refer to diagrams (Vellodi 2014). Where for the former this represents a form of icon (Knappett 2005:89), Deleuze and Guattari (2004:157) reserve a special role for the diagram as the virtual structure or abstract machine that defines an assemblage (Deleuze 2006a:30; Harris 2017).

3

DISCUSSING RELATIONS

Typology, difference, and change

Introduction

Relations have been an emergent theme in archaeology over the last 25 years. In Chapter 2, Ollie argued that despite this increasing importance, we have not yet done enough to define what we mean by relations and to distinguish between the different ways in which archaeologists use this term. In this chapter, the authors debate how relations work and explore connections with other traditions of thought, including Indigenous religion and object-oriented ontology (OOO). We also make space for a deeper interrogation of Deleuzian concepts like the virtual, the actual, and differentiation. These concepts, especially in contrast to Actor-Network Theory (ANT) and OOO, allow us to explore how we can think about change in more helpful ways. Before we discuss these issues, however, we begin by thinking about whether Chapter 2 offered a typology of relations, or not, and what some of the issues and problems with typologies are more generally.

A typology of relations?

SOPHIE: Ollie, I found your chapter really helpful in terms of clarifying the differences between various types of relational approaches used by archaeologists, but I think it was useful to me precisely because I was using it as a *typology of relations*, something that you say wasn't your aim. Could you explain to me why I shouldn't use your chapter in this way?

OLLIE: Well, of course you can use the chapter in any way that you find useful. There are several reasons I don't see it as a typology though. I think first of all, whilst typologies can be useful, even essential, archaeological tools, they're often limiting (Boozer 2014; cf. Fowler 2017). As soon as you have a typology, you're forced to place things into singular boxes. A pottery vessel is either a Grooved Ware pot or a Beaker. An artifact is ideotechnic, socio-technic, or technomic (Binford 1962). These typologies thus tend to make us divide things up regardless of what they might have in common. Second, typologies allow essences in by the back door, so they are fundamentally non-relational. Although we might think to ourselves that of course there is no essential "Beaker pot" out there, no Platonic ideal of this material form, the reality is that typologies rely upon the idea that there is, and it is against this which we measure the pots we find on our sites. Such an approach is not only essentialist, but it also limits our understandings of difference. If difference is just a mode of comparison (how different is one kind of pot from another, one individual pot from its ideal), then it is always negative, and objects are always slightly poor copies of some original ideal (Deleuze 2015:270). The kinds of difference I discussed in the chapter seek to celebrate difference, to see difference as an affirmative force that produces bodies through relations.

Chris Fowler (2017) and Gavin Lucas (2012) amongst others have used assemblage theory to rethink typology, and Fowler in particular has made a powerful argument for rethinking typologies in relational terms. I find these useful arguments for destabilizing the typologies that we rely on as archaeologists, and making them more productive. I am, however, wary of us setting up new typologies.

SOPHIE: Ok, so if it's not a typology of relations, than what is it?

OLLIE: The way I try and think of the terms in the chapter is as a series of adjectives. This has a number of advantages. First, it allows us to mix and match. I am not arguing that some relations have affective qualities and some are about difference. These aren't two types of relations; I'm saying all relations work through affect and difference. I'm not saying there are intensive and extensive types of relations, rather that relations have intensive and extensive qualities. In effect, I am arguing that we can provide a set of dimensions to relations along which we can begin to describe them. In what ways is a particular relationship intensive? How do its specific intensive qualities produce change in bodies? How does a relation extend those changes through space?

RACHEL: I see what Ollie is doing here as deeply Deleuzian in the way that he deploys "and" (Deleuze and Parnet 2002:42; cf. Braidotti 2019c:67). Relations are not *either* intensive or extensive but always both in varying ways. The use of "and" avoids simple classifications where something is one thing *or* another, it allows us to step beyond binaries and a Hegelian dialectic and appreciate the complexity of the world. It is part of why traditional typologies can be damaging because they always seem to want to place things in a singular box. They make difference from the ideal into a negative state of being.

SOPHIE: So intensity becomes a tool for describing relations and how relations allow flows of affect to shape engagements between bodies. But what about your use of Charles Sanders Peirce's terms, icon, index, and symbol. Aren't they different types?

OLLIE: Those terms are probably the closest I get to different types in the chapter, although you'd have to ask Craig whether type is the best term from a Peircean perspective. What I was trying to do with those terms, however, is use them to describe certain processes, the comparative levels of territorialization, reterritorialization, and deterritorialization at play in each. These form shorthand descriptions, as well as a useful way of bringing different traditions of thought together. If we started trying to fit all our relations under these three labels, then it would have formed an essentialized typology and that is something I would definitely try and resist.

CRAIG: My understanding of Peircean sign modes is much closer to Ollie's thinking about relations than it is to traditional archaeological typologies. Peirce provided a framework that is anti-essentialist and context dependent. The modes you mention are fluid and overlapping. A sign can function iconically, indexically, or symbolically or in all three ways at once. In short, to use Ollie's language, the sign modes are like adjectives, or to use Rachel's language, there is always room for an "and" when discussing Peirce.

But this makes me wonder, do you think that most archaeologists casually discussing "types" harbor essentialist motives or are they more open to relational thinking than their terminology lets on? I agree that we should always be open to asking what some taken-for-granted aspect of our thinking does in the world. Yet I also agree with Sophie that it is a real challenge to talk archaeology and avoid the notion of types. From a practical angle, what language should we use?

OLLIE: One of the issues with archaeology more generally is that it is a child of the Enlightenment in lots of ways; our practices, terms, language, and so on, all emerge in a world of typologies and modernist bifurcations – Julian Thomas (2004) traces this in his excellent book *Archaeology and Modernity*. So when we try and think outside of these categories, outside of types and outside of dualisms, it's always a challenge. It's also the case that types have been extremely helpful in bringing order to the past; it's almost impossible to imagine how archaeology could have begun without typologies. So I recognize the tensions here. To answer your question more directly, Craig, I guess I don't know what is in most archaeologists' heads, I suspect most of the time types form a helpful shorthand that we all rely on, but that many of our colleagues are sympathetic to relational ways of thinking (at least I hope so!). However, the real issue isn't what do archaeologists believe, so much as what do archaeologists *do*? So the question is, when you are writing about the past and you invoke a typology, what effects does it have? Does it make your reader presume that ideal types existed, linked no doubt to fixed and bounded people, or are you using it as a convenient shorthand to signal something else? My worry is that unless we work hard to emphasize the issues with typologies, we might tend toward the former too often.

SOPHIE: That's really interesting Ollie, and I recognize the tension between taking a relational approach that actively rejects fixed categories and describing those relations as fitting within a typology. I still can't help but think of typology as a useful tool though, even an essential one. The way I understand, knowledge relies on categories. What I like about relational thought is that it reminds me that my categories do not necessarily overlap with those of others. Relational categories, particularly the "black boxes" of Bruno Latour that I talk about in Chapter 6, demand recognition that they are situational and can be reconfigured depending upon the context.

I appreciate that the distinction between the different sorts of relational thinking you describe is in what they're doing, rather than what they are. When we use typology in archaeological practice, it's all too easy to allow the types we assign at an early stage of analysis to become reified. Is this what you mean by essentialism creeping in by the back door?

OLLIE: In part, yes, I think reification is definitely one danger.

SOPHIE: Rather than thinking of this chapter as a helpful typology of relations, which, as you rightly point out, carries all of that baggage of fixed, essential types, I wonder if I can reframe the way I think about this as a relational taxonomy. Where typologies are based on conceptual difference, taxonomies rely on empirical evidence (Bailey 1994). This might fit better with looking at groups of ideas for what they are doing at any given time, rather than trying to assign them to predefined types. Both taxonomy and typology are just different means of describing things by putting them in categories though, so I imagine you'd reject either just as strongly!

OLLIE: Not necessarily – I don't think we can reject categories, I just think we need to treat categories as assemblages in themselves, which are always shifting and becoming. Anything can be part of more than one category, but it is much harder to make something more than one type. Obviously, we have to break the archaeological record up to understand it, just as we also have to bring it together and synthesize it. The question is, by doing so do we suppress difference in favor of similarity, or allow difference and multiplicity to emerge?

LINDSAY: Picking up on some of the comments made by Ollie here about the damaging effects of typologies, I'd like to interject with a brief example from the North American Southwest. Southwest archaeology has provided some of the most persistent and well-known typologies in North America. Indeed, the very foundation of archaeological research on Pueblo communities in the Southwest lies in Alfred V. Kidder's Pecos classification, which he presented at the first annual Pecos Conference in 1927. Generations of archaeologists have used Kidder's typology, or variations of it, to sequence Pueblo sites based on ceramic and architectural styles. While typologies like the Pecos classification are useful for creating concise interpretations out of messy fragmentary data, they are inherently reductionist. As Rachel notes, typologies place things in singular boxes (for example, decorated black-on-white pottery = 900–1150 CE = Pueblo II period) and in doing so limit our understanding of the associated social relations and processes.

Matt Liebmann (2012) has made a similar argument regarding the Pecos classification and how it aggregates the 400-year period after Spanish colonization in New Mexico into a single homogeneous era called Pueblo V. The Pecos system essentializes Indigenous experiences in the recent past while presenting the precolonial past as dynamic (Liebmann 2012:31). Although Kidder could never have imagined how the Native American Graves and Repatriation Act (NAGPRA) would radically alter archaeological praxis and theory in the Southwest, nonetheless, his typology has important political implications for Indigenous Peoples today. Specifically, by assuming that "Pueblo" material culture and social systems ended with the arrival of Europeans, the Pecos typology reinforces an essential divide between contemporary Tribal Nations and their ancestral communities. This typology perpetuates a harmful set of binaries, Indigenous prehistory = dynamic versus Indigenous history = static, which undermines the cultural connections between living Indigenous people and their ancestors and has deleterious effects on the ability of tribal communities to make cultural heritage claims. The overarching point I want to make here is simply that while typologies are intellectually helpful from an archaeological perspective, they can be legally disenfranchising.

Ollie, could you comment a little more on why you view typologies as dangerous and how this might vary in different contexts? I'm also curious as to how a relational approach focusing on categories might address the political issues I described for the Pecos classification.

OLLIE: I think typologies in almost every context have the same broad philosophical issues that I listed at the start of the chapter: they essentialize and reify particular things; they homogenize; and they produce a negative rather than positive view of difference. Typology often becomes not a means but an end in itself – I once had a famous archaeologist tell me that a site I had excavated couldn't have a ditch around it because "those types of monument don't have ditches." However, these shared philosophical issues clearly can have differing political implications. Breaking up my kitchen crockery so that plates go in one cupboard, bowls somewhere else, mugs in one place, glasses in another has all those philosophical flaws but little in the way of political consequences. This is clearly not the case with the Pecos classifications you set out earlier. This is because assemblages – including typologies – always exist within wider sets of relations. So the typologizing of Pueblo ceramics can never be cut off from the relations between Indigenous people, archaeologists, state and national agencies, the broader consequences of colonialism, and so on. This has consequences for archaeological typologies in other contexts too. So if I uncritically accept the pottery typology commonly put forward for Neolithic Britain, it may not immediately have the same political implications that the Pecos classification does in the Southwest. But because all archaeology is relationally interlinked, a failure to challenge typology in one context helps to sustain it in another: it reifies it as a "fact," which is then seemingly challenged in other places for *solely* political reasons. Thus, we need to be critical of how we use typology in a British context not only because it is philosophically problematic but also because of the wider web of disciplinary connections to which it is linked (see also our discussions of "prehistory" in Chapter 5). In fact, maybe I do need to go home and rearrange my kitchen cupboards . . .

So can we develop alternative ways of categorizing the same material differently? One set of categories does not have to replace another, they can coexist and be recognized as working differently from various perspectives. I wouldn't want to comment on whether there is anything of merit at all in the Pecos classification, but the distinction of British Neolithic pottery categories has some useful elements to it (it helps us organize our data, helps us think about shared processes of making, the visual links through decoration that tied people and different kinds of material culture together, and so on). It also tells us about a real historical process, one that produced material things that have enough in common for archaeologists to want to place them in a single group (cf. Beck 2018; Fowler 2017). What we need to get much better at doing is attending to this historical process, the process of people working with materials that made objects, the ongoing relational processes that objects *are*. I wonder if, much like the adjectives for describing relations I developed in the last chapter, we might want to think about developing terms for objects that try and describe their processual and relational qualities, that attend to their histories and attend to what these material bodies do, and use these to identify what it is that two or more objects share.

On the origins of relations and the importance of difference

RACHEL: Discussing different kinds of relations, or better, different ways of describing what relations do, is something I think we need to see much more of in archaeology in order to add more nuance and detail to our narratives and, as Ollie highlights in Chapter 2, to stop them from becoming meaningless. Different thinkers though do not necessarily agree on where relations emerge from. As noted in Chapter 2, Tim Ingold's (2011) now classic debate about ANT and SPIDER is one such example: Ingold argues that in Latour's ANT we first have nodes and then connections emerge – i.e., that we have a world of actants and that relations between them then emerge. He contrasts this with his own meshwork thinking where we can imagine a meshwork of lines from which knots can emerge – i.e., that we have worlds of relations that come together in specific ways to make things (including people, animals, plants, landscapes, etc.) later emerge. Ollie, can you outline and explain your position on whether relations are primary or secondary?

OLLIE: This is definitely an important issue. In my chapter, I put forward the argument that relations are fundamentally in-between, that is, they are always in the middle as Gilles Deleuze and Félix Guattari (2004) remind us. I tried to contrast this with Ingold's (2011) claims that relations are primary, and with Ingold's claims about Latour that relations are secondary to the things themselves (cf. Fowler and Harris 2015). In Graham Harman's terms that I used in the chapter, Ingold's approach *undermines* objects, whereas Latour's *overmines* them. Deleuzian approaches, such as the one I argued for, normally get accused of the former (e.g., Harman 2011:9), but Deleuze, as ever, is a bit more tricksy than that. Relations for Deleuze do not preexist the terms they relate, nor do they relate preexisting terms. Instead, they emerge in parallel with them. The notion of parallel emergence, or expression, is a really key bit of Deleuze's (1988, 1990) thinking that he takes from Spinoza. This means there isn't some "primordial soup" of relations, to quote the online anonymous philosopher FT (2018), from which things emerge like the first complex life-forms climbing onto land (i.e., the SPIDER situation for Ingold). Nor, however, do we have transcendent forms of object, life, or whatever, dwelling in their Platonic cave and hoping to be asked to join the party (i.e., the ANT situation). Instead, relations and the things they relate are immanent to each other.

Ok, this is a lot of philosophical meandering, how does this actually work in practice? Take the Viking boat burial discussed in the previous chapter. One way of thinking about it would be to see all the different elements (the boat, the body, the sword, and so on) preexisting the burial itself, and that the burial emerges as a result of these different objects coming together. Here the constituent parts, and their relations, constitute the burial – we have *undermined* the burial in Harman's terms. In contrast, we could argue that people decided to bury their dead comrade, and gathered together various things to deposit in the grave with them. Here the relations between the objects emerge because they are part of the burial – we have overmined them, their context determines what they are. However, the better way to think about this is how these emerge in parallel with one another, the burial emerges through the bringing together of these objects, and they in turn emerge as grave goods through being buried. We cannot start either with relations or entities, but instead have to recognize how they are caught up with one another from the start, they are different modes of a singular substance (Spinoza 1996).

RACHEL: As ever, Deleuze offers us a way to avoid binary explanations. Relations are not either primary or secondary to things but in parallel with them.

LINDSAY: I would quickly note that to me the question of primary versus secondary origins of relationships itself reflects what Ollie referred to as the "Enlightenment" groundings of much of archaeological theory. The Deleuzian solution to the ANT versus SPIDER debate – that relations are immanent and external to their terms – resonates with some of the ideas that Vine Deloria (2003) discusses in *God Is Red* regarding Native "religion," a term that is perhaps more in line with Western understandings of philosophy than

Indigenous belief systems. Deloria argues that the origins of relations as laid out in Native philosophies are actually far less important than understanding the relationships themselves and the actionable implications of these relations. As he notes, "The task of the tribal religion, if such a religion can be said to have a task, is to determine the proper relationship that the people of the tribe must have with other living things and to develop the self-discipline within the tribal community so that man acts harmoniously with other creatures" (Deloria 2003:87). The implications of this comment for our discussion are that archaeologists ought to pay attention to how "things appear to mesh to provide a whole tapestry" rather than on the constituent things themselves or the sequence in which they are combined (Deloria 2003:87). The resonances between Deloria and Deleuze's thinking are striking to me. Two scholars from fundamentally different cultural contexts are articulating similar approaches to relatedness. Where the parallel breaks down is in what to do with this understanding of relations. In the sphere of Native "religion," the goal is to develop a moral structure for action, while Deleuze's intentions seem more abstract and universalizing.

Ollie, this draws me back to your discussion of relations as metaphysics and the ways in which symmetrical approaches draw attention to the ontological importance of relations. As you point out, symmetrical understandings of relations focus on current assemblages, while new materialist approaches draw our attention to the historical processes that create contemporary relations. In this sense, Deloria's explication of relations is much more akin to a new materialist lens in its emphasis on connecting the past to the present.

OLLIE: That's a really interesting comparison. The only thing I would add is that whilst Deleuze is definitely more abstract, in the end, he too is trying to figure out how people can live in different ways, especially in his work with Guattari (Deleuze and Guattari 2004, 2013). He wants to find ways for people to live that are meaningful and creative, ways that deny fascism, ways out of the repression of sexuality and commodification of desire.

CRAIG: I hope you don't mind if I jump in here. I can't help but connect pragmatism (e.g., Cipolla 2013a; Preucel and Mrozowski 2010) with many of these themes, including your earlier points about looking at what typological thinking *does* in the world. Ollie already brought up Peircian semiotics and this is generally how archaeologists employ Peirce's writings, but it is important to note that his semiotic theory was only part of his broader commitment to pragmatism. Pragmatism asks about *what things do in the world* – about the differences that they make. This includes asking about what differences typological thinking might make for contemporary Pueblo Peoples and what differences assemblage thinking might make for our world today. Scholars are just beginning to explore the many connections between pragmatism and Deleuzian thought (e.g., Bowden et al. 2014). This is an appealing new line of thinking. It begins to bridge what some archaeologists might see as a gulf between theoretical debate and actual archaeological practice and it underscores the importance of the parts that we play in the world (not just practicing archaeology in a vacuum). As we discuss later in Chapter 11, this also relates to our specific place in the world, to our situated knowledge.

OLLIE: The intersection between Deleuze and pragmatism is one I think that can be really useful, both by helping us to understand in more detail two prominent ways of approaching archaeological theory and by helping people like me understand the influence of pragmatists on Deleuze's thought from the very start (e.g., Deleuze 1991a:99).

CRAIG: I also have some questions about different relational approaches. Ollie, as I read your chapter, one of Graham Harman's classic critiques of ANT jumped to mind. He often compares Latour to the ancient Megarians, who made no room for what you refer to as the virtual (Harman 2009:28–9, 2016a:9–11, 2018:49–51). Harman often explains this point in relation to a person who is a skilled house builder. That skill, of course, is developed through repetitive experiences in the world – including, most importantly, *building actual houses.* Yet, according to the ancient Megarians, once asleep, that builder possessed no special building skills. In short, this approach defined the world only in terms of actual relations at any one point and time. This likely sets off alarm bells for many archaeologists because they seek models that deal with the passage of time and that recognize how certain entities endure relational shifts.

Such an approach leaves no room for what Harman might refer to as a reserve or a withdrawn essence. According to him, thinkers like Alfred North Whitehead and Latour replicate this problem through overmining. Leaving the specifics of Harman's work aside for the moment, I would be interested to read more on how your relational approach accounts for capacities that aren't currently expressed. For example, we still need models that recognize the capacities of the ceramics and stone tools we find, no?

OLLIE: I don't always agree with Harman, but I do find his work on Latour very convincing, not least because even when he is being critical, he is always fair [and for anyone trying to find a way into Latour's work, I think Harman's *Prince of Networks* (2009) is an absolutely excellent text]. So I would agree with Harman that Latour (1999:122), who defines something by what it effects in any particular moment, has an issue when it comes to thinking through potentials that are not currently being expressed – the skills of the sleeping house builder, as you put it, or the ability many humans have to read even when not actually reading.

As you suggest, the main solution I would offer to this is Deleuze's notion of the virtual, which he develops especially through his reading of Henri Bergson (Deleuze 1991b, 2004). I only managed to squeeze this in as an endnote in my chapter, so thanks for giving me the chance to expand on it here! Deleuze argues that all assemblages, all elements of the world, have both a virtual and an actual aspect. In the case of your house builder, at the moment they are digging foundations, or laying concrete, or building walls, their house building skills are "actual." The virtual captures those things when they are not in use. The virtual here, importantly, is just as real as the actual (Deleuze 2004:260). An empty saucepan has the capacity to hold liquid, and this capacity is definitely real, and more than that, you cannot understand what a saucepan is unless you understand that element of it – the virtual as well as the actual. I think this is really important for archaeologists, as it allows us to think about different elements of the sites we dig and the objects we find, not just what there is at one moment, but the potentials that object or site holds now and held in the past. Another way to think about this is how Manuel DeLanda (2006:10) distinguishes between capacities and properties in the same manner. A knife on the tabletop has various actualized properties, including length and weight, but it has other capacities – to cut and to threaten – that are not currently happening but are absolutely real nonetheless. Elsewhere I've tried to use these concepts to help us as archaeologists think about cities (Harris 2019) and scale (Harris 2017). We can use this to think about the capacities of the ceramics and stone tools we find, the things they could do, even if they're not doing them right at that moment. In her Ph.D. thesis, my former student Emily Banfield (2018) wrote about the forms of potential and anticipation that are present in flint nodules and flint cores that have yet to be exhausted. When we find them in the ditches of Neolithic monuments, we can think very differently about them if we embrace these *virtual* aspects.

CRAIG: Interesting. I feel the same as you about Harman; I don't always agree with his OOO perspective, but I still find his writing fair and useful. So, how exactly does your discussion of virtual capacities and actual properties relate to Harman's thinking on essentialism? Is the virtual a different way of referring to Harman's reserved essence? I still find merit in his argument that no object is exhausted by its relations, but I don't think this is the same as agreeing with his anti-relational position (which I don't). What about you?

OLLIE: I think there are some real differences between Deleuze's ideas of the virtual and Harman's notion of essence. First, we need to acknowledge that the virtual shifts and changes – it isn't fixed. Up until the middle of the twentieth century, a piece of organic matter did not have the capacity to help archaeologists discover when it died – that changed with the advent of radiocarbon dating. The capacity to date a fragment of bone changed at that moment, new virtual capacities emerged. Before this, archaeologists often threw away animal bones as they had no future purpose. The recent ability to study isotopic signatures or ancient DNA has also changed the virtual of these parts of archaeological assemblages. Deleuze (2004:258) calls this moment, when something new becomes individuated in the virtual, as differentiation (in my paper I used this in a general sense, here I am using it specifically as Deleuze employs it). So the virtual is differentiated, and structured, it is shaped by what Deleuze calls a diagram. Deleuze (2004:258) uses the term *differenciation* for when things get actualized, that is put into practice, when you actually send your bone off for carbon-14 dating and get back a specific date. So the critical process of difference making I referred to in the chapter is actually two separate things, differentiation and differenciation. For our skilled house builder, the years spent learning to build houses have differentiated them in a particular way, it has shaped their virtual capacities. This is relational in that it has emerged through relationships with the world, and transforms the person's capacity to affect things, to affect the building of a house, and to be affected, to know when a house build is going well, or when to alter something. This capacity endures even when the house builder is asleep, in their memory, in their muscles, in the way neural connections have formed in their brain. When they actually build a house, they and the house emerge through a process of differenciation. This requires a whole set of relationships once again, this time with wood, stone, landscape, or architectural plans perhaps. To me, the notion of a virtual shaped by history allows us to think about how capacities to act endure (cf. Fowler 2013; Fowler and Harris 2015), without having to reject the relational existence of the world. I agree with Harman that no object is exhausted by its (actual) relations, but what the affective qualities of the virtual capture is precisely the capacity for something new to come about – without having to evoke an ahistorical essence.

Differentiating change

CRAIG: Your discussion of the relational (rather than essential) status of the virtual is really helpful here. Given archaeology's subject matter, how does all of this fit into discussions of change? More importantly, how does this help archaeologists differentiate all historical changes from one another, that is, in terms of their ability to affect futures?

OLLIE: So as soon as we start talking about change, I have to flag up here that I have learned a great deal from Rachel (Crellin 2017, 2020), and she will probably want to correct me in a moment. I think you are definitely right to bring up this critical issue, though. One of the points Harman (2009:104) makes about Latour's networks is that because they have no capacities in reserve, any change to the network results in an entirely new network coming into existence. This is very different from the kinds of relations that new materialists write about which are always shifting, always in the process of becoming. Because relations are external to their terms (Deleuze 1991a:66; see Chapter 2), these can shift and change without the whole assemblage *necessarily* being dramatically altered. For a new materialist, change, through processes like entropy and erosion, is the norm, and whilst it varies in terms of intensity and extension (how fast it is, how widespread it is), and it can be slowed through processes that bind things together, it is basically the world's default setting. This, however, raises a second critical question about change. If things are changing all the time, how do we differentiate between different degrees of change? Which changes matter? When do small changes amount to more significant ones?

DeLanda (2002:18) argues that we can identify moments of change that amount to what he calls "phase transitions." The easiest example to explain this with is to go back to our saucepan. Imagine you are heating water on the stove; as you do so, the particles in the water start moving more and the bonds that hold them as a liquid begin to weaken. As the temperature rises and reaches 100°C, the water begins to boil, it goes through a phase transition and changes from one kind of thing (liquid) to another (gas). The difference in temperature between 10°C and 20°C is in some ways no greater than between 95°C and 105°C. However, one change leads to a phase transition, the other doesn't. Even the phase transition isn't instantaneous though, your water doesn't change into gas in an instant; it takes a while to boil away. Nonetheless, these changes bring about something new, and they emerge in the connection of different forces – they are genuine events in the sense Deleuze (2015) writes about.

As archaeologists, we can think about the kinds of changes that amount to particular phase transitions, and how they can build up over different lengths of time (Crellin 2017; Harris 2014). We can think about how building a new monument in a place alters and how it will be engaged with from that point, even if people had been previously living on the site. That process of living might have shifted all the time, but never amounted to something as dramatic as the construction of a new kind of architecture. Similarly, processes of environmental degradation can take place through tiny daily activities, but amount to whole landscapes being transformed over the long term. Here change itself is slow, but nonetheless amounts to a singularity, a point of focus around which things shift (Deleuze 2015). It is still radical, it still creates something new.

RACHEL: Ollie has very effectively captured lots of my thinking on this topic (Crellin 2020). When I first started thinking about change, I envisaged using a Latourian approach but found the way his networks vanished as a result of change very problematic from an archaeological perspective: Harman (2009) refers to Latour as an occasionalist for this very reason. It was these problems that led me to begin to engage with Deleuze and DeLanda, as well as Jane Bennett (2010). As Ollie says, a new materialist stance makes change the norm not the exception, and I think this has some really useful consequences for archaeology. As archaeologists, we often operate in what I term a "block-time approach" where we posit periods of relative stasis that are interspersed with moments of rapid transition when we move from one period to another (Crellin 2020:Chapter 1). For example, we might present the Neolithic as relatively stable and then talk about the onslaught of changes that emerge in the Chalcolithic as a transition that then brings about the Bronze Age. Or, similarly, we posit that Indigenous people lived relatively stable lives and then point to the process of colonization as bringing about a significant shift. When we bring in a new materialist approach, where change is constant and ongoing and is not limited to humans, we can begin to move beyond this model. Saying that change is constant and ongoing does not mean, however, that it is always happening at the same pace everywhere. I look at a mountain range and it looks pretty stable to me, but geology reveals that in fact mountains are always changing and on the move – just at their own pace. Phase transitions help us to demonstrate that change happens at different paces. I also think an important point to note here is that we often do lots of work to mask change, to make change appear to slow down: so we could think about cleaning where we live to mask the daily changes that go on, or getting a haircut to reduce the appearance of the passage of time. Change is ongoing but ongoing at many different tempos and often humans and non-humans work to produce the appearance of stability.

LINDSAY: Rachel, I'm intrigued by your approach to time and its potential implications for rethinking how Southwest archaeologists approach Indigenous history, particularly in the deep past. As you note, archaeologists tend to break history into blocks of time, a tendency that creates the impression that the past was characterized by long periods of relative stasis punctuated by moments of radical change. In the Southwest, these moments of change have often been identified through major shifts in demography, with population explosions accompanying the development of agriculture and the rise of hierarchy, while population declines are interpreted as "collapse." As I discussed earlier, change has also traditionally been marked in the Southwest by shifts in pottery types or architectural style, for example, the transition from pit house to room-block is associated with intensive agricultural production. In contrast to Basketmaker (I, II, and III) and Pueblo periods (I, II, III, IV), which are divided into multiple time blocks based on demography, architecture, and ceramics, the approximately 9,000 years of history prior to agriculture is largely discussed in terms of one homogeneous phase called the "Archaic." Although changes in projectile point styles have been used to carve the Archaic into broad technological periods (Early, Middle, Late) typically lasting anywhere from 1,000 to 3,000 years, the overall impression is one of relative stability. Sure hunter-gatherers were developing different strategies for hunting, targeting different types of resources, and moving to different locations overtime, but really at the end of the day they were hunting and gathering.

As you lay it out, the new materialist proposition that change is happening all the time and at different tempos seems to offer a productive means of deconstructing current archaeological models that emphasize what in hindsight seems like "important" shifts, but are in reality just the most archaeologically visible changes. Instead of thinking about change as peaks and troughs in human ingenuity or population numbers, we might instead think of Indigenous societies (and perhaps all human societies?) as constantly in the process of changing, ebbing and flowing so to speak. In addition to challenging the imposition of Western metrics of "development" onto the past, this approach goes a long way to displacing European invasion as the final and most definitive moment of Indigenous change, this is something we explore more in Chapter 9.

Conclusion

OLLIE: The notion of Indigenous societies ebbing and flowing is a good place to bring this chapter to a close, emphasizing as it does how any relational approach to the world must embrace change over stasis. This is one example of the consequences of taking on a relational approach, and how relations impact many different areas of the work we do as archaeologists. From standard archaeological concepts like typology, to how we conceptualize change, moving toward relational approaches puts many of these things up for grabs. It also demonstrates how broad ideas about the "ontological turn" or the "relational turn" cover up all sorts of important differences. There may be connections between new materialism and OOO, but they start from quite different assumptions. The aim of this chapter, and the last, has been to open up a dialogue about what relations are, the intellectual resources we can employ to conceptualize them, and the impact they may have on how we work as archaeologists. Many of these topics return later in the book. One issue that has started to raise its head here that is of more immediate concern is the question Lindsay has posed about the relationship between Indigenous paradigms and the debates this chapter has focused on. In the next chapter, she develops these issues further.

4

INDIGENOUS ALTERITY AS ARCHAEOLOGICAL PRAXIS

Lindsay M. Montgomery

Introduction

In his now famous manifesto, Lakota scholar Vine Deloria Jr. pointedly criticizes the way in which anthropologists, albeit unintentionally, have removed American Indians from the realm of real-world politics arguing that "Abstract theories create abstract action. Lumping together the variety of tribal problems and seeking demonic principles at work is intellectually satisfying. But it does not change the real situation" (Deloria 2014:86). In essence, Deloria is arguing that anthropological theory-making has transformed people into Things. This process of "Thing-ification" is made possible by the alterity of Indigenous people as ontologically and culturally different from non-Indigenous people. Once transformed into Things, rather than human actors with wants and needs, Indigenous people can become interesting case studies for the production of abstract principles about humanity, culture, and history. The anthropological fixation on documenting, categorizing, and theorization about American Indian culture, behavior, and beliefs has allowed the scholarly world and the larger public to ignore the structural imbalances created by Western colonialism. Systemic imbalances continue to limit the ability of Indigenous people to exercise a set of basic rights, including access to land, health care, religious freedom, employment, and legal representation.

Despite disciplinary shift toward an ethical form of praxis centered around descendant communities and public outreach, archaeology remains largely informed by positivist principles of abstraction. The aDNA testing of human remains from Pueblo Bonito, a massive 650-room structure in New Mexico's Chaco Canyon, offers one example of how Indigenous concerns and values have been rendered secondary to anthropological interests (Figure 4.1). In 2017, an interdisciplinary team of 14 researchers published an article in the journal *Nature Communications* documenting their findings based on extracted

FIGURE 4.1 Pueblo Bonito, Chaco Canyon, New Mexico.

Source: Photograph by Mike Adler, 2019.

mitochondrial DNA from nine individuals buried in room 33 at Pueblo Bonito (Kennet et al. 2017). Housed at the American Museum of Natural History (AMNH), the room 33 remains were determined to be "culturally unidentifiable" in June of 2000 following protocols established under NAGPRA (Balter 2017a, 2017b). Prior to approving the new DNA research, the AMNH failed to consult with contemporary Pueblo groups or the Navajo Nation, all of whom are recognized as having an ancestral connection to Chaco.

This recent case reflects elements of Deloria's commentary, made nearly 50 years earlier, in several ways. First, the question. The researchers sought to prove the sociocultural relationships between the early residents of Chaco and contemporary Indigenous peoples. They also wanted to provide evidence for a general theory about the development of social status in "complex" societies. These questions, to which many Pueblo and Navajo Peoples already have well-established answers, largely reflect archaeological investments in theorizing about social transformation and political organization rather than Indigenous interests or questions. Second, the ethics. While the AMNH had fulfilled its legal obligations under NAGPRA, the research team's failure to consult with tribal leaders prior to studying the human remains reflects a clear disregard for the concerns of descendant communities and reaffirms the asymmetrical relationships between anthropologists and Indigenous communities. Both of these points gesture toward the ways that anthropologists continue to create abstract theories about Indigenous peoples that render them mute in contemporary discourse.

This disciplinary history of turning Indigenous people into Things to be studied and theorized about begs the question: Is it possible for anthropological theory to engage with Indigenous alterity in ways that do not render actual Indigenous people and problems invisible? From one perspective, the answer to this question is a resounding no. The very act of studying Indigenous people, even when doing so collaboratively, requires some level of abstraction, which can have alienating effects. Alternatively, other scholars have responded to this question by turning to Indigenous worldviews as a source of culturally grounded theory-making (see also Chapter 10). While there is certainly a growing consideration of Indigenous worldviews within archaeology, this approach draws forth another essential question: Is it possible to write Native histories that employ Indigenous understandings of the world? Although somewhat dismaying, Deloria (1972:31) may be right when he said that writing a history of Indigenous people, "in terms of a universe that is alive and not dead is asking too much of the American people." Indeed, it is one thing to try to understand another way of thinking, but it is a very different enterprise to reason in the style of the Other's worldview (Meyer and Ramirez 1996:92). This chapter struggles through these questions by tracing out how anthropologists have typically approached Indigenous alterity and the implications of taking up Indigenous alterity as a theoretical framework.

Indigenous alterity and anthropology

Within the social sciences, alterity has largely been conceptualized in one of two ways: alterity as Other and alterity as radical difference. An understanding of alterity as Otherness reflects a long-standing and broadly held practice among all humans to define themselves in relationship to what they are not. Alternatively, alterity as radical difference reflects a theoretical move situated within the ontological turn (discussed further in Chapters 10 and 11), which positions Indigenous worldviews within the same intellectual plane as Western theory.

Within the discipline of anthropology more particularly, Indigenous alterity has served as a mirror for the Western self. Specifically, the concept of "culture" has provided anthropologists with a vocabulary for discussing various forms of alterity (Venkatesan 2010:181). For early anthropologists, non-western people could be differentiated from westerners and from one another based on a set of qualitative criteria, including their ceremonies, values, and material culture (Grinde 1995:215). In an effort to document Otherness, nineteenth-century anthropologists sought out groups who had radically different lifeways from the West, a practice that reflects the discipline's ties with European imperialism and settler colonialism (Said 1978). This was a deliberately comparative enterprise, the intent of which was to develop functional, symbolic, cognitive, and even biological explanations for cross-cultural differences (Bertelsen and Bendixsen 2016:9).

Early anthropological approaches to alterity as difference took an explicitly anti-historical stance toward Otherness. While the Western self was understood as universal, cosmopolitan, global, and constantly changing, the Indigenous Other was understood to be static, timeless, rooted in place, and ruled by tradition (Shepherd 2017:34). These perceptions were informed by a linear logic that placed non-Europeans (i.e., "primitives") outside of time and excluded them from modernity, a category conflated with "civilization" (Linke 2012:191). This discourse continues in various forms into the present and perpetuates the notion that Indigenous science and philosophy represent cultural failures (Whitt 1995:250).

Since the 1990s, alterity has taken on new dimensions in anthropology. The reconceptualization of alterity as radical difference is situated within a broader turn toward ontology. The essential intervention of the ontological turn has been to "recalibrate the level at which analysis takes place" (Course 2010:248). This represents a shift away from explaining why cross-cultural difference exists to engaging in experimental conceptualizations that may enable us to understand these fundamentally different vantage points (Holbraad 2009:439). While the traditional approach to culture draws on Western analytical concepts to understand the behavior, beliefs, and practices of the Other, the ontological approach insists that attending to data should transform our analytical concepts. Scholarship within this paradigm acknowledges profound cultural difference, rather than distortion, and offers a refreshingly honest recognition of cultural misunderstanding. Although she would not have positioned herself within the ontological turn, Indigenous philosopher, Viola Cordova (Apache), makes a similar point: "A dialogue with an alien other requires, first of all, an acceptance that there is the possibility of an other as *other* (and not simply a distortion of oneself)" (Cordova 2007:75).

Much of anthropological writings within the ontological turn reference the work of Arjun Appadurai. In *The Social Life of Things*, Appadurai (1986) traces how commodities act as powerful symbols that express and define social relations, influence the development of technology, determine the legitimacy of political systems, and provide ways for people to conceptualize their world. Drawing on this work, anthropologists now seek to challenge some of the basic assumptions surrounding human exceptionalism and difference (Bennett 1994, 2010; Bertelsen and Bendixsen 2016:19; DeLanda 1997) while embracing the idea that agency is distributed across species, social domains, and material contexts (Gell 1998; Gosden et al. 2004; Knappett and Malafouris 2008; Latour 2005a).

Following this broader trend in anthropology, archaeologists have increasingly turned to the work of Appadurai (1986) and others who have problematized the subject–object divide. Accompanying these critiques has been a renewed attention among archaeologists to ethnography, a methodological shift embraced by scholars interested in non-anthropocentric examinations of human–animal relations, material culture, animism, and the body (Alberti 2016a). Among some North and South American archaeologists in particular, there seems to be a growing interest in using Indigenous ontologies as analytical frameworks rather than as data (Alberti and Marshall 2009; Cipolla et al. 2019; Laluk 2017; Viveiros de Castro 2014). This interest reflects postcolonial challenges to the authority of Western thought as well as efforts to engage with the traditional subjects of anthropological inquiry on more ethical and politically grounded terms. The growing interest in radical alterity as theory also reflects the emergence of Indigenous archaeology as a decolonizing paradigm and the greater incorporation of Native voices and scholars into academic and heritage management positions. These developments mark a move away from Indigenous knowledge as reflecting Otherness and toward a recognition of local Indigenous knowledge as theory in its own right.

The ontological turn in archaeology has led to a new line of inquiry that seeks to understand what things "do" in the world (Fowles 2016:21). This line of questioning has taken on several different forms, including those who follow Alfred Gell's (1998) conceptualization of object agency in terms of its relationship to human actors and that of more radical anthropologists like Tim Ingold (2013) who view non-humans and humans as ontological equals. Here I am largely concerned with the latter iterations (Henare et al. 2007; Latour 1988, 2004; Mitchell 2005; Olsen et al. 2012; Witmore 2006). In the North American context, the renewed interest in things was also a response to critiques of anthropology leveled by Deloria in the 1960s. These critiques along with Indigenous activism have produced legislation, such as the National Museum of the American Indian Act and NAGPRA, which have limited and redefined archaeological research on Native Americans (Fowles 2016:16). The cumulative effect of these trends has been a move away from treating Indigenous people like things and toward treating things like quasi-humans.

The adoption of object agency approaches by some archaeologists has resulted in what I consider a dangerous transference of the critiques of Eurocentrism, the ongoing Western colonial project, and the place of the subaltern from human subjects onto things. This transference is dangerous precisely because it erases the alterity of Indigenous ontologies in a well-meaning attempt to let the subaltern speak. In doing so, scholars may unwittingly decenter the social, political, and economic struggles of Indigenous people from the study of their objects. This is precisely the problem that Deloria commented on at the start of this chapter. Cordova has said something to a similar effect, "while the Native American, as an artifact, is undergoing a resurgence of popularity, the Native American as he actually exists is ignored" (Cordova 2007:163). My goal here is not to present intellectual interest in agency or Indigenous thought more broadly as bad practice but rather to point out the importance of politics and praxis to the application of these concepts.

The call for anthropology to be a politically relevant discipline is not new and can be traced back to the writings of early ethnographers like Bronislaw Malinowski during the twentieth century (see Gellner 1995:99). However, over the past 20 years, there has been an increasing sense of urgency to conduct research that helps to identify blind spots in the dominant system of world politics, society, and economics (Froystad 2016:230). This intellectual resolve has taken many forms, including efforts to question the theoretical supremacy of Western frameworks and the creation of counter-memories that challenge dominant historical narratives. Indeed, anthropology's long-standing interest in alterity makes it particularly well-suited to deconstruct encompassing notions of humanity and present compelling alternatives (Hage 2012:290).

The main issue at hand is not that anthropology as a discipline has failed to be concerned with politics, but rather that current applications of Indigenous thought within archaeology have generally been apolitical. This trend in part reflects the particular contexts in which Indigenous ontologies have been applied. For many archaeologists, Indigenous thought has served as contextual data to be used in reconstructing past behaviors or – in line with the ontological turn – has served as the inspiration for theories of object agency, animism, and landscape use. In the former iteration, Indigenous theory is used to answer questions framed within a Western approach to knowledge production. In the latter case, Indigenous thought is abstracted from the social and political contexts that inform it. While it is certainly important to understand Indigenous philosophies on their own terms, it is an entirely different project to "recognize the legitimacy of Indigenous philosophies when they purport to defend strong forms of Indigenous rights, sovereignty, and nationhood" (Turner 2006:116).

My primary contention throughout this chapter is that archaeologists must undertake the uncomfortable task of attending to politics when drawing on Indigenous worldviews as theory. This is because ontology directly informs Indigenous cultures and identities – identities shaped by the very real impact of colonial systems of power and legislation. The nearly 500 years of European imperialism experienced by Indigenous peoples has forged a collective sense of identity across geographically and culturally disparate groups. These shared historical experiences are at the core of Indigenous assertions – rather than anthropological attributions – of alterity. This is a claim that Indigenous people have and do make for themselves in so far as most Indigenous peoples proclaim a form of difference that Euro-Americans do not possess and contend that this difference necessitates formal intellectual, legal, and political recognition (Turner 2006:99). Archaeological efforts to incorporate Indigenous ontology will therefore have to address the historical impacts of colonialism on Indigenous people. They will also need to address how Indigenous alterity and identity are negotiated within our current political system.

Critical Indigenous philosophy as archaeological praxis

Indigenous worldviews serve as the building blocks of tribal identity politics. Archaeologists may address this connection through anti-political or alter-political scholarship. Anti-political approaches challenge the existing social order, while alter-political writing imagines radically different alternatives to the existing social order (Froystad 2016:230; Hage 2012, 2015). An alter-political stance is in line with what Dale Turner (2006) has labeled as critical Indigenous philosophy. Actualizing this approach entails a three-step process: (1) defining the principal features of Indigenous alterity, (2) identifying dominant modes of defining Indigenous alterity, and (3) proposing alternative theories of knowledge and rights based on future-oriented archaeologies.

First, there is a need to define Indigenous alterity by identifying the specific ways that Indigenous groups conceptualize their ways of knowing and being. The concept of radical alterity mentioned earlier can provide a pathway for defining features of Indigenous thought. These efforts are in line with what Cherokee sociologist Eva Marie Garroutte defines as "Radical Indigenism," the study of Indigenous:

> Philosophies and their assumptions, values, and goals not simply as interesting objects of study (claims that some believe to be true) but as intellectual orientations that map out ways of discovering things about the world (claims that, to one degree or another, reflect or engage the true).
>
> *(Garroutte 2003:10)*

In many ways, Garroutte's definition describes the work of anthropologists like Eduardo Viveiros de Castro (Viveiros de Castro 1998, 2004, 2012) and others who seek to generate analytical frameworks derived from non-western ways of being. In the Amazonian context, Viveiros de Castro (1998) has referred to this project as *perspectivism*, the idea that there are multiple other ways of imagining how to be and act in the world. While I tend to agree with reactions to perspectivism, which critique this approach for potentially detracting from the real-world politics (see Harris and Cipolla 2017:185), I do not believe this means we should abandon the idea of radical difference entirely. For me, understanding how Indigenous groups construct the world is not only an interesting and helpful tool for reconstructing past practices and beliefs, but it is vitally important for understanding and advocating for Indigenous ways of being in the present.

Critics of this approach have also pointed out (e.g., Harris and Robb 2012) that perspectival theory-building may run the risk of universalizing particular ontological positions. These critics contend that there is a troubling tendency within the ontological turn to essentialize and de-temporalize Indigenous people in an attempt to break down the nature–culture divide (Froystad 2016:231). Indeed, the existence of over 5,000 distinct Indigenous nations worldwide suggests that characterizing an "Indigenous" theoretical approach, even if restricted to the 573 federally recognized Tribal Nations within the United States, is empirically tenuous (Whitt 1995:225). As Simon Brascoupé (Mohawk/Algonquin) has pointed out, "'mining' the knowledge of Indigenous people, without considering the cultural context does not provide a sufficient understanding of that knowledge" (Brascoupé 1992:11). Indigenous cultural diversity demands that archaeologists thoughtfully consider the particularities of each Indigenous community's knowledge system (as well as diversity within these communities) and to clarify the conditions under which certain Indigenous theories do or do not apply (Holbraad 2009:436). If the goal of relational ontology is to describe non-western thought without distortion, then we must acknowledge that in some – perhaps many – cases an Ojibwa theory of agency may not accurately capture Pueblo approaches to objects, for example. That being said, there are several theoretical principles that can be found in some variation or another within most North American Indigenous ontologies and which may serve as the basis for Indigenous assertions of a shared alterity.

Principle I. **The world is circular**. In *The American Indian Mind in a Linear World*, Donald Fixico (2003) argues that Indigenous philosophy is circular and requires the observation of cycles. As Black Elk (Oglala Sioux) noted, "You have noticed that everything an Indian does is in a circle, and that is because the Power of the World always works in circles, and everything tries to be round" (Hill 1994:xi). To understand the world in circular terms is to recognize that all things are related. The universe is a complex interdependent system made up of sets of relationships. Indigenous philosophers posit that the natural world, including humans and non-humans, is "connected by a complex web of interdependencies and feedback loops which maintain the system in a delicate balance" (Stevenson 1992:302–3). Analytically, this emphasis on interconnectivity suggests that archaeologists should seek to identify and disentangle relational networks (B. Deloria et al. 1999:52–3). One version of this conclusion has already emerged within the discipline via Actor-Network Theory (ANT) and entanglement approaches (Hodder 2012; Ingold 2008; Latour 2005a).

Principle II. **The universe is alive**. In other words, there is no hierarchical relationship between animate and inanimate beings. This non-anthropocentric approach applies to the biological world and extends to intra-species communications. As Deloria observes, by expanding "our understanding of the sense of being relatives, we discover that plants, birds, and animals often gave specific information to people" (Deloria 1992:38). Similarly, philosopher J. Baird Callicout has argued that, "the Ojibwa regarded animals, plants, and assorted other natural things and phenomena as persons with whom it was possible to enter into complex social intercourse" (Callicout 1989:209). This is not anthropomorphism. Rather, this principle is based on a fundamentally different perception of personhood. Western understandings of personhood are drawn largely from the work of Immanuel Kant who describes persons as rational human beings who act on universal moral principles. Underlying this concept of personhood is the belief that humans being are "above all mere things of nature" (Kant 1964:106). In contrast, Indigenous philosophy recognizes the equality of human and non-human forms of life within nature and perceives personhood as a value-laden concept (B. Deloria et al. 1999:50).

The notion that animate and inanimate beings exist on a shared plane in some ways mirrors claims by archaeologists within the ontological turn – although this parallel has often gone unacknowledged (Reyes-Foster 2016; Todd 2016). Despite this shared rejection of anthropocentrism, there exists a critical slippage between archaeological applications of this principle and Indigenous philosophy. First, the relational approach to human–object agency has often been applied as a universal logic, an intellectual position that conflicts with the dynamic nature of Indigenous principles of interconnectedness. To say that all things are related is not the same as saying that hierarchy or difference does not exist within the natural world. The analytical impact of this stance is exemplified by A. Irving Hallowell's conversation with an Ojibwa man concerning the capacity of stones and other "inanimate" objects to speak to humans. According to Hallowell, he "once asked an old man 'are all stones we see about us here alive?' He reflected a long while and then replied, 'No! But some are'" (Tedlock and Tedlock 1992:147). As the statement by Hallowell's informant makes clear, human and non-human things can and often do have varying degrees of power or agency. It is this more nuanced conclusion that should be incorporated into archaeological applications of Indigenous thought.

Furthermore, the scholarly desire to produce generalizable statements, in this case about agency, reflects a fundamental difference in the goals of Western and Indigenous efforts at theory-building. Within an Indigenous philosophy, the principle of relatedness operates as an ethical code demanding attentiveness to one's relations. As a result, the primary application of this principle is not to answer questions about the nature of an object's agency (e.g., Gell 1998), but rather to inform everyday practice.

***Principle III.* Nothing is transfixed**. This principle recognizes that knowledge is constantly changing, experiential, and contextual. Furthermore, knowledge is both individually and communally circulated. In other words, all relationships have the capacity to evolve over time, and these patterns can be used to make predictions about the future. While linear conceptualizations of time have a way of distancing the past, within a circular view of change, "the past is a part of the present such that history is a continuum without a beginning or an end" (Fixico 2003:45). This fluid way of thinking resists attempts at measuring time or making definitive Truth claims. Instead, Indigenous philosophers posit the dynamic nature of Truth and argue that all data must be constantly considered and reconsidered, thereby denying the possibility of anomaly (B. Deloria et al. 1999:46).

Encompassed within this principle is a basic respect for alternative ways of knowing the world and gaining access to the perspectives of the other-than human. This approach can be summarized as a *commitment to epistemological pluralism* (Whitt 1995:246–7). This pluralism is exemplified by the practice of teaching Pueblo children to hold in their minds the concept of both being human and simultaneously being Katsina while performing Katsina dances (Tafoya 1987:3). One result of this pluralism is a recognition that knowledge can come from many different sources and take many different forms. Epistemological fluidity allows for the existence of a general, although not fixed, set of ideologies that Indigenous groups share while also accommodating diversity in the application and particular meanings of those principles.

***Principle IV.* The universe follows a spatial logic.** All relationships are manifested in particular places and spatial arrangements (B. Deloria et al. 1999:55). As Deloria has pointed out, the ontological centrality of spatial relations contrasts with the importance of time within Western thought:

> Western European peoples have never learned to consider the nature of the world discerned from a spatial point of view. And a singular difficulty faces peoples of Western European heritage in making a transition from thinking in terms of time to thinking in terms of space.
>
> *(Deloria 2003:62)*

Accordingly, learning to think in terms of space requires embracing a radically different set of ideas about how the world works and what sorts of relationships are important.

In essence, particular locales across the landscape are central to Indigenous identity, epistemology, and ontology. This is a phenomenological claim in that knowledge about the world derives from bodily acts of traversing and dwelling in particular places. Individuals and communities gain and share this knowledge about the world through storytelling, ceremonies, singing, visions, and dreams. These modes of knowledge transmission are not easily reduced into factual propositions, nor can they be readily tested or replicated. As a result, Indigenous principles are often seen by the dominant knowledge system as "tainted with a normative and spiritual component" (Whitt 1995:236).

Archaeologists seeking to draw on these principles (and other propositions laid out by Indigenous philosophers that I did not discuss here) must embrace a transformative Indigenous philosophy. According to John Taber, transformative philosophy is a distinct type of philosophy that, "does not stand on its own as a theoretical edifice but requires a certain transformation in the student to be intelligible, which transformation it in turn finalizes" (Taber 1983:65). In this sense, anthropological descriptions and approaches to Indigenous alterity will require a conversion of consciousness, or what Meyer and Ramirez (1996:105) have called a *gestalt switch*. As Cree scholar Shawn Wilson has argued, "*if research doesn't change you as a person, then you haven't done it right* [original italics]" (Wilson 2008:135).

In addition to the descriptive work of explicating key aspects of Indigenous alterity, scholars must delineate the dominant cultures' philosophical paradigm. A philosophical paradigm provides the "criterion for choosing problems that, while the paradigm is taken for granted, can be assumed to have solutions. To a great extent these are the only problems that the community will admit as scientific or encourage its members to undertake" (Kuhn 1962:37). Understanding the peculiar ways of characterizing who Indigenous people are as humans and as political entities is an anti-political endeavor that critically engages with European methods, theories, and ideas in order to demonstrate how these ideas have distorted and marginalized Indigenous voices (Turner 2006:106, 114).

The dominant Western knowledge system draws on a linear view of history. Along this trajectory, Science – as defined by Western Enlightenment thinkers and their predecessors – represents the pinnacle of human knowledge systems and the final stage of human development (Weber 2005:13). The preeminence of Science has facilitated the advancement of archaeological and biological knowledge over Indigenous epistemologies (Whitt 1995:237). Archaeologists can contribute to an anti-political project by reflecting on the ways in which standard practices and theories buttresses this dominant system of knowledge production. Of course, this critique is not unprecedented, nor has it gone unheeded. Largely building on the work of Michel Foucault (1978, 1979, 1980; Rabinow 1984), archaeologists within post-processual and postcolonial camps now recognize the culturally constructed nature of knowledge (Liebmann and Rizvi 2008; Lydon and Rizvi 2010; Meskell and Preucel 2004; Pagan 2004; Wilcox 2009; Wilcox 2010). Whether one identifies as processual, post-processual, post-processual plus (Hegmon 2003), or none of the these, all archaeological paradigms are in some way informed by a standardized method of inquiry, specific modes of quantitative and qualitative verification, and a commitment to the generalizability of knowledge, although to varying degrees. Ultimately, most archaeologists interpret their material data using established categories of ethnicity, temporality, and culture, determined or vetted by other Euro-American scholars.

Although many archaeologists now recognize the validity of post-processual critiques, logical positivism remains the dominant paradigm within North American archaeology. This methodological approach to Indigenous material culture is particularly ingrained within Cultural Resource Management, which describes the vast majority of archaeological work in the United States (Smith 2004). Positivism is premised on the principle of value-neutrality; the idea that knowledge claims are independent of individual or group social and cultural values (Whitt 1995:232). The upshot of this philosophical paradigm is that artifacts can be abstracted from their Indigenous meanings and translated into theories, human behaviors, or historical processes. In other words, the notion of value-neutrality directly contributes to the thing-ification of Indigenous people.

Whether we like it or not, the broader public interprets the published results of archaeological inquiry as historical "truths." These historical "truths" about Indigenous people are not confined to the lecture halls of the university or to the pages of peer-reviewed publications bur rather circulate within a Eurocentric legal system used to arbitrate treaty rights, land tenure, and political recognition. In producing such "truths," archaeologists have often excluded, denied, and invalidated other forms of knowledge. The effect of this philosophical–intellectual–legal system is the consolidation of power in the hands of the dominant society and the subordination of Indigenous ethics.

The concept of value-neutral theory goes against the very basic belief among Indigenous groups that all things are related. The principle of relatedness "always remains the critical interpretive method of understanding phenomena" within an Indigenous philosophical tradition (Arola 2011:3; Deloria 1992:40). This interrelatedness applies to cognitive and ethical virtue as well as describing the indivisibility of the human, natural, and spiritual worlds (Whitt 1995:240–1). In short, the principle of relatedness is an ontological, intellectual, and ethical maxim that denies the division between morality and scientific discourse. The link between valuing and knowing compels scholars to be aware of, and act within, the political and social worlds in which their work is situated.

Instead of producing unbiased historical accounts, the goal of scholarly inquiry within an Indigenous philosophical framework is to determine the correct way of behaving and acting in the present and future (B. Deloria et al. 1999:46). To actualize this principle means adopting ethical modes of questioning. This approach to inquiry has parallels within the Western tradition. For example, in *Nicomachean Ethics*, Aristotle argues that the goal of ethical inquiry is action rather than knowledge or explanation of practice (Anagnostopoulos 1994:67–8). This approach to inquiry shifts the orientation of archaeological questioning away from developing explanatory models of specific cultural and historical phenomena. Instead, we are compelled to ask questions about the *moral* content of entities, their role and function in the natural world, and their relationships (B. Deloria et al. 1999:47). Adopting this framework also requires broadening the types of information that we consider relevant and embracing anomalies as data in and of themselves rather than as abnormalities within an established pattern in need of explanation and testing.

An Indigenous framework also demands that archaeologists acknowledge and respect the inaccessibility of some knowledge. While Western science posits that knowledge is something attainable by all rational beings, most Indigenous knowledge systems are not so egalitarian and therefore the question of when, where, and who accesses information about the past is of paramount concern. Chip Colwell and T.J. Ferguson (2004) have offered up the notion of *Virtue Ethics* as a method for structuring archaeological practice in a way that respects the core values of Indigenous groups. A virtue-based approach promotes the adoption of research that draws on Indigenous moral behaviors (e.g., humility, caution, generosity, honesty) and uses these values to determine what questions to ask and how to disseminate the answers to these questions.

The concepts of respect and reciprocity are key features of a culturally grounded virtue ethics approach (McPherson and Rabb 2011:89). Respect mediates all relationships, including human–human interactions and human interactions with the natural world and its non-human inhabitants (Whitt 1995:243). This perspective runs up against the Western belief that nature has no intrinsic value and therefore respect is reserved exclusively for human beings. The Western approach suggests that non-human inhabitants and the land lack significant moral standing, a belief that leaves them vulnerable to systemic abuse (Whitt 1995:245). Within the Western tradition, the association of Indigenous people with the land has made them into second-class citizens within the natural order, thus opening them up to the same forms of exploitation as non-human elements. As Winona LaDuke contends, "as the land suffers, so suffer the people. Whether they are citizens of the natural or the synthetic order, in the end there is no escaping this basic link" (LaDuke 1983:iv). The centrality of respect and reciprocity in Indigenous philosophy has two important implications for archaeology. From a practical standpoint, this principle demands that archaeologists learn about the value systems that govern human (and non-human) interactions among descendant community members. Second, this ethical principle implores archaeologists to incorporate these principles into the analytical process at all phases of inquiry.

Finally, a critical Indigenous philosophy must use Indigenous ontologies to assert an alternative theory of rights, sovereignty, and nationhood. Realistically, this means broadening the philosophical base from which the language of rights is drawn, rather than trying to dictate (because this is unlikely to happen) how Indigenous rights are conceptualized and implemented (Turner 2006:121). Paul Nadasdy (2007) makes clear the important role that anthropology plays in upholding and potentially deconstructing Western political–legal practices. In discussing the hunting practices of First Nations communities living throughout the Yukon, Nadasdy notes the way in which wildlife management agencies and land claims judges continue to ignore Indigenous conceptions of human–animal relations despite well-established ethnographic evidence regarding these practices. Anthropology and social theory, more broadly, has been complicit in maintaining the ontological divide between humans, animals, and objects, a divide that directly contributes to the political marginalization of Indigenous people and thought (Povinelli 1995). If we as scholars are committed to incorporating Indigenous knowledge into management and development processes (which I am), then we must abandon such engrained ontological assumptions. As Nadasdy points out, this will take more than simply suspending our disbelief about what Indigenous people say and will instead entail a combination of agnosticism and a "willingness to treat extraordinary experiences as data and take them into account in our theory making" (2007:37).

Archaeologists are well-positioned to contribute to the production of an alternative theory of rights by challenging the current legal framework upon which Indigenous alterity is adjudicated. Contemporary Indigenous people are recognized by the dominant society as legally, culturally, and ontologically outside of the modern Western nation state. The explicit link between alterity and legal status was made clear by the Supreme Court in the *1913 United States v. Sandoval case*, in which the court determined that Pueblo People were still "Indians" by nature of their race, customs, and domestic government and therefore, comprise an "inferior people . . . requiring special consideration and protection like other Indian communities" (Wiseman n.d.:2). In order to claim this alterity in a court of law, Indigenous people must prove that they are sufficiently and substantially outside of Western culture.

Indigenous groups have used archaeological investigations along with ethnographic research and oral histories to demonstrate their alterity in order to gain political power within the Western legal system. In some instances, archaeological evidence and Indigenous claims align. A recent example of this is the

Thomasina E. Jordan Indian Tribes of Virginia Federal Recognition Act (H.R. 948) passed in January of 2018, which granted federal recognition to the Chickahominy, the Eastern Chickahominy, the Upper Mattaponi, the Rappahannock, the Monacan, and the Nansemond tribes. The passage of this bill was directly facilitated by several scholars at William & Mary College (e.g., Gallivan 2016) whose work provided archaeological and historical evidence for the long-term occupation of eastern Virginia by these six newly recognized communities (McClain 2018).

While Indigenous communities may marshal anthropological evidence proving their alterity in order to win rights-based legal cases, archaeology has also served to undermine Indigenous claims to political recognition. The current legal framework requires Indigenous people to establish a relatively consistent form of alterity over time. Archaeological discourses, which posit a radical disjuncture between past and present peoples, undermine such attempts to demonstrate continuity. As has been noted by several scholars, the archaeological habit of dividing the past into prehistory and history reifies the notion that the arrival of Europeans in the Americas was the definitive moment in Indigenous history (Lightfoot 1995; Scheiber and Mitchell 2010). The continued use of this temporal division within the discipline perpetuates the implicit belief that Western colonialism represents a cataclysmic moment in Indigenous history – a moment that resulted in a fundamental break between contemporary Indigenous groups and Indigenous people in the distant and deep pasts. For example, archaeological cultures, such as the Hohokam (1–1450 AD), have been made into temporally bounded anthropological Others who are perceived as distinct from their living Indigenous ancestors, the O'odham who are in turn positioned as legally different from the federally recognized Pima tribe (Wilcox 2010:16–18). In this particular scenario, archaeological conceptions of time and history run counter to Indigenous assertions of alterity based on a sustained engagement with a particular landscape and a set of cultural practices. Within this framework, living Indigenous people occupy a position of alterity vis-à-vis their ancestors, placing them in a double bind.

Returning to the Virginia case already discussed, one of the barriers to federal recognition for these six tribes had been the intense focus by archaeologists on the British colonial site of Jamestown and subsequent Indian–White relations, most popularly the John Smith–Pocahontas mythology. Scholarly bias toward the post-European period of settlement in the northeastern United States has facilitated the erasure of a precolonial Indigenous past in the region. Commenting on recent archaeological excavations at the Indigenous settlement of *Werowocomoco*, Chickahominy Chief Stephen R. Adkins challenged the idea that "American" history began with Jamestown. In a 2013 press conference, Adkins argued that new archaeological evidence has "ripped to shreds the Anglo-centric term 'pre-history' as it relates to the history of this land and its Indigenous people prior to the arrival of the invaders in 1607" (McClain 2018).

In summary, the prehistory–history divide hinders the development of an alternative theory of rights and Indigenous assertions of sovereignty. It does so by presenting contemporary Indigenous people as fundamentally different from Indigenous actors in the past. By creating and reifying this position of alterity through scholarly discourse, archaeologists undermine Indigenous claims to a direct and sustained connection between themselves and their ancestors. In essence, the Western legal systems have granted archaeologists the power to legislate when and who can claim alterity. This power has been used to both support Indigenous claims to political Otherness and sovereignty and undermine the basis for such claims. Until the dual construction of Indigenous alterity is addressed, archaeological contributions to an alternative theory of Indigenous rights will be limited.

Many archaeologists have recognized the problematic nature of the prehistory–history divide – although perhaps for different reasons – and have sought to dismantle it by reframing Indigenous actions as continually negotiated processes of adaptation and persistence that continue into the present (Liebmann 2012; Panich 2013; Silliman 2009, 2010). Another means of contributing to the articulation of an alternative legal framework is by conducting research on Indigenous conceptions of ownership, rights, and arbitration and advocating for the incorporation of these constructs into the legal system. One ramification of taking this position ought to be the displacement of "scientific" expertise as the only legitimate body of evidence in legal cases pertaining to Indigenous alterity and a more consistent recognition of the value of oral histories and personal narratives.

Conclusion

To conclude, I would like to return briefly to the question posed at the beginning of this chapter: Is it possible for anthropological theory to engage with Indigenous alterity in such a way that it does not render Indigenous people and problems invisible? Although this will be a difficult task requiring a dramatic reorientation in the analytical basis of anthropology, I believe that the answer to this question is yes. Despite areas of incommensurability, it is possible to use radical Indigenous alterity to inform archaeological praxis. Embracing Indigenous ontological alterity deliberately moves against scholarly attempts at "color blindness," an approach that views elucidating difference as promoting prejudice and therefore something to be avoided (Grinde 1995:215). Alterity also serves as an important counterbalance to liberal leanings toward "multiculturalism" – inclinations that reinforce Eurocentric notions positing the superiority of Western civilization.

While non-Indigenous intellectuals certainly have a role to play in developing these alternative paradigms, Indigenous scholars are central to actualizing this alter-political approach. In *This Is Not a Peace Pipe*, Turner uses the term "word warriors" to describe Indigenous intellectuals "who engage the imposed legal and political discourses of the state guided by the belief that the knowledge and skills to be gained by engaging in such discourses are necessary for the survival of all Indigenous people" (Turner 2006:922). The growing number of Indigenous archaeologists who are educated in European legal, historical, and political discourses have taken up this role as word warriors within the discipline of archaeology (for some examples, see Atalay 2006; Laluk 2017; Martinez 2012; Panich and Schneider 2014; Watkins 2000; Wilcox 2010).

Incorporating Indigenous ontologies into archaeological practice has far-reaching implications for the methods archaeologists employ and the questions they ask. For example, archaeologists ought to move away from universalizing models of object agency, which displace postcolonial critiques onto objects. Embracing Indigenous critical philosophy will also entail adopting new modes of inquiry that are guided by Indigenous values and an attentiveness to ethical praxis (Denzin et al. 2008). Finally, Indigenous alterity demands that archaeologists attend to politics, either in the form of critique (anti-politics) or in an effort to imagine an alternative system (alter-politics). This entails not only explicating Indigenous ways of thinking but also creating bridges between Indigenous philosophy and the dominant language and ideals upon which the Western legal system is based (Kymlicka 1989:154). Ultimately, thinking deeply about Indigenous difference offers a pathway for unraveling nationalistic narratives that seek to unify a diverse set of people across a vast geographic territory by claiming historical and cultural unity. These narratives ignore the rich histories, social institutions, and, indeed, power of Indigenous societies in the past in order to avoid the painful and uncomfortable task of explaining how Indigenous power has been repressed in the present (Grinde 1995:203).

5

DISCUSSING INDIGENOUS DIFFERENCE

Translation, ontology, and the future of European prehistory

Introduction

In this chapter, the authors debate some of the issues arising from Chapter 4. The relationship between Indigenous knowledge and the kinds of debate in archaeological theory with which this volume wrestles is critical here. Beginning with object agency, this chapter asks about the similarities between, for example, the relational approaches that characterize posthumanism and some elements of Indigenous knowledge. Is it helpful to compare these things at all, or does that undermine the status of the latter by casting it in terms that are not its own? How do we translate and articulate different approaches, and could this lead to new forms of archaeological practice? What are the implications and risks of Indigenous knowledge spilling out past the boundaries we set up as archaeologists? In this context, the critical term metaontology comes to the fore, raising the issue not only of our own ontologies, but also how these relate to one another, and the kinds of knowledge claims they make. The chapter finishes with a debate about "prehistory"; should this concept be used in Europe in the light of its critique in North America?

Object agency

OLLIE: Lindsay, one of the things I really like about your chapter is how clear you are that we need to attend to the local differences between Indigenous perspectives. For example, you point out that Ojibwa theories of agency and Pueblo conceptions of objects may be very different from one another. Once you give this a moment's thought, of course, this makes perfect sense: after all, these are people who live different kinds of lives, in different environments with different histories. This also certainly problematizes the idea that

"Indigenous thought" exists as a category of thinking that can be compared with "Western thought" as well.

One of the questions I have about your chapter, however, is about the way you use the term "object agency." In your paper, you identify two forms of object agency approaches, those associated with people like Alfred Gell, and those that make a stronger argument about the equivalency of humans and things. You are critical of the second group, in particular, for sometimes appropriating the language of postcolonial studies, talking about "subaltern" things and so on (e.g., Olsen 2003:100), and of object agency approaches in general for homogenizing Indigenous views and flattening the difference between people and things. However, I wonder if I could press you a little more on this. Do you see any claim that accords vibrancy to the material world as similarly problematic? Or does this relate either to the specific language of symmetrical archaeology (that things are subjugated, etc.) or to the specific claim that objects have agency?

LINDSAY: Ollie, I don't really have any quarrel with the basic proposition that objects have agency. To give one example, to me Jane Bennett's concept of thing-power offers an important way of understanding the relationship between human and non-human actors. As Rachel notes in Chapter 8, Bennett's (2010) concept is based on the idea that humanity and non-humanity have always been in dialogue and that thing-power constitutes an animating force that works through individual actants. As I discussed in Chapter 4, the notion that humans and non-humans have a constantly evolving dialogical relationship informs much of Indigenous philosophy. My primary critique is not aimed at the concept of material vibrancy, but rather at how symmetrical archaeology has adopted a politicized rhetoric without attending to the politics of that rhetoric. What I mean is that I find it problematic to use terms like "subaltern" and "subjugated," which derive from a decolonizing discourse on power relations without also explicitly addressing the implications of using such terms. Basically, I am calling for some more self-reflexivity in symmetrical archaeology. We need to understand the ramifications our vocabulary choices have on the living communities whose objects we are theorizing about.

CRAIG: Sorry to jump in here, but I completely agree with you. It seems to me that using the term "subaltern" in the style of symmetrical archaeology belittles Indigenous experiences of colonialism and settler colonialism. This reminds me of Audrey Horning's (e.g., 2014) critiques of comparative colonialism in which she points out that archaeologists must use caution when labeling different groups involved in British colonialism (e.g., the Irish versus the Powhatan) in such a way. Is the Powhattan experience really equivalent to the Irish experience? Horning would argue that it is not due to a range of factors. I'm sure she would also take exception to appropriating this term to discuss colonized *things* (cf. Cipolla 2017a, 2018; Fowles 2016).

Translation and transportation of ideas

OLLIE: It seems as soon as we start exploring issues of the relationship between Indigenous and Western thinking, we get into some fairly controversial waters. For example, we have seen Zoe Todd (2016) raise a powerful critique of how Bruno Latour in particular and the ontological turn in general have adopted ideas from Indigenous groups without acknowledgment. Alternatively, Darryl Wilkinson (2017b) has argued that there are significant differences between current trends in posthumanism (broadly defined) and the kinds of thinking he detects amongst past and present Indigenous groups.

More generally, your chapter and these debates raise questions for me about the place of Indigenous thought outside of the specific contexts from which it emerges. As someone who works with the European past, I find myself in a bit of a quandary here. On the one hand, I have no difficulty in accepting that drawing on ideas from an Indigenous context could be very powerful for opening up different ways of thinking about life and death in the past, especially if we treat those ideas not as *analogy* but as *theory*. This difference is really key, after all there is a long history of ethnographic analogy in European archaeology, where non-western presents are equated with western pasts and used to fill in the gaps in our understanding (e.g., what if Neolithic Britain was like modern-day Madagascar or Melanesia?). Treating Indigenous thought as theory would be quite different, as Benjamin Alberti and Yvonne Marshall (2009) have argued. This would mean not making an analogy, but rather approaching Indigenous thought as a form of philosophy, in the sense that it can provide a means for understanding the world with every bit as much intellectual cachet as ideas generated by western thinkers. This could potentially, it seems to me, represent a powerful tool for elevating traditions of thought that are too often ignored when we talk about the canon of ideas, and create dynamic new interpretations of the past.

On the other hand, I worry that if I were to employ such ideas, I would be doing violence to the contexts from which they originated. Even if I get better at my citational practices (a topic we touch on in Chapter 11), does using Indigenous theory mean I will always be severing it from the very contexts in which it gains its power and efficacy? Indeed, is archaeology simply taking yet another resource from Indigenous people to use for its own ends? Does designating Indigenous thought as philosophy simply domesticate it to Western categories of thought, and suppress its vibrancy and difference? Finally, can we use Indigenous thought in non-Indigenous contexts in a manner that doesn't suppress the differences between European pasts and non-western presents? Or are we doomed to a world of animist shamans across Paleolithic and Mesolithic Europe, partible persons in the Neolithic, and so on? That, it seems to me, risks misrepresenting the

European past and – more worryingly – de-historicizing and primitivizing the non-western present.

LINDSAY: I think you are right to trouble over the potential pitfalls of transforming Indigenous thought into theory. I agree with your critique that applying Indigenous thought in "non-Indigenous" and non-local contexts may end up de-historicizing and de-contextualizing ideas, which are best left culturally grounded. By universalizing Indigenous knowledge, we may simply be engaging in a form of intellectual appropriation that undermines efforts to "decolonize" the discipline of anthropology. It strikes me that terminology plays a pivotal role here. In many ways applying terms like "theory," "philosophy," and "science" to Indigenous thought is unsatisfying. These terms actually end up doing violence to Indigenous knowledge systems by filtering their meanings through the language (and associated worldviews) of an English-speaking colonizer. This critique can be applied more broadly to other non-English-speaking research contexts (e.g., Africa, Australia, Asia) in which scholars are compelled to filter their research through the dominant language of the academy in order to be read and recognized as legitimate.

It seems to me that one way to address this linguistic problem is to adopt an ethno-philosophical approach, actively seeking to use alternative terminology drawn from Indigenous vocabularies. This requires a certain level of knowledge about the structure of a given Indigenous language. In many cases, Indigenous principles may simply not translate into English (Turner 2006:100). This poses a problem not only for non-Indigenous archaeologists but also for Indigenous people, some of whom are not fluent in their respective Indigenous languages as a result of colonialism. However, this dilemma is not insurmountable. As Dennis McPherson and J. Douglas Rabb (2011:141) contend in *Indian from the Inside*, Native philosophy can, with some difficulty, be studied first in English, although it will eventually be important to become culturally immersed.

While I agree that there are differences between posthumanist critiques and Indigenous thought, continuing to dwell on these comparisons undermines the validity of Indigenous philosophies as stand-alone frameworks that do not need analogies in the Western canon to be valid. Placing Indigenous thought on the same level as western theoretical frameworks can go some way toward undermining the primacy of Western systems of knowledge production. This is an empowering approach for Indigenous people in so far as it provides them with an alternative tool kit for explaining their pasts, presents, and futures. In this sense, Indigenous theory-building provides an important mechanism for combating the erasure of Indigenous peoples and voices under the continuing power asymmetries within settler colonialism.

OLLIE: The issue of how we constantly mistranslate terms is definitely one that raises its head not just between Indigenous and non-Indigenous contexts but in all acts of translation – see, for example, the ongoing debate about how we should translate the term *agencement* in Deleuze and Guattari's (2004) work, that is, whether the term assemblage or arrangement better captures the original sense of this term (e.g., in archaeology, see Hamilakis 2017). However, I want to press you a little further on the issue of using Indigenous concepts in other contexts. Are you arguing that, should a scholar become "culturally immersed," it would be possible to employ a concept taken from (say) a Pueblo society to understand (say) the Neolithic in Europe? Or perhaps do you think it would be productive to get Indigenous archaeologists to engage with other historical contexts to see what effect these concepts might have? What might the outcome of these kinds of collaboration be? The closest example I can think of the latter in Europe is the development of the argument that Stonehenge was built for the ancestors by the archaeologists Mike Parker Pearson (British) and Ramilisonina (Malagasy) (Parker Pearson and Ramilisonina 1998). This was explicitly pitched in terms of analogy, rather than elevating Malagasy perspectives to the level of theory, but it has been enormously influential – I wonder if that article was written now with the kinds of decolonizing practices that have become more influential since the late 1990s, how much further that collaboration could have been developed as an explicit challenge to the dominance of "Western" theory in archaeology.

LINDSAY: As you point out, the issue of translation is only one hurdle that scholars encounter when engaging with different perspectives. Before responding, I want to hedge the following comments by saying that I feel there is no satisfyingly straightforward way of determining if and how Indigenous knowledge should be incorporated into archaeological thought. I think this difficulty arises from the diversity of Indigenous modes of thought, the constantly evolving nature of Indigenous (indeed all) cultural systems, variable experiences of colonialism, and the different ways contemporary communities have engaged with archaeology and Western knowledge systems more broadly. In short, because Indigenous thought is so variable, it is difficult to make generalizable statements about its use.

Turning to the issue of cultural immersion, in order to avoid misappropriating or altering the core meaning of the term or idea when applying Indigenous concepts as theory, I believe that it's important to gain a deeper understanding of the cultural and linguistic frameworks that surround that concept. Essentially, I am arguing against ontological cherry-picking. For example, the Hopi concept of *niyah* refers to a traditional system of shared labor in which groups of men work together to plant each other's fields (Polacca 2016). Niyah, as a theory of labor practice, could be used to describe and explain a range of shared work systems outside of a Hopi cultural framework. However, in applying this construct to other social scenarios, we must be careful not to disassociate the terminology from its larger set of social meanings, including notions of clan-based identity, the reciprocal relationships between humans and the physical world, and collective social responsibility. In my opinion, the burden is on us (the researchers) to prove that there are enough parallels between niyah and let's say a European Neolithic agricultural context to make using a Hopi conceptual framework a valid analytical choice. This type of parallel argumentation is of course much easier to muster in contexts with robust ethnographic or historical evidence to fill in the cultural blanks so to speak. Ultimately, I am saying that we should take as much care in applying a western (often subconsciously capitalist or Marxist) concept of "labor" to describe Indigenous practices in the past as we do in applying Indigenous constructs of "religion" to Paleolithic cave art.

To your other point, I agree that it would be productive to engage Indigenous peoples, as archaeologists or collaborators, in research related to non-Indigenous peoples and historical contexts. At a basic level, increasing the representation of Indigenous people within the field, whether they work in Indigenous contexts or not, is essential to making anthropology a more inclusive and diverse discipline. This argument resonates with the writings of Sonya Atalay (Ojibwe) who has argued that the theories and methods developed within Indigenous archaeology are both relevant and valuable tools for archaeologists working in a variety of contexts (Atalay 2007:250; Nicholas 1997). One example of this type of methodological cross-pollinating is Atalay's research at the Neolithic site of Çatalhöyük in which she applies a collaborative framework derived from Indigenous archaeology to community-oriented research in Turkey (Atalay 2010, 2007; Atalay and Hastorf 2006). While Atalay is a proponent of applying Indigenous traditional knowledge, such as the Ojibwe notion of *gikinawaabi* (practices surrounding communal access to knowledge) in a global context, this type of transference is largely methodological rather than interpretive (Atalay 2006). The point I'm trying to make here is that yes, Indigenous perspectives offer interesting analogies into other contexts (as your Pearson and Ramilisonina reference demonstrates), and yes theories and methods informed by Indigenous politics can be used in different contexts (as Atalay's work shows). However, I remain wary of applying Indigenous thought as theory in these alternative temporal or regional cases.

Translating ontology

SOPHIE: Turning to another of our key themes, would it be helpful to elevate Indigenous concepts to the same ontological level as European ones?

LINDSAY: Although I very much like the underlying sentiment of your question, I find the notion of "elevating Indigenous concepts" to the level of western theory a problematic on two fronts. First, unlike Western theoretical frameworks, which deliberately aspire toward universalism, most Indigenous constructs were/are not intended to be applied outside of the community. While some concepts may be more easily expanded to fit a generalizable framework, in many cases universalizing Indigenous concepts to make theory fundamentally alters those concepts. In my mind, this may do more harm than good. Second, most efforts to apply Indigenous worldviews as theory reinforce dominant Western epistemologies rather than deconstructing them. Note that we talk about raising Indigenous thought to be on par with western thought; we do not talk about altering Western forms of knowledge production to align more closely with Indigenous frameworks. Decolonization is fundamentally about power; specifically, it is about creating a more equitable distribution of power. If archaeologists begin to take up Indigenous thought as theory and apply it to their own research contexts, whether they are Indigenous or not, I wonder if the epistemic power dynamics have really changed all that much?

CRAIG: This whole discussion seems to tie back to a few of the overarching tensions that have characterized and shaped the history of archaeological thought. In my opinion, these questions speak to the ongoing tension between the historical/particular and the processual/general, but also to the tensions between relativist versus universalizing theories (cf. Hawkes 1968; Hodder 1982; Trigger 1970). On the one hand, Lindsay's argument centers on local knowledge and perspectives; in short, we should avoid situations where we simply laminate one group of people's concepts over some other people's history and/or land. We don't want to intentionally force these foreign concepts (or ontologies) in places where they don't belong. Ollie, on the other hand, seems more concerned with how knowledge of these different concepts might force him to see the world in different ways. As he notes, he isn't *trying* to find Melanesian personhood in Scotland in the Neolithic, but his confrontation with that different mode of personhood might change how he sees his own world, including the archaeology that he does, and force him to ask new questions. I suppose that this all goes back to the idea of metaontologies (which we can define as an overarching ontological position that a person holds; explored further in Chapters 10 and 11), but couldn't we also frame this discussion as trying to move beyond the dualisms of historical/processual, general/specific, relativist/universalist?

As discussed in a number of places in this book, Alberti and Marshall (2009) urged archaeologists to move beyond the classic anthropological model where the western observer assumes that there is *one world* (ontologically speaking) and *multiple worldviews or epistemologies*. They and others before them (e.g., Deloria 1997) noted how this approach typically assumes a closer correlation between Western science and reality than between different Indigenous knowledge systems and realities. The anthropologist speaks with the informant about the informant's worldview, but subsequently explains away that difference to tell us "what's really going on" from a Western vantage (again assumed to be superior). I certainly agree with Alberti and Marshal and others that this is a major problem. Where I disagree is in their proposed solution, which is inspired by perspectivism.

As someone who works with Indigenous communities frequently, I feel that it is important to emphasize that I can learn many things from my collaborators and colleagues, but I can never fully grasp those different perspectives. This isn't because I inherently disagree with them or because I find them unsatisfactory. It's because I don't have a choice – I already have a metaontology that was shaped by my experiences in the world; this means that my encounters with difference will always be colored by my western and settler colonial position – it never goes away, so I can't simply step out of it when I choose. My rather boring solution to all of this is to note how I maintain my own metaontology even though I recognize other ontologies and strive toward some means of avoiding explaining them away and translating them into Western academic "common sense." Here, I think that a perspectivist solution – that is, as indicated by Lindsay, attempting to question how Western common sense gets things *wrong* – is a good idea even if it isn't wholly achievable for someone ensconced in Western modes of knowledge production. Going back to the idea of dualisms, I think Alberti and Marshall leave us with an unattended dualism between the observer and the observed; I just want a slightly less rigid model where we recognize that our metaontology persists even though it can and does change as we encounter difference, particularly when we remain open-minded (as perspectivism encourages).

RACHEL: Like Ollie, I have found myself torn about what exactly I should do with regard to Indigenous ontologies. I adopt a posthumanist, new materialist position because I see Western Cartesian thinking as actively damaging in our world. Working in the Neolithic and Bronze Age in Europe, I have no Indigenous thinking to draw upon and so I have reconciled myself to adopting a metaontology that I think does more good than harm (for now at least). I've avoided adopting terms like "bundling" and "doing" because I worry about the damage I would do to them by placing them in a European context (cf. Harris and Crellin 2018). Lindsay's earlier point about the need to turn things into theory has made me reflect again, on whether my need for a metaontology is colonial, and I wonder if there is a decolonizing way to move away from metaontology in my own work. I like to think that starting from a flat ontology can allow alternative ontologies to emerge for me and I think Craig's recent point (Cipolla 2019; see also Chapter 10) that it is very hard to actually ever escape my Eurocentric perspective is a salient one. Lindsay's argument here is one I am going to dwell on for a while; can I make a decolonial move to a position where I no longer need my metaontology to help me study the Neolithic and Bronze Age in Europe? Or is this an impossibility, and the best I can do is acknowledge that I have a metaontology, work to make sure it allows other local, alternative ontologies to emerge, and treat other ontologies as equally real and valid? I've got no closed answer for where this leaves me at the moment.

LINDSAY: Rachel, you bring up some important and difficult issues here and, in response, I find myself turning to the words of Black feminist scholar Audre Lorde: "For the master's tools will never dismantle the master's house. They may allow us temporarily to beat him at his own game, but they will never enable us to bring about genuine change" (Lorde 1983:96). What I take Lorde to be saying is that working from within dominant systems of knowledge production, as we archaeologists do, inherently limits our ability to create genuine change. This is because the sanctioned methodologies and ontologies that inform our archaeological praxis are intrinsically narrow and therefore only allow for the slightest disciplinary reforms. In other words, radical decolonization is impossible from within the Western academy. The implication of Lorde's comments for your question in particular I think is that whatever ontological framework we pull from our tool kit comes with its own unique limitations: a point that both you and Craig have already drawn to our attention. In this sense, it is impossible to make a "decolonial" move that would remove the need to acknowledge one's metaontology and the intellectual baggage that comes with it.

That being said, acknowledging and clearly tracing out differences in our metaontologies is essential to dismantling dominant ontological schemas, or what Lorde refers to as the Master's House. So, rather than disentangling ourselves from the tensions that exist between various ontologies, I would suggest that dwelling on these differences may provide an alternative decolonizing pathway. This process of dwelling entails placing different metaontologies in a non-hierarchical relationship with one another. This is to say that we must create an intellectual space in which our epistemological, ontological, and experiential differences can coexist and are assigned the same value. Decolonization also requires acknowledging the interdependency of these non-hierarchical differences. Thinking over the tensions between Cartesian dualisms and "bundling" and "relational" approaches can generate new and creative ways to "be" and "think" in the world. For me, this work requires the uncomfortable task of constantly reiterating and reexamining my metaontology and our ontological differences.

RACHEL: I love that Audre Lorde quote, and this is a salient place to bring it up. Part of the process of assigning the same value to our differing ontologies, epistemologies, or experiences, for me, comes from a reframing of difference. Penny Bickle (2020) has recently written eloquently about the need to rethink Western gender difference in Deleuzian terms drawing on the work of Rosi Braidotti (2011a, 2013). Traditional European views of difference see them as a negative difference from a norm or standard; so, for example, women suffer from a *lack* of what men have (a penis, leadership skills, strength, etc.). Deleuze (2004) urges us to recast difference not as negative but as a positive and productive force in the world. Women are not less than, just different, and that difference is a positive force in the world. The colonialist European position was that Indigenous ontologies and epistemologies were wrong, they lacked the enlightening hand of "science," and were therefore *less than* western thinking. This is obviously a deeply mistaken, problematic, and damaging position. By seeing difference as productive and affirmative, we can move western thinking away from the top of the intellectual hierarchy and recast it alongside other ways of thinking, all of which are assigned the same reality no matter their differences. Difference here is not negative but productive. In this kind of intellectual thinking, it does not matter if we adopt different ontologies necessarily, because they allow the emergence of productively different narratives about the past and are a product of our own specific context.

I recently spent some time in Germany debating archaeological theory and philosophy and I was very much struck by the strength of the German archaeologists caution around engaging with archaeological theory and particularly theory (like my own) that has an explicit politics. Following the German experience with the work of Kossina and the application of his thinking by the Nazi party, and the thinking of Heidegger, they are rightly cautious. I was questioned about how I could be comfortable with taking an explicitly political stance and whether I worried that my ideas might be used for damaging or dangerous purposes. My reply was in two parts: first, that I do not think there is an archaeology that is either atheoretical or apolitical, so I felt it best to make my politics and theory explicit. Second, that I have spent time reflecting on the politics and ethics of posthumanism and I adopt it because I think it is a *better* way of thinking than the dominant ways of thinking in Euro-America at present. I see current thinking, rooted in ideas of difference as negative, in dualisms and binaries, and in anthropocentrism, as actively damaging and therefore want to move away from them. I also think it is important not to be static in our thinking but to be open to critique and to change.

My experience in Germany made me reflect though – we need to treat different ways of thinking as equally ontologically real but that does not mean they have the same value. There are clearly deep damaging and problematic ways of thinking – the rise of populism in Europe and America is evidence of that. So, of course, we need to treat Indigenous thinking and ontology as equally real as Euro-American. I also think we have to treat the kinds of thinking and philosophy we find damaging and dangerous in the same way – as equally real. Simply dismissing populist thinking does nothing to combat it. We have to engage. So we treat all these ways of thinking as equally real but that does not mean we necessarily value them equally. How we come to value them is, in my opinion, rooted in their politics and ethics and what they actually do in the world (i.e., rooted in pragmatism). In that process of assessing their value – far right and populist thinking is clearly deeply damaging, but so are some kinds of more mainstream thinking too – anthropocentrism and Cartesian dualisms from my perspective. This position, of treating them all as equally real but valuing them differently, also allows us to address aspects of some Indigenous ontologies we might find problematic – the sacrifice of the Aztecs or the torture of the Huron. It also allows other Indigenous ontologies where the emphasis is on being in good relation and avoiding anthropocentrism to be elevated not only to the same status as different western philosophies but also beyond them.

I think there is also something important about how sustaining and developing both feminist and decolonial critiques necessarily involves discomfort. We have to *stay with the trouble* (to adapt a phrase from Haraway 2016) when it makes us uncomfortable. We have to accept that crafting a better world for more of us to live in comfortably together involves not shying away from the difficult stuff but highlighting and dwelling in the discomfort and tension. Being prepared to, in Sara Ahmed's (2017) term, be the "killjoy" and then also at times know that we might have done things that have been damaging to others (and need our own joy killing!). Dwelling in the discomfort is something that may be new and challenging to Euro-Americans and western thinkers, but because of the history of colonialism, it is something that sadly Indigenous communities have been doing for centuries now in the face of colonialism.

CRAIG: I think this is absolutely spot-on, Rachel. This reminds me of the first time, as an archaeology student, I stepped on a Native American reservation. An elder addressed the group of archaeologists and, when even imagining what it might be like for a group of (non-Indigenous) archaeologists to walk on the reservation by themselves, i.e., without Indigenous accompaniment, he wept. Nothing prepared me for this moment and for what it would teach me about different orientations to archaeology. There was a discomfort to it, of course, but I think of this moment as foundational – it forever changed my approach to archaeology. Since that time, that elder passed away, but I think of him, that moment, and the several years we got to work closely together regularly. We absolutely need to remember instances like this one in North American archaeology because it shows us that we need to do better (and that we have lots of work ahead of us).

LINDSAY: I think you make a lot of really good points here Rachel about the difference between acknowledging the reality of alternative world views while valuing them differently. This discrepancy strikes me as one of the problematic outcomes of what I will call liberal multiculturalism, the idea that multiple groups and ideas can coexist peacefully side by side. While certainly a nice sentiment, this warm and fuzzy type of politics creates a false sense of equality, which obscures the very real disparities in our world, how value is determined, and who ultimately gets to determine that value. By its nature, social theory is often disconnected from actual social processes (e.g., decolonizing approaches within the discipline of archaeology versus tribal willingness to participate in archaeology). As both you and Craig point out, it is worthwhile to slow down and attend to how our theories affect life on the ground, before racing onward to develop new ones.

Prehistory?

RACHEL: Taking things in a different, though related, direction: Lindsay's chapter made me reflect on my job title: *lecturer in later prehistory.*[1] This title reflects my specialism in the Neolithic and Bronze Age in Europe (particularly Britain and Ireland). In Europe, some archaeologists would argue that there is a significant and important divide between prehistory and what follows because with the emergence of writing and the spread of the Roman Empire, we undergo a significant and important transformation. Others might suggest that retaining the term "prehistory" in Europe allows us to demonstrate that Europe had a time before writing, and that we can use our prehistoric narratives to demonstrate the richness, complexity, and diversity of ways of life at this time. Other archaeologists still might argue that it highlights a key difference in methodology: that we study a time before texts when archaeology (and in some contexts oral histories) provides our data. I can see the deeply damaging nature of the term outside Europe (see also Schmidt and Mrozowski 2013); despite this, I realize, I have retained the term in my own work: I teach modules in "prehistory," I've published books with "prehistory" in the title, and I use the term to explain what I do to the general public. Schmidt and Mrozowski (2013:5) largely let European prehistorians off the hook by writing that they: "respect the embedded identities of prehistorians working in Europe and outside the colonized world" – effectively saying if you do not work in the colonized world, we understand why you want to retain the term. I now wonder whether we should be abandoning the term entirely – because for any good it might do within Europe, it is also doing much more damage elsewhere.

LINDSAY: I agree that the concept of "prehistory" is truly hard to get away from, both inside and outside the colonized world. Even though I am a staunch advocate for doing away with the history–prehistory divide, I find these terms slipping into my own writing, and especially speaking, more often than I would like to admit. I think part of the reason for this is that as a discipline, archaeology has not come up with any viable alternatives for talking about these different temporal periods and their salient evidentiary differences. This is something that we will need to do if we are serious about actually moving away from "prehistory."

CRAIG: Great points! This brings to mind some recent work on the limitations of how archaeologists in North America classify and essentialize different periods. Lee Panich and Tsim Schneider (2019) convincingly demonstrate how the standard set of classifications (e.g., prehistoric, protohistoric, historic) used in professional archaeology limit archaeologists ability to "see" Indigenous histories in the western United States after the start of European settler colonialism. They looked at almost 900 archaeological sites recorded in a particular county in northern California and showed how these classifications misrepresent the archaeological sites they typify. For example, a number of sites labeled "prehistoric" also included settler colonial-era deposits – sometimes dating well into the nineteenth century. In the end, Panich and Schneider recommend using calendrical dates when classifying archaeological sites and, of course, being more diligent about noting when sites are multitemporal. I bring this up because it shows just how dangerous certain broad labels are when used haphazardly. What about simply employing smaller, more specific scales when typifying titles and research foci?

LINDSAY: Panich and Schneider's study is a great example of how a critical approach to the gray literature can shed light on the constructed nature of the archaeological record, and I totally agree with their suggestion to use specific periods and titles in our work. Furthermore, I have to disagree with Schmidt and Mrozowski's stance that prehistorians in Europe can play by different rules than scholars working in the colonized world. My objection to this exceptionalism is that it fails to acknowledge that contemporary Europe remains entangled with the colonized world and continues to experience economic benefits and sociopolitical privileges, which are the legacy of hundreds of years of colonialism. In this sense, European prehistorians can never really be "outside" the colonized world. If we acknowledge that the intellectual landscape of Europe, just like Africa, Australia, New Zealand, and the Americas, has been intricately impacted by colonialism, then the question shifts from "is prehistory an appropriate term to use in current or former colonies?" to "is the term prehistory analytically important for framing the past or not?" This is a discipline-level question, not a regional issue. Although I am sure many people will disagree with me, I think that continuing to use the term "prehistory" in the European context assigns a special status to Europe and reifies the legitimacy of this term. We should stop doing that.

RACHEL: What a necessary study you mention there Craig – providing that kind of quantitative evidence for erasure is really powerful. My continued use of the term prehistory *is* damaging, it relies on a form of exceptionalism, and it denies the central role of Europe in colonization. My initial reaction to the suggestion to stop using the term prehistory was "but that is what I do, that is who I am" – dwelling longer in my discomfort I realize I need to abandon the term. Since our meeting in Syracuse, I've been beginning to reshape my practice, but I am very much a work in process. I've noticed how often I use the term, how easily (as you note, Lindsay) it slips out, and I'm working toward replacing it. As part of a larger decolonial project at Leicester, we are busy renaming modules, and Ollie and I are teaching a seminar in one of our courses that specifically asks whether the term prehistory is colonial so that we can engage our students with this issue. I've had disagreements with some colleagues when I've mentioned that I am trying to no longer use the term.

To return to the earlier point, about dwelling in the discomfort, Europeans need to think about the damage the term prehistory does and the pain it causes; but we cannot stop there. Drawing again on Braidotti's (2019a:470–1) feminist thinking, she talks about the need for an affirmative ethics, that we have to confront the negative and the pain and then not see that as the end task but the one that leads on to the next task: creating new positive possible futures. So yes, I do not want to use the term prehistory anymore – but as you recognize Lindsay – we now need to take the next step and work out what other language we can use instead. As Panich and Schneider point out, I think that within the discipline we already have the terms to move beyond it by being more specific in our language: "I study the Bronze Age and Neolithic," "I specialize in the period 3000–1500 cal BCE." Where I find it more challenging is with the general public; at university open days, "prehistory" is the term I rely on to explain what I do, and I know that for many people the phrase "Bronze Age" might be quite meaningless. I wonder if the key with this kind of interaction with non-specialists is for archaeologists to take the extra time to explain what, where, and when we study even if that does mean we do not get as much time to do the detail as we might like.

CRAIG: This is a good point, Rachel. When I address visitors in the museum, I come across similar challenges with discussing the past. Instead of referring to "prehistory" versus "history," I try to talk in terms of how many years before present. I also increasingly reference "long-term" histories as a way of encompassing both Indigenous "prehistories" and "histories." This opens up the conversations to *continuities* across this divide and to the fact that Indigenous "prehistories" are just as dynamic as more recent Indigenous histories.

Conclusion

LINDSAY: Over the course of this discussion, the issue of translation emerged as a central topic of debate. We discussed specific definitions of terms like object agency and theory as well as the legitimacy of using particular concepts, like "prehistory". While all the authors agreed that the term "prehistory" has damaging effects for Indigenous peoples in North America, we debated whether it can and should be used in the European context. Should archaeologists working outside of the colonized world have to play by the same theoretical and rhetorical rules and how do we convey these debates and theoretical shifts to a public audience? The question of literal translation also emerged in this discussion; can Indigenous concepts be conveyed properly in English? The topic of translation emerged yet again in our debate over whether Indigenous thought can or should be used in non-Indigenous contexts. While some authors argued that applying Indigenous philosophy to alternative temporal and cultural cases, for example, Neolithic Europe, might do the important work of placing Indigenous thinking on par with western theory, others discussed the potential dangers in such acts of transference and the problematic nature of generalization.

The topic of decolonization was also at the heart of many of our conversations. Authors working in both Europe and North America questioned how they might decolonize their own work and what role metaontology might play in this process. What emerged from this discussion was the notion of dwelling in discomfort – the idea that critical self-reflection is an important step toward coming to terms with the colonial baggage of anthropology and working to undermine, if not undo, the harm this colonial legacy has enacted. In the next chapter, Sophie takes this call for self-reflection in a new direction sparked by her experiences with aphantasia and the implication this cognitive disposition has for thinking through how and what theories archaeologists apply to peoples in the past. Through a case study on Byzantine song, she lays out the particular implications of using phenomenological and Actor-Network Theory based approaches to understand embodied experiences in the first millennium CE.

Note

1 Since we wrote this dialogue, I have changed my job title to "lecturer in archaeology."

6

A SONG OF BYZANTIUM

Sophie V. Moore

Introduction

Imagine yourself in a little basilica church somewhere between the fourth and seventh centuries CE. You are singing music you have heard your whole life, music appropriate for the time of year and place in the liturgical cycle, music that you learned through repetition and deep familiarity. The words are in a language you understand (Greek), even if it's not your first language, because it is the language of the church, the administration, and the Empire that you still think of as Roman. All around you in the large open space of the nave, other people are also singing, holding the same known notes in monophonic unison; the shape of the space and swell of people singing around you steals your voice from your ears and makes it hard to tell where you begin and end. Instead, you are part of a whole, the community of the church, and you feel perhaps a shadow of what you expect paradise to be, with the self cast aside to become part of the kingdom of God.

In any context, singing is embodied practice (Figure 6.1). The right note in the right place can shake your core and reverberate within you. Shared music can ground you and lift you up. It is no coincidence that the vast majority of religious traditions have a chanted or sung element. It is impossible to sing well while tense, so singing creates relaxation and the haptic feedback is deeply pleasurable; neurologically speaking, singing produces endorphins. This is true both today and in the past context that I am interested in exploring here: Late Antiquity or the very early Byzantine period.

What kinds of theoretical approaches can offer us the toolkit we need to explore a moment like this? We need tools that allow us to consider the embodied experience of a particular moment and to attend to the material qualities that shape the precise acoustic moment. This chapter argues that we need to combine seemingly different approaches within archaeological theory if we want to develop a

FIGURE 6.1 Singing in the chapel of St Mary, Cennet ve Cehennem, Silifke.
Source: Photograph by Alexander Sangster.

holistic understanding of Byzantine song. Specifically, I seek to combine phenomenology, which draws us into a consideration of human experience, with the Actor-Network Theory (ANT) of Bruno Latour (e.g., 1999). This latter approach allows us to reconsider the role of the non-human, to consider how networks get taken for granted and through this, via Latour's analysis of belief, to take the specifics of God seriously in Byzantium. These approaches may appear to be incompatible at first, but in this chapter I argue that the ways in which they overlap to produce a useful toolkit are more important than the differences between them. Because both of these theoretical approaches are relational and non-dualistic, they provide useful lenses that reveal differing elements of the complexity of past worlds. I am less concerned with theoretical purity than I am with the outcome of the analysis and the insights that emerge. I begin with phenomenology as a theoretical approach to the past that centers experience, before developing my own relational and non-anthropocentric position drawing on ANT.[1] I will then explore some of the tensions between these approaches before applying them to an extended case study from the world of Byzantine song.

Phenomenology: resituating human experience

In a book dedicated to exploring the latest cut and thrust of the relational and ontological turns, how does phenomenology fit in? Outside of its reworking by Graham Harman (e.g., 2011) and its use by archaeologists interested in object-oriented ontology (OOO) (e.g., Olsen 2010), it is often absent from the forefront of archaeological debate. Phenomenology gained traction in archaeology in the 1990s as part of the development of post-processual thinking. In particular, archaeologists studying British prehistory used phenomenology to produce new ways of thinking about monuments and landscapes. Most famously in the work of Christopher Tilley (1994), phenomenology theorized the nature of human experiences through encounters with landscapes and monuments in the present. Tilley's approach offered both a theory and a methodology. Based on the suggestion that human bodies, past and present, had much in common with one another, Tilley (1994) argued that all human experience was mediated through the material body. Thus, he noted his own embodied experience when visiting Neolithic monuments and used this as a proxy for the experiences of people in the past. This approach has been the subject of significant emulation (e.g., Cummings and Whittle 2004) and critique (e.g., Brück 2005a; Fleming 2006), but it remains what most archaeologists think of when you bring up phenomenology.

Phenomenology in the style of Tilley is by no means the only option. Around the same time in the mid-1990s, both Julian Thomas (1996) and Chris Gosden (1994) drew explicitly on the philosophy of Martin Heidegger to make a wider argument about the relationships between people and things. Drawing on Heidegger's (1971) critical insight that things could be understood as gatherings of relationships, Thomas (1996), for example, explored how objects in Late Neolithic Britain brought people into existence relationally, as much as the other way around. In parallel, Gosden (1994) argued that archaeologists could use Heidegger in various ways to reconceptualize notions of time in the archaeological record.

Although phenomenology was widespread in the archaeology of the 1990s and 2000s, two elements have combined to lessen its current impact. The first was the critique put forward by Joanna Brück (2005a) that undermined claims that the human body was a source of universal shared experience. Brück (2005a) convincingly showed that different bodies – of women, of children, and so on – have different experiences. She also argued that bodies too are emergent historical phenomena and so cannot be essentialized. While this critique focused primarily on the phenomenological methodology that Tilley had developed, it helped to undermine the broader philosophical claims as well, at least in the eyes of many archaeologists.

Second, archaeology as a whole has seen a turn away from accounts that focus primarily on human experience. Variously classed as the material turn, or as non-anthropocentric approaches, many current theoretical ideas try to decenter human beings from analysis, the very opposite of what much archaeological phenomenology has attempted to do. As such it is perhaps little surprise that despite its centrality to the emergence of relational approaches in archaeology more widely (see Harris and Cipolla 2017:Chapter 6), fewer archaeologists are explicitly using phenomenological approaches than during earlier waves of relational thought in the discipline. Here, however, I suggest that we cannot appreciate something like Byzantine song holistically without describing human experience in all its relational complexity; phenomenology is precisely what we require for this. To set this in context, let me offer a brief history of phenomenological philosophy, which should help to explain how it is that specific elements can fit in with relational theories.

The three main branches of phenomenology are transcendental, perceptual, and hermeneutic, all of which were developed in the late nineteenth and early twentieth centuries (Lewis and Staehler 2010). Here I focus on the distinction between transcendental and hermeneutic phenomenology as these are the two traditions that have been most influential within archaeology. Perhaps the most important early development of this philosophy was Edmund Husserl's (1970) transcendental phenomenology, built on Kant's separation of the world into phenomenon and noumenon, or the experience of the thing and the "thing itself" (Welton 1999:367). Husserl's phenomenology began the process of deeply interrogating the phenomenon side of this dualism. Husserl searched for a pan-human experience and saw the mind as "transcendental," a constant that relates to the world in one single way (Welton 1999:135). This approach underlies critical elements of Tilley's archaeological applications discussed earlier. These too depend on a transcendental vision of human experience in the world, where specific experiences in the present can be used as a fairly direct proxy for experiences in the non-modern past.

The problem with working from a position where minds '"transcend" time and space is that we cannot be certain that people in the past experienced or thought about things in the same way that we do today. In fact, it is highly likely that they did not. It is increasingly obvious that even people who live in the same time and place do not start from a position of shared experiences. An example of this is a condition called *aphantasia* – a particular type of cognitive disposition where individuals essentially have no mind's eye and are completely lacking or unaware of mental visual imagery (Keogh and Pearson 2018). After reading a newspaper article about the condition that seemed eerily familiar (Lavelle 2019), I started to ask questions of friends and family along the lines of "but do you *really* see things when you imagine them?" I think I am aphantasiac, but I was unaware of this until I read about it, and still find it difficult to believe that my own inner life is so different from the majority of people around me. Until reading about aphantasia, I assumed that whenever other people mentioned seeing images in their minds, they were speaking metaphorically. As I have never been able to conjure even so much as a color, I was working from the baseline assumption that all other internal human experience reflected my own. With respect to internal visual imagery, I had essentially internalized a transcendental approach to the human mind.

Husserl's early work operated within the Cartesian model of mind and body. It differs significantly from how Heidegger developed phenomenology through the twentieth century. Unlike transcendental approaches, hermeneutic and perceptual phenomenology move away from positivism and Husserl's focus on objectivity. A total review of Heidegger's phenomenology is well beyond the scope of this chapter, but his hermeneutic phenomenology holds a number of concepts that are, I suggest, integral to relational archaeologies. To begin with, Heidegger's phenomenology is directly anti-dualist (Thomas 1996). In place of the oppositions of mind and body, and person and world, which underlay Husserl's investigations, Heidegger (1962) argued that human beings could never be separated from the world in which they lived. His term *Dasein* captured this inseparability; Dasein is always Being-in-the-world. Because Dasein is *thrown* into the world, there is no essential human prior to specific historical contexts, humans are always located in the flow of time; Being-in-the-world is thus a historically situated position (Heidegger 1962:78–86).

In addition to being non-dualist, Heidegger was a rigorously relational thinker – something he has in common with ANT, despite Latour's occasional snarky asides about him (Latour 1999:176). Heidegger (1962) emphasizes the need to move from thinking about bounded objects opposed to human subjects, toward acknowledging a position where the two are relationally constructed within a shared Being-in-the-world. Critically, for Heidegger, things (rather than objects) are *gatherings*, a term he develops tracing the etymology of the German "Ding" (Krell 1977:294). This is a theoretical move shared by both Heidegger (1962) and Latour (2005b) (see Harris and Cipolla 2017:Chapter 8 for a discussion of how "first wave" symmetrical archaeology makes a similar move). The relational nature of things allows Heidegger to identify two modes in which things are disclosed to Dasein: ready-to-hand and present-at-hand (Heidegger 1962:91–102). When things are ready-to-hand, we do not think about using them; whereas when things break, or we do not know how to use them, they are brought into sharper focus and become present-at-hand. To clarify this, we can imagine three stages of riding a bike. To begin, we have to think closely about the haptic knowledge that goes into learning to balance and propel ourselves forward; a novice bike rider is paying close attention to balance and the road surface, and these thoughts are close to the surface of their consciousness – in Heideggerian terms the practice is present-at-hand. As our cyclist gains proficiency, the physical act of riding a bike becomes second nature and the relations between balance and road, speed, weather, and self are smoothed out and appear as one single act: cycling. In Heideggerian terms, cycling is now ready-to-hand; it is embodied knowledge that requires little thought. If a part of our bike breaks – the chain slips, the caliper breaks wear down, or we suddenly get a flat tire – the bike returns to being present-at-hand.

Phenomenology affords us terminology that can be used to describe the nature of human experience as deeply relational and embedded in the world. The collection of different philosophical perspectives that we label phenomenology goes far beyond a claim of universal human subjectivity. In its hermeneutic form, stemming from Heidegger's reworking of Husserl's key concepts, it shows us how we can attend to the disclosure of particular historically specific forms of Being-in-the-world that revel in and foreground human experience without denying relations or imposing dualisms. This is what Thomas' (1996) *Time Culture and Identity* did for Neolithic Britain. Nevertheless, phenomenological approaches to the past focus on human experience, and because of that, a purely phenomenological approach does precisely what many of the approaches discussed in this book ask us not to: it sidelines the rest of the world. In the next section of this chapter, I will argue that we can further strengthen our theoretical toolkit by combining Heideggerian insights with the relational approach of Latour.

The black box of belief: raiding Latour

The thought and writing of Latour has had enormous impact across the humanities, not least in archaeology where his work has inspired both applications of ANT (e.g., Jervis 2014; Van Oyen 2015, 2016; Whitridge 2004b) and the emergence of symmetrical archaeology (e.g., Olsen 2003, 2007; Olsen et al. 2012; Shanks 2007; Webmoor 2007; Webmoor and Witmore 2008; Witmore 2007). His work emphasizes how the world comes into being through relational networks of people and things, in which agency is distributed and emergent. The key point I take from Latour is that non-humans play a critical and active role in the networks that make up our world. Instead of viewing them as merely the repositories of human intentionality, or as simple enhancements to human existence, this approach affirms that it is through specific relationships involving people and things that events happen. Put more succinctly, actions emerge out of relations.

In the now classic example, Latour (1999:176–7) discusses the relationship between people and guns in a useful illustration of the proposition that actions emerge out of relations between humans and non-humans. Latour characterizes the two sides of this debate as moralist and materialist. For the National Rifle Association in America, for example, whose unofficial slogan is "guns don't kill people: people kill people," the state of a person is either moral or amoral, and the presence of the gun does nothing to change them. From this perspective, the natural aim of a killer is to kill, whether or not she has a weapon. Contrasting with this position, Latour identifies the materialists (slogan: guns kill people) as holding the position that people are transformed by the materials in their possession. From this perspective, it is a truth universally acknowledged that an angry person in possession of a gun must be transformed into a killer. For Latour (1999), it is neither the moral/amoral intention of the human nor the potential of the gun to fire that kills a person, it is the network of human–gun–everything else that can combine to produce the emergent property of a network – someone who has been shot. Thus, Latour uses the term actant, rather than agent or person, to identify any entity in the world capable of having an effect through its relations. It does not matter to Latour what the entity is, it can be a human, a thing, a landscape, an animal, a god, or a picture. This specific insight is crucial because it broadens our analysis of the networks in which Byzantine song emerges beyond the singers to consider the role of churches, architecture, materials, and, indeed, God himself.

Beyond Latour's non-anthropocentrism, I want to outline two further specific elements of his work that we can add to our theoretical toolbox: blackboxing and his discussion of belief. Latour's use of the term black box developed through his work on ANT, and it is outlined in detail in his book *Pandora's Hope* (1999:174–215). Latour uses the term to describe any network of humans and non-humans that has become so stabilized as to be taken for granted (there is a clear similarity here with Heidegger's ready-to-hand, we will explore the key difference shortly). A good example of a black box is a well-functioning computer. When your computer works, you do not need to know how the microprocessor and the hard drive are interrelating, you just take their work for granted. Being aware of the process of blackboxing allows us to take seriously the role of non-humans in producing the conditions necessary for specific actions or even producing actions themselves.

I suggest this concept of the black box is useful for considering how networks of humans and non-humans stabilize in ways that allow us to ignore their constituent parts and take them for granted. Where Heidegger's concept of ready-to-hand allows us to understand how individual human beings experience the process of things being blackboxed – the computer just working, or the experienced cyclist zipping downhill with very little effort – Latour's broader notion reveals how this process underpins a much wider range of relations in the world. When you purchase an apple in a supermarket, it is not just your relation to the production of the apple that you gloss over, important though it is, it is also the wider network of consumers, tills, farmers, fertilizers, barcode scanners, trollies, and shipping containers that are being blackboxed. As we will see, these wider networks, and the societal and personal specifics of what the "taken-for-granteds" or blackboxed elements of a network are, add a critical dimension to our understanding of the experience of Byzantine song.

A final critical tool Latour offers us is more nebulous in his research, but helpful in mine, and that is his analysis of belief. This is essential to an examination of Byzantine life because in a context without vocal atheists, whether or not people "believed" in Byzantine varieties of God is no longer the question; relational enquiry instead enables us to ask how people's knowledge of God and the otherworld affects their networks. From the vantage point of a society with a large and vocal secular component, we might spend time questioning the faith of Byzantine people in God. Did they *really* believe in God? Did God *really* exist? Latour's work shows us that these are unhelpful questions. For Latour (1999:122), whether or not something exists is dependent upon the effects that it has on the network in which it is caught up. In a Byzantine context, Latour asks us to take seriously believers when they worship. In looking for relations that produce action, we can put aside entirely the question "did God exist?" Instead, our questions become specific to the context. Were churches built? Yes. Did people worship? Yes. It is clear, therefore, that God was having an effect, and consequently needs to be accounted for in our discussions of Byzantine experience.

Latour (1999:270; Latour and Weibel 2002) also demonstrates that it is the effects of God, rather than God's existence, that matter in his discussion of iconoclasts. Iconoclasts are people who destroy or deface icons (in Jewish, Christian, and Islamic contexts, these movements against figurative art tend to come from the Old Testament commandment prohibiting the worship of false idols, Deut. 5:8–10). Latour's discussion of iconoclasts is particularly interesting for a Byzantine context, as the seventh and eighth centuries in Byzantium are known as the iconoclast period, which ends with the "triumph of orthodoxy" in 843 CE. When Latour (1999:270) discusses iconoclasm and belief, he argues that iconoclasts (by whom he means those who subscribe to a modernist division of the world into fact/fiction, nature/culture, object/subject) create belief by being intent on its destruction. From a Latourian perspective, without people to object volubly to belief, it is no different to knowledge. In a context without vocal atheists, there is little difference between how people know that the sun will come up tomorrow, how Byzantine people knew that there was an afterlife, or, given the basic level of my knowledge of aerodynamics, the way that I know that an airplane I am entering will remain airborne. For Latour, the iconoclasts create disbelief and therefore the possibility of belief as distinct from knowledge. In Latourian terms, it is the iconoclasts who create "fetishes" because they separate beliefs from facts (Latour 1999:266–92). In a context that has a conceptually clear divide between sacred and secular, belief takes on a completely different role from the way faith operates in a world that has varieties in theology, but in which God is accepted knowledge, as in Byzantium.

If we take this line of argumentation to its logical conclusion, by thinking about "belief" in the past, we are retrofitting our conception of the world to create a past in which people "believed" in God (cf. Latour 1999:145–73). When we ask what people believed in the past, we are doing them a disservice, and should instead be asking what they knew and what they had faith in (cf. Alberti and Marshal 2009:344). This may seem a semantic difference, but I think that this small shift acts to put back together the fact and fetish of the modernist settlement into what Latour (1999:272–5) terms a "factish." A factish describes how facts are also fabricated. This places belief in gods I might question on the same plane as the science, which I believe in. A Latourian God in Byzantium is a factish: fabricated and therefore real. To return to the concept of blackboxing, introduced earlier, the workings of belief and faith are blackboxed both to us in the present and to Byzantine worshipers in the past. The specific workings of individual experiences of God are unimportant compared to the effects that God had, and continues to have, in the world.

These two key points of understanding – all knowledge as socially constructed with the ability to affect change (factish) and the broadening out of Heideggerian ready-to-hand to include non-humans in the concept of blackboxing – offer us a set of tools that enhance our phenomenological account of experience and allow us to effectively and sensitively approach the topic of belief in a way that does not focus on objectivity or "scientific fact" but instead embraces the facts on the ground. This is critical for our analysis of Byzantine song.

Developing theoretical axioms

From the earlier discussion, I suggest we can take a number of critical axioms:

- Archaeological studies include humans, even if they are not the sole or central focus. This makes experience, and therefore phenomenological approaches, crucial for relational studies of the past.

- Experience is not transcendent, but rather historically located, and an integral part of any network in which it is engaged.
- Non-humans play a central role in all networks and we can usefully think about them as either ready-to-hand or present-at-hand.
- Actions emerge out of relations, and things exist if they effect other things, even if they are immaterial things like faith.

While ANT is normally contrasted with phenomenology, I believe we can helpfully combine them. Although the analysis of a black box or a network reveals the distributed nature of agency, phenomenology can give us insight into the different human components: the surprise and disruption of routine for humans and human-adjacent animals when the normally ready-to-hand things they depend upon disappear. ANT and the forms of phenomenology I employ are both relational and anti-dualist (cf. Harman 2009; Thomas 1996, 2004); combined together, they offer us insights into different dimensions of events, operating at a variety of scales and including a host of different actors. I suggest the combination of these approaches can open up new understandings of Byzantine song and the development of an understanding of God as composite, and it is to this that I now turn.

Making music matter: a song of Byzantium

It is a deliberate distinction that I am making in writing about Byzantine song, rather than Byzantine music. It is the practice of singing, rather than the codification of music or the writing of lyrics that interests me here. The field of Byzantine musicology is an active one and tremendous work is being done to tease out a sense of experience from the script of *kontakia* and from monastic foundation documents (e.g., Arentzen 2017; Dubowchik 2002). This chapter, however, is much more in line with the work that has been done on acoustic spaces, most notably by Bissera Pentcheva (2010, 2011, 2017, 2018), Sharon Gerstel (Gerstel et al. 2018), and others, in that it takes a phenomenological angle on music, albeit one aided by concepts taken from ANT.

In this case study, I will use my theoretical toolkit to bring three aspects of Byzantine song into relief. First, that singing and listening to song was a bodily experience that Heidegger's concept of ready-to-hand helps us to understand. Second, that in order to fully grasp the nature of this experience, we must consider the role of non-humans. Third, that one of the critical non-humans within this network is God who is understood as unquestionably real in the terms already defined. Highlighting these three aspects allows me to open the black box of Byzantine song and demonstrate the utility and value of these theoretical tools.

Experiencing song

The perspective, typified by the statement of Jorgen Raasted (1986:54) that the understanding of "the effect of Byzantine religious music on the mind of worshippers" is reliant on textual sources, is dominant in the discipline. My phenomenological approach pushes me to ask: but what of the body? The somatic experience of singing at the outset of the practice is not accessible through text. Orthodox hymns variously take the form of congregational chant, kontakia and troparia existed as early as the fourth century CE (Arentzen 2017:1), but we only have extremely fragmentary textual records prior to the ninth century CE (Lingas 2013:315). How then, does the combination of phenomenology and ANT change analysis for our understanding of Byzantine song prior to the middle Byzantine period? Building on recent work in the discipline (Pentcheva 2018), I start by looking for the ready-to-hand. Rather than asking about the concept of music for Byzantines, or the intention of the composers or transcribers, we can ask instead about how the majority of people experienced music in religious spaces. In doing so, we ask ourselves about one single network, one single imagined moment, a Latourian black box. This relational approach to practice can add to our understanding of how religious music, specifically the group experience of hymns sung in part by the congregation, may have "worked" for Byzantine worshipers.

The early Byzantine musical tradition grew out of the secular and ritual chants of Late Roman Paganism and the religious traditions of Judaism and the Syriac tradition of madrasha (Arentzen 2017:1). To an extent, it misunderstands early Christianity to separate psalmody – the singing of religious chants – from liturgy; they were closely enmeshed from the beginning of the practice. The earliest traditions are interpreted by Alexander Lingas (1996:26–7) to reflect Paul's exhortation to "pray without ceasing" (1 Thess. 5:17), and took the form of psalms chanted in sequence, occasionally interrupted by spoken prayers and readings. There is a distinction to be drawn between monastic and lay experiences and the development of the Sung Office (Taft 1992); although the central point of this case study is relevant to both spaces, I am choosing to focus on the communal gatherings of the laity in dedicated spaces that occurred throughout the Byzantine empire from the fourth century CE onward (Lingas 1996:29). A church "service," such as it was in the fourth century cathedral tradition, involved fixed psalmody, litanies, prayers, and a blessing. The psalmody (chanting or singing of psalms) that is our focus here was probably sung by a soloist, with refrains in which the congregation could join (Lingas 1996:29). The general point I am making holds for lay participants in services until at least the eighth century, and in some situations, significantly beyond that date.

Within the early church, the vast majority of the audible aspects of services were sung (or earlier, chanted) (Wybrew 1990:27–46). The inaudible aspects of a service include prayers delegated to individuals and the scents of incense and interplay of light, metal, textile and glass that formed the network of worship and the building itself (cf. Harvey 2006; Nesbit 2012; Pentcheva 2010; Jeffery 2018). It is likely that, as in later periods, the early tradition maintained a strict hierarchy of soloists, cantors, and choirs, who sang different sections of worship (Lingas 2013:312). Although we cannot know for certain, it is widely assumed that by the time Romanos the Melodist was composing in the sixth century CE, the entire community was expected to respond with short memorable sung verses within kontakia (Arentzen 2017:5). These verses are known as troparia (although that term also refers to other things), and it is this aspect of call and response on which I focus. The kontakion became a fundamental element of the Sung Office by the sixth century CE, although our first fully notated version of it is from the tenth century CE (Arentzen 2017:1). The development of the tradition of monophonic chant (one melodic line) passed back and forth between professional choir, the *psaltis*, and the congregation, with a drone maintained by the *ison* or five drone singers, must have been in place long before then, given the variety of music recorded with the innovation of neumes (a form of musical notation) in the mid-Byzantine period (Lingas 2006:137). Kontakia start with a soloist and the psaltis picks up the theme, which is then echoed by the congregation.

In order to begin to fully appreciate the varieties of experience of Byzantine song in religious spaces as it emerges out of Late Antique heterodoxy, we must pay attention to specifics as they were experienced. How did people learn music? How was it written down and communicated? Which elements of musical practice were ready-to-hand for the communities using them and which were up for debate, or present-at-hand? In answering these questions, we must also account for the non-humans who are playing a crucial role within the production of song, as I will discuss in the following.

From the 4th to approximately the seventh century CE, the Byzantine sung office was an oral tradition, and remained so for the illiterate in society for the whole period (Dubowchik 2002:281–3; Troelsgård 2018). The invention of musical notation in the Christian Orthodox tradition began here, but even where psalmody was written down, the system of recording used did not convey what we might think of as the "tune" of the music; it was adiastematic, which means that it was incapable of conveying precise intervals between notes (Lingas 2013:316). Instead, the system of notation called *neumes* communicated nuance – the order of psalms, inflection, acoustic affects, tempo: in theatrical terms the notation provided stage directions but not the script. By the ninth century CE, this semi-oral (or completely oral, if you were one of the congregation) method of learning music had developed into Byzantine "round" notation, which is a much more complete system; between the ninth and twelfth centuries, we have more than 1000 extant musical texts (Dubowchik 2002:277).

The shift in codification of music that began as early as the eighth and ninth centuries coincided with Iconoclasm, a period of intense theological debate and revisionism. The revisionist histories of the iconoclastic period, and the explosion in composition and textual recording of musical texts, markedly increase our technical knowledge about the nature of Byzantine music after iconoclasm. An academic consequence of this is that there is considerably more discussion of Byzantine music from after the ninth century CE, and the scholarship focuses on the technical aspects of the music, as well as the theological implications (building on the foundations laid by Tillyard 1935 and Wellesz 1961). Critical here, however, is that the network of actors in a middle Byzantine church is significantly different to those in the proto-textual early Byzantine church congregation, and a phenomenological approach can add extensively to our understanding of this latter context.

When considering the experience of singing, it is worth thinking about how people learned to sing. As already noted, the early Byzantine tradition of music was largely an oral one. Even after the development of neumes, melodies must be transferred from practitioner to practitioner by ear to maintain the knowledge of psalmody embedded in the community. Troelsgård (2018:83–4) has persuasively described this as an aural rather than an oral tradition, to move the emphasis away from performance and toward experience, but here I stick to "oral tradition" as an accepted term. The congregation was taking part in a rite that was a known constant, something that was ready-to-hand. Sung responses were required, not prompted or scripted, a significantly different experience to the majority of modern musical religious practice that involves either diastematic modern notation, which, if you can read it, gives you an exact note on which to start, or waiting until you've got the hang of a tune, reading the words, and matching up the two. The passing on of oral traditions of song creates a specific type of knowledge born of familiarity among the initiated that was altered radically by the proliferation of melodies and prayers that occurred in middle Byzantium. This proliferation could be considered an emergent property of the relationship between diastematic notation, increasing literacy, and the elaboration of the annual cycle of middle Byzantine worship.

Non-humans also sing

Beyond the texts, other non-humans also played a role. Early Byzantine churches have particular acoustic properties. Pentcheva's (2017) work on the *Icons of Sound* project attempts to reconstruct the acoustic space of Hagia Sophia to discuss the auditory appreciation of the sung rite. Her work has produced an appreciation of the depth of echo produced by the marble spaces and placements of different groups contributing to the sung office (Pentcheva 2014). The dislocated nature of sound produced in Byzantine churches was entirely deliberate, she argues. Churches were designed with clever manipulations of acoustic space and concealed choirs to build a soundscape that was uncanny and mysterious. Acoustic spaces were, therefore, constructed with an eye to crafting religious experiences: the non-humans play as much of a role here as the humans. Pentcheva's work is explicitly phenomenological, seeking to reconstruct experiences of worship in the sixth century CE church of Hagia Sophia by using the material conditions of the church, to suggest how experiences were codified. To an extent the acoustic methodology of Pentcheva's work actively privileges the intention of the architects in constructing artistic spaces, which for me grants too much agency to individuals involved in the design of the building rather than its use. There is no denying that Byzantine acoustic space was crafted, but the intention of the people is not the only actant that needs to be considered here. A broader phenomenological account guides the analyst to consider the dominant experience, which would have been that of congregation members, rather than the composer and the architect. It is the addition of ANT that pushes us toward exploring the role of the non-human, not only at the point of construction, but as part of the networks that sing.

God acts in Byzantium

Perhaps the most important non-human in Byzantine religious song is the one I have not yet discussed: God, the Byzantine concept of the divine, as a "thing" in the Heideggerian sense. God the actant was in a network, alongside other actants.

A large part of Byzantine theological practice revolves around making the absent, present (Buchli 2015:Chapter 2). This trait is visible in contentious debates revolving around the nature of Christ, and in the eventual iconoclastic controversy of the eighth and ninth centuries CE, but the persistent desire to make tangible the intangible is also present in material culture. Importantly, I do not say "represent" the divine, as this would be to significantly misunderstand Byzantine modes of mimesis, where essence rather than image is copied from object to object (Pentcheva 2006).

This idea of making the absent, present, or of producing experiences that cite the unrepresentable is a consistent theme throughout Byzantine religious art and material culture. For example, the flatness of Byzantine icons is deliberate, rather than an artistic failing, allowing people to use icons as conduits to saints (Cormack 2018:75–6). Pentcheva has argued that repoussé icons, which might depict something like the Archangel Michael, play with concepts of space within image; Michael's wings do not fit within the frame, not because the artist was incompetent, but because it is impossible to contain the divine nature of angels within an earthly representation (Pentcheva 2006:632).

A later example of deliberate techniques of confusion as a trope emergent within Byzantine religious experience are the middle Byzantine apocrypha worked on by Jane Baun (2007), particularly the apocalypses of Anastasia and the Theotokos. Apocalypse here refers to a journey to the other world, undertaken by a saint near death. The tropes that are relevant to us here are the collapsing of time and space in the narrative to produce an everywhere and everywhenness that reflect the continuous present of the divine (Baun 2007:145). Although these texts (as most of our sources do) date to the mid-Byzantine period, it is not the specifics of middle Byzantine otherworldly narratives, but rather the likely development of a Byzantine understanding of God as mysterious, unknowable, and ever-present that are useful to an understanding of the development of song from the fourth to the eighth centuries CE.

Methods of citing the unknowable nature of God are present in Early Byzantine narratives concerning churches as heaven on earth (Wybrew 1990:84). Materially, this shows up in the use of light within liturgical spaces, typified by its shifting quality (Nesbit 2012). In the same way, the experience of churches was shaped by lavish decoration such as the use of gold applied to facetted surfaces, the canny placement of windows acted to simulate radiance, and the importance of the color experience we translate as "purple," said to resemble the shifting quality of the sea. The absent is phenomenologically present in the emphasis placed on imprint and haptic vision. The deliberately layered and non-representational materializations of God in the Byzantine world could easily be considered vibrant matter in Jane Bennett's (2010) sense. Instead, it may be better to think that in a world with no divide between belief and knowledge that God falls into the category of ready-at-hand. As for Latour in his discussion of iconoclasm (1999:270), God is an actant among other actants.

Phenomenology, non-humans, and god: endnote

Bringing together the phenomenological elements of song with an understanding of the role of non-humans, including God, allows us to move away from literary debates and to appreciate song in a more holistic manner. This is perhaps best exemplified if we return to the opening of this chapter, and our imagined experience of singing in a Byzantine context. The church spaces had acoustics that created echoes. These echoes were dislocated by the structure of the churches, their sources were therefore unknown, and the result was disorienting (Gerstel et al. 2018). The singer became part of this dislocation themselves through singing monophonic lines along with a crowd of others, allowing their own voice to become part of the overall sound. Given that the early church is envisioned as prefiguring heaven on earth, and that the route to heaven is framed as becoming one with the body of Christ (being within the community of the church), I suggest that opening the black box of the Sung Office allows us to appreciate more fully how singing acted to create an embodied experience that also prefigured heaven as the subsuming of self within an other-worldly experience.

Conclusion

Some of the archaeological theory discussed in this book takes an approach that foregrounds materials and decenters humans. In this chapter, I have sought to highlight human experience through an approach grounded in phenomenology. This allowed me to think through in detail the experience of Byzantine song as a historically located element of Being-in-the-world. By drawing on ANT, I have demonstrated that in order to fully appreciate the nature of embodied phenomenological experience, we must also consider the role that non-humans play in the world. This includes considering how specific forms of architecture produce particular auditory experiences, and the manner in which we learn music and the non-human forms of notation involved are fundamental to the experience of singing. Finally, I have suggested that Latour's approach to belief allows us to resituate God in the Byzantine world as a factish. In turn, this facilitates a recognition of my own historically situated place in a society where the concept of "secular" makes sense, and thus a recognition that my experience of belief is not a transcendental aspect of human experience. In order to think through the full implications of Byzantine song, I need to think through the tangible effects that God had on a Byzantine world.

My concern in this chapter was not to dwell on whether every intricacy of phenomenology is compatible with ANT; phenomenology is too broad a church for that to be possible, it is not a consistent theoretical position but rather a set of methods and approaches that focus on experience. Nor have I exhaustively measured these theoretical approaches against other available relational varieties. Rather, I have chosen to focus on what combining different tools together, to form a new toolbox, allows us to do. In my case, it has allowed me to think about how the development of Byzantine song in the early church may have impacted a common understanding of theology at the time, producing an embodied understanding of paradise as oneness through the shared experience of singing.

Note

1 I am not alone in combining the insights of phenomenology and ANT (see Harman 2009). Indeed, it forms one element of Symmetrical Archaeology, particularly in its "second wave" (Harris and Cipolla 2017; Olsen 2010). However, in contrast to the object-oriented ontology of Graham Harman, I seek to maintain the thoroughly relational elements of both Latour and Heidegger and thus reject Harman's argument for withdrawn essences.

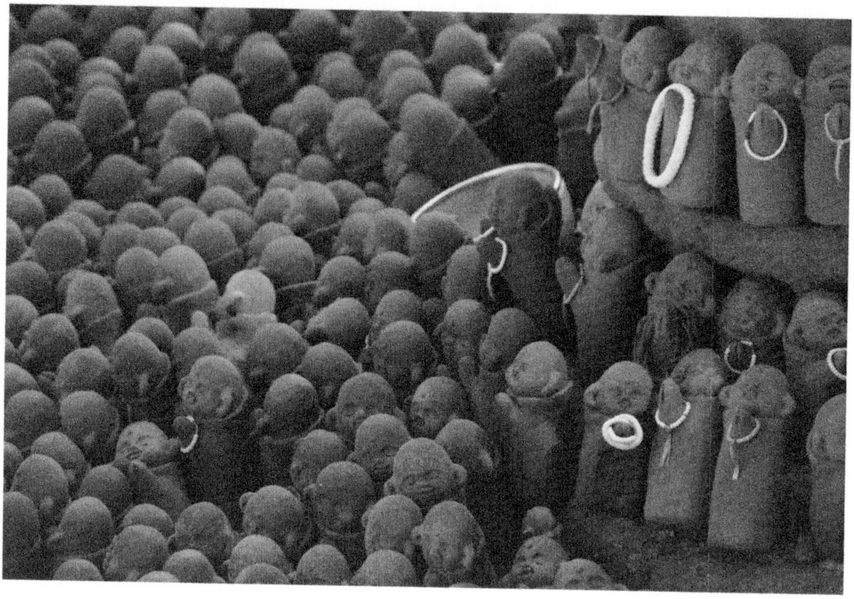

7

DISCUSSING PHENOMENOLOGY AND POSTHUMANISM

Experience, assemblages, and beliefs

Introduction

In this dialogue, the authors build on the previous chapter's discussions of phenomenology and Actor-Network Theory (ANT) and explore how these themes connect to the other theoretical approaches of the volume. The first topic centers on how phenomenology deals with the experiences of Others: other people and other things. Can you use phenomenology to think about Indigenous contexts, or to explore post-anthropocentric narratives? From there the discussion moves to consider ANT in relation to concepts of assemblages and new materialism that are dominant elsewhere in the volume (especially Chapters 2 and 8). How different are these ideas? Does Bruno Latour count as a new materialist? The chapter finishes by turning to the final critical issue raised in Chapter 7, that of belief and how this connects to the thorny issue of the metaontologies, raised in Chapter 5 and discussed further in Chapters 10 and 11.

Thinking through experience

LINDSAY: Sophie, I want to pick up on the particular critique that you and others have made in reference to the universalizing claims of the transcendental strain of phenomenology. As you point out, it would be difficult to say with any confidence that people in the past thought about things in the same way as we do today (cf. Brück 2005a). I agree, and would add to this my own critique: imagining a common human experience of the world becomes difficult in the Native North American context (and in the context of many other groups with non-western worldviews). The universalized body posited by phenomenology democratizes access to the past and allows the archaeologist's experience of the landscape in the twenty-first century to stand in for the experiences of people in the past. While some may feel comfortable with this comparison for the Neolithic in Britain, the idea that archaeologists can gain insight into the consciousness of Native peoples in the past through the mimetic act of walking the same trails in some ways suggests that living Indigenous people do not need to be a part of this analytical process. In other words, the notion of a transcendental human body runs the risk of making the lived experiences, oral histories, and personal narratives of Indigenous individuals supplementary data. Furthermore, this particular version of phenomenology seems to ignore the various ways in which Western colonialism has influenced and continues to structure Indigenous engagements with space and place. As I discuss in Chapter 4, it is this clear lack of attentiveness to power dynamics and the ongoing impact of these dynamics, which is perhaps the most troubling aspect of most phenomenological and relational applications within archaeology.

SOPHIE: I think your comments on the problematic and colonial nature of transcendental phenomenology are absolutely on point Lindsay, and it's something I worried about a lot when starting to think through the experienced nature of song in a Byzantine context. I am never sure if I am doing a disservice to the people that I'm studying when I try to talk about experiences that are not my own, even when I am actively rejecting a transcendental phenomenology. The compromise I have reached with myself is that trying to talk about the experienced past is important because the sort of everyday experiences in my analysis of Byzantine Song are not present elsewhere, and center the lives of people who are not present in the textual sources and therefore usually rather peripheral to discussions of the Byzantine world. I think the specific networks with which Byzantine people engaged are essential to thinking through their bodily experiences. This is especially true given that I'm starting from a point where their experiences cannot reflect my own in any straightforward manner.

The space between transcendental and hermeneutic phenomenology makes a world of difference to the ethics of phenomenology. The contrast between these things is the difference between Christopher Tilley (1994) taking shared human experience as a starting point when looking at Neolithic monuments (which is not what I'm doing) and Julian Thomas' (1996) hermeneutic approach to the past, which is more similar to my own approach. I have not tried to put myself in Byzantine shoes (give or take imaginative exercises like that at the start of Chapter 6) but rather to use phenomenology to think relationally about how moments of song were constructed, which elements of the musical tradition were ready-to-hand and which present-at-hand, and how they interacted with non-human actants to produce particular emergent properties.

LINDSAY: Sophie, I think the distinction that you are making here between Tilley's and Thomas' approaches to phenomenology is an important one, and my initial critiques are more directed toward the former framework rather than the latter. Your comments have made me think about how your adaptation of Thomas' hermeneutic approach would work for Native North American dance and song (Burton 1993; Heth 1992; Scully 1975). Some potential points of difference I see include audience, space, and the intended effect of these performances. For example, in your chapter you discuss the relational effects of soundscapes within the confined space of the church and between the clergy and congregation. The scope of this performance contrasts with many forms of Indigenous "doings" (Fowles 2013), such as the dances and songs performed by Pueblo People as part of patron saint feast day activities. In the Pueblo context, dances and songs are intended to have an effect on both the world in here (the intimate space of the performance, including the performers and audience) and the world out there (the larger Pueblo universe including its natural and cosmological elements).

These are bundled events, in that each element of the performance has a purpose – to ensure the physical, cultural, and spiritual prosperity of the community – which is only realizable through the combination of each element. This "bundling" takes both immaterial and material forms. For example, the fringe on the white sashes, representing rain, worn by Pueblo men reinforces the message of the songs sung during these dances (Frisbie 1980; Sweet 1983, 1992). The significance of these elements is inextricably linked to place and movement. Pueblo dances typically begin in the plaza – the central space between the two moieties in each village. The four cardinal directions are usually acknowledged through a gesture at the beginning of the performance, connecting this center place to the wider landscape. The Latourian relational perspective that you outline in your chapter, particularly the idea that "actions emerge out of relations" would seem like a good analytical parallel to this idea of bundled performances.

SOPHIE: Starting from the hermeneutic perspective that we all experience the world quite differently, not only opens up different avenues of analysis but also perhaps raises issues concerning ethnographic analogy. I think it's very easy to take for granted how we ourselves experience the world (like I did with aphantasia), and actually very difficult to imagine different ways of being or realize how many aspects of our own experience are not shared cross-culturally, or even between individuals in the same society.

RACHEL: Shifting the argument in a different direction, I want to consider the prospect of a non-anthropocentric phenomenology – is that even possible? Phenomenology is a relational approach and paved the way for the emergence of the new theoretical frameworks we have seen in the past decade, but it is also fundamentally concerned with the nature of human experience. Can we have a non-anthropocentric phenomenology?

SOPHIE: I think this is a great question Rachel, and one that doesn't have a yes/no answer. In the phenomenology of Heidegger (1962) that I discuss a little in my chapter, the human subject is absolutely given center stage. This is clearly an anthropocentric way of thinking about the world.

Similarly, if we look at how phenomenology was used by archaeologists in the 1990s, the human experience is still very much at the center of phenomenological analysis. The question becomes how far we are willing to stretch the definition of phenomenology. If we take its common use-meaning within archaeology, which I suggest is "a mode of enquiry focused on experience," then the center of phenomenological analysis is limited by the variety of things we are willing to accept as having experiences; so if we are willing to accept non-humans as having experiences, then we can potentially write this sort of study. You could argue that phenomenological modes of thought will always frame analysis within the Cartesian dualism, centering "experiencing subjects" (which to date are traditionally human) as opposed to non-experiencing objects. It is this element of opposition between experiencing subject and experienced object that threatens to undermine my proposition that phenomenological approaches can be used in tandem with relational theories that do not immediately privilege human beings.

OLLIE: Maybe we can push this further, in fact. It is clear that traditions emerging from Heidegger have gone in non-anthropocentric directions. Graham Harman's (2011) object-oriented ontology (OOO) uses Heidegger to think about how objects always withdraw from each other. Interestingly, his reading of Heidegger's ready-to-hand is very different to the one you use Sophie – he would see ready-to-hand as non-relational. As an example from within archaeology, Bjørnar Olsen's (2010) *In Defense of Things*, which is one of the least anthropocentric archaeology books ever written, cites Heidegger extensively in developing his version of symmetrical archaeology. We've also, of course, had Ian Bogost's (2012) *Alien Phenomenology*, which explores the idea that any kind of thinking about experience of another is fundamentally different to our own, whether that other is a person or an object.

SOPHIE: Absolutely, and there are also approaches to experience that do not emerge from phenomenology. Two bodies of non-anthropocentric work that deal explicitly with experience are Eduardo Kohn's *How Forests Think* (2013), which draws on Peircean semiotics, and Suzanne Simard's (2009) work on the diffuse communication that occurs between trees through rhizomatic [literally, although perhaps also in the Deleuzian sense (cf. Deleuze and Guattari 2004)] networks of mycorrhizal fungi. Kohn's (2013) work is an explicitly non-anthropocentric ethnography of the Ruana of Equador's Upper Amazon. His work is framed around the concept of selves as thinking, experiencing entities, or experiencing subjects I suppose, although that carries baggage that I think Kohn's work escapes. Through this approach, Kohn leads his reader to think about an ontology where experience, the nature of Being-in-the-world, is not axiomatically human, particularly through considering the nature of consciousness and how forests think.

Simard's work, popularized as the "wood wide web" through TED talks, and the controversial and emotive work of Peter Wohlleben frame a way of thinking about communication between trees (Simard 2009; Wohlleben 2016). This branch of forestry is beginning to demonstrate how trees share resources and experiences such as attack from pathogens or insects that they then communicate to other trees that are able to preemptively respond to the threat (Simard 2009).

Neither of these bodies of work are phenomenological, but both have commonalities with the elements of Heideggerian phenomenology that I find useful for archaeological investigations. Both Kohn and Simard are thinking and writing about stimulus, experience, and response; I think these relate to the concepts of "Being-in-the-world" (*Dasein*) that I talk about in Chapter 6, and the "thrownness" of experiences that I don't, but which emphasizes the always already nature of being (Heidegger 1962:223).

To return to your original question, which was about non-anthropocentric phenomenology, it is clear that neither of these thinkers are doing that. There's a trap to be avoided in calling things phenomenology, which have shared points of departure in centering experience, but which come from other traditions of thinking similar to the concerns expressed by Zoe Todd (2016) that I came to through reading Craig's work in Chapter 10 of this volume. Todd discusses how in talking about Gaia without acknowledging any of the Indigenous traditions that engage with sentient environments, Indigenous thought is appropriated by the Western canon. I think the way forward for me is probably not to try to produce a non-anthropocentric phenomenology but probably to broaden out how I think about and write about the experienced past beyond the Western philosophical canon.

CRAIG: Sophie, what immediately jumped to my mind when I read your chapter is Karen Barad's work (e.g., 2003, 2007), which incorporates posthuman feminism and new materialism with the philosophy of the Danish physicist, Niels Bohr. Barad's writings on physics – often cited in relation to her theorizing of the wave/particle debate – make heavy use of the term "phenomena" and certainly draw upon phenomenologists like Merleau-Ponty. Although Barad's work builds upon some of the important insights that you outlined earlier, the phenomenological focus on "conscious subjective experience of the individual human subject" (Barad 2007:155) is what led her to identify her approach with a different moniker; she uses the term "agential realism," which seems to share much in common with your approach. Agential realism works on the notion of "intra-action," Barad's way of eschewing simplistic notions of eternally bounded entities or bodies that preexist their relations (cf. Chapter 2).

For her, as with a general phenomenological approach, subjects and objects are not fixed; and, as with the distinction between ready-to-hand and present-at-hand, there are different types of relations possible, depending upon the status of the terms that they relate and the broader context (including things like habit, as your bike example in Chapter 6 demonstrates). She offers an example of a person in a dark room with a stick (Barad 2007:154–8). She notes two mutually exclusive ways for the person to intra-act with the stick. First, the person might grip the stick firmly so that they can use its tip to "feel" what they cannot see or reach with their hands – the stick is part of the subject in this case (cf. ready-to-hand). Second, the person might grip the stick loosely as to feel the texture of its surface – the stick is what she calls the "object of observation" in this case (cf. present-at-hand). Unlike many phenomenologists, however, Barad's main concern is not the person's experience, it is the "different material configurations of ontological bodies and boundaries, where the actual matter of bodies is what is at issue and at stake" (Barad 2007:155). To return to themes explored in Chapters 2 and 3, we might say that Barad's main interest is in how assemblages territorialize and deterritorialize. She frames this as a realist approach. First, how do you situate your work in relation to that of Barad? Second, how does your phenomenological approach sit in regard to realism?

SOPHIE: As you point out, Barad's main concern is not personal experience, whereas in my chapter I was specifically interested in how we can write about different human experience in the past. One could absolutely approach Byzantine song as an example of a phenomenon in Barad's terms. There is no question that the intra-action, to use Barad's term, of people, church, sound, notation, belief, and God produce something new. This is critical because singing collectively, within particular forms of architecture, resonates – literally – within your body: the boundaries between bodies, buildings, and sounds shift during that experience. I would argue that Barad offers us a different set of theoretical tools to answer different questions, there are overlaps with what I was trying to do in Chapter 6 but fundamentally I feel that an emphasis on phenomenology always brings me back to human experience – the primary focus of my research.

With regard to realism, I do accept that the world really exists outside of human beings' knowledge of it. The world does not depend on human beings (DeLanda and Harman 2017:28). However, the worlds I am interested in are ones involving human beings, and I am asking about human beings' experiences of those worlds. Here the kind of realism I am drawing on is closer to Barad's description that realism "is not about representations of an independent reality but about the real consequences, interventions, creative possibilities and responsibilities of intra-acting within and as part of the world" (Barad 2007:37).

Actor-Network Theory

OLLIE: Moving on from the question of phenomenology and realism, Sophie, I'm interested in the other big theoretical influence on your chapter: Latour. When it comes to talking about the roles of non-humans, I lean toward new materialist approaches rather than the work of Latour, as I tend to see the latter's networks as fairly static and not much use in explaining change (Crellin 2020). You cite Jane Bennett (2010) in conjunction with Latour in your chapter. Do you see a clear connection between Latour's vision of actants, on the one hand, and new materialism on the other?

SOPHIE: I definitely think there are overlaps between Bennett and Latour. Bennett, for example, adopts Latour's concept of actant; it is an important component of her work on vibrant matter, which I see as squarely new materialist.

RACHEL: I think historical context is important here. Bennett's key work is published in 2010, and in this she combines the vibrant materialist concepts we now so readily associate with new materialism, with Latour's actants. Latour's language gives her a way to ontologically level things and people, and to help meet her aim of shaking the "adamantine chain" separating the organic and inorganic (Bennett 2010:57). In today's context, we might see her work as combining two different strands of thinking, the emphasis on things themselves that Latour brings from his ANT with the focus on flow and process that she takes from Deleuze and Guattari. I personally see Bennett as a posthumanist thinker but I do not see Latour in the same light.

OLLIE: I think that's an interesting point. The posthumanist philosopher Francesca Ferrando (2019) defines posthumanism as having three core tenets: post-humanism (that is the attempt to move past humanism); post-dualism (that is to get out of binary oppositions of the Cartesian kind); and post-anthropocentrism (that is to remove human beings from the ontological apex (Bennett 2010:ix)).[1] Although Ferrando (2019:161–2) disagrees, I think Bennett's work matches these definitions. Latour is pretty clearly post-dualist, *We Have Never Been Modern*, is a central text here. However, we might wonder if he is post-humanist, and if he is post-anthropocentric?

RACHEL: I don't see Latour as post-anthropocentric because whilst he clearly shifts the focus away from human beings, he doesn't broaden the canvas that much. We get plenty of discussion of things, especially when they encounter human beings, but the wider world of animals, plants, and weather are often ignored. Even microbes only get to play their role after human beings have discovered them, even if this leads to complex readings of time (Latour 1999).

OLLIE: Yes, I think I agree, even if things like soil sometimes get to play a role when they encounter scientists (Latour 1999:Chapter 2), and his more recent work on the anthropocene is broadening the picture he paints (e.g., Latour 2018). Similarly, I'm not sure he is really post-humanist. Latour rarely deals with questions of gender, or power, or what or who counts as human. Being post-humanist, contra many of its critics, is absolutely not about ignoring the complexity of human beings. Far from it, it is about opening up that complexity for rigorous examination for the first time, outside of the assumptions about it we normally hold.

CRAIG: This discussion is quite interesting when you step back and think through some of the major critiques levied at archaeologists who experiment with these various thinkers (e.g., see critiques from Barrett 2016; Hodder 2014; Van Dyke 2015). I've grown increasingly frustrated with the tendency to lump Latour, Bennett, Deleuze, Harman, and many more together under the general banner of "posthumanism." I think it's important to note that this frustration and the need to further parse posthuman theories in archaeology are what partially motivated some of us to write this book! I'm glad to read more on your views about how someone like Latour differs from Bennett. And, echoing what Rachel discusses later in Chapter 8, it's important to continually dispel the rather strange accusations of the critics who essentialize this diverse body of theory and equate it with things like stopping us from discussing humans or adopting an intractable and never-changing flat ontology (this, of course, is just the opposite of what various thinkers using the term actually mean, see Cipolla in review a).

On this note, I wanted to return to Ollie's earlier question – about the rigidity of Latour's approach when it comes to dealing with change (see also Crellin 2020). I think Ollie is right; Latour's ANT focuses on the network at any one moment in time, but seems ill-equipped to consider history. Perhaps, Sophie, that deficiency doesn't necessarily matter to your rethinking of Byzantine song. I imagine that you would need to add other theoretical tools to your kit if you were to take on a different set of questions focused on long-term change, no?

SOPHIE: First, I would argue that I do think about change through time. In my chapter I tried to set out some of the differences in Byzantine song at different points in history. These differences emerged through different forms of singing, the role of different singers, and changing methods of musical notation. What the combination of Latour's emphasis on networks and the non-human and phenomenology allows me to do is to describe, in detail, the changing roles of non-humans and the changing experiences for human beings. Singing in the ninth century CE and singing in the twelfth century CE were not the same.

A reasonable criticism of this, that someone like Rachel would make, is that this approach produces a block-time narrative and does not actually describe the detail of how change emerges in the world. This may be true, but on the other hand it allows me to describe clearly how differences in practice existed in the past and avoids the risk of reducing change to an ever-shifting blur of undifferentiated flow.

RACHEL: Block-time approaches are very hard to avoid. I argue that they are often necessarily the starting point for analysis, we have to know the rough shape of the periods we study and the differences between them (Crellin 2020). I go on to argue though that we should not stop here but should instead seek to paint a more nuanced picture of change through time. For me drawing out the process of change, with all its small continuities and shifts is what is important. Your description of the risk involved in the painting of nuanced pictures of change producing "an ever-shifting blur of undifferentiated flow" is something I have thought about. In my work I use the concepts of a phase transition, drawn from the work of Manuel DeLanda (1997, 2006) to explore how bigger changes can emerge from smaller ones (see also Chapter 3).

CRAIG: Fair enough. Perhaps my question wasn't about change versus stasis but rather about different scales of change.

Black boxes and assemblages

Sophie: I think the relationship between Latour, Bennett, Barad, and posthumanism is interesting, but to me what really matters is how these ideas work as tools when we think about the past. For example, I use the term black box because I find it a useful tool in conceptualizing how objects are made up of elements that are not immediately obvious. If for me, ready-to-hand is a useful way of describing human experience, black box acts as a more general way of describing a similar process. Rachel, why do you prefer to use the term assemblage rather than black box? For me they do more or less the same thing.

RACHEL: From my point of view, assemblage captures not only how things are made from multiple components but also how these persist through time. Latour's black box, like his network, doesn't provide a sense of how the world is constantly in process, as we discussed in Chapter 3. More importantly, assemblage theory and new materialism offer a fully posthumanist approach that provides us with concepts to build both better pasts and better futures.

SOPHIE: I can see your argument that Latour is not a posthumanist, but is he a new materialist? He is often referred to as an example of new materialism in parts of the literature. Why doesn't Latour count as a new materialist?

OLLIE: Sometimes debating who is or who is not a new materialist can be seen as very niche question, after all the differences between say Latour and Bennett, or between Latour and Deleuze are not as significant as between classic archaeological theorists like Lewis Binford, say, and Christopher Tilley. Nonetheless, I think this does matter, not least because if you want to lump these approaches together, you also need to think about the differences that you are losing and the consequences of that (we discuss this further in Chapter 11). For me, Latour and archaeological approaches derived from Latour like symmetrical archaeology are not new materialist because they do not emphasize the importance of materials themselves, as opposed to things, they do not take an approach where the world is constantly in motion, and they do not deal with change through time. These are critical elements of new materialism. The differences are even stronger between what Craig and I termed second-wave symmetrical archaeology and new materialism (Harris and Cipolla 2017). The former draws on Harman's OOO to argue that objects withdraw and are non-relational. For new materialists, relations always emerge in parallel with objects (as we discuss in Chapter 3). Whether an object is relational or not is a pretty major philosophical difference.

SOPHIE: That's helpful. In a recent paper, Christopher Witmore (2014) discusses archaeology and the new materialisms. In this paper, Witmore argues that things are assemblages (sounding very new materialist in your definition) and that things are things (sounding more like what you call second-wave symmetrical archaeology). Is there a tension here then?

OLLIE: Yes, I think there is. As Harman (2016b:34–5) points out, you can't have your cake and eat it too. If we are talking about the relationship between these different perspectives, they are not all identical, we'll return to this more in Chapter 11. This doesn't mean that one approach is better than the other, necessarily; as you would say it depends what you want to do with them. Are they useful tools for thinking new thoughts? But it does matter that we don't present these perspectives as the same, because it allows critics to cherry-pick particular elements, and use them to attack all the different perspectives that are represented (e.g., Barrett 2016; cf. Crellin and Harris in review).

Our beliefs/their beliefs: negotiating a way forward

CRAIG: I wonder if we might take this discussion in a slightly different direction now. As I discuss later in Chapters 10 and 11, I feel that we, as archaeologists, have to continually recognize our metaontologies – the broadest scale at which we speculate on the nature of reality, including our understanding and engagement with other perspectives on reality. Like Barad and many phenomenologists, I find it crucial to recognize the parts that *we* play in the pasts that emerge through our relations with the world. Barad discusses this within her theory of agential realism and intra-action, specifically in her discussion of the inseparability of the observer and the observed, or, to use her terminology, the object and the agencies of observation (2007:188). For me, this concerns who I am as a white male settler colonist practicing archaeology on Indigenous lands with Indigenous peoples. I have spent a great deal of time thinking through and writing about these relations and this ties back to Rachel's discussion of discomfort and "staying with the trouble" in Chapter 5. Of course, these differences between me and my collaborators are *productive* – they lead us collectively to think in different ways than we do when practicing archaeology apart from one another. As I read your chapter I was reminded of your atheism – mentioned in Chapter 1 – and wondered about how this dimension of identity factors into your engagement with past religious practices such as the singing that you discuss. In other words, what role might this type of speculative difference – between you and the people of the past that you write of – play in the pasts that emerge through your archaeology?

SOPHIE: I absolutely take your point about the inseparability of observer and observed. My atheism is completely relevant to my discussion of Byzantine religious practice. At the beginning of my doctoral work, I found it hard to take Byzantine orthodoxy at face value because it felt very different to my own understanding of the world. The Latourian concept of factish is really what helped me take Byzantine belief seriously, but the speculative difference you mention here is fundamental to my mode of enquiry and the productiveness of my scholarship (Latour 1999). As an archaeologist and an atheist, I am coming from quite a different place than the majority of scholarship in the field of Byzantine theology that is largely rooted in current Greek Orthodox practice. There is a deep-seated tradition within the Greek orthodox church that the church itself is unchanging, that the rules set at first council of Nicea in 325 CE structure belief – this shows up in continued use of ethnographies of nineteenth- and twentieth-century Greece as proxies for Byzantine practice (e.g., du Boulay 1974), particularly in the mortuary sphere, which is not supported by the archaeological evidence. I am by no means alone in working on a particularist history of Late Antique belief, but I do think that my outsider's perspective can be useful, and certainly I find the speculative difference helpful in broadening out my understanding of meaning and belief.

RACHEL: There is a real honesty in this response Sophie. Archaeologists working with Indigenous people, for example, might be uncomfortable admitting that they struggled to take seriously the different forms of knowledge at play. One of the powerful lessons we can all learn from the kinds of collaboration that Craig practices is how to make these differences in thinking productive. These kinds of approaches allow me to think about how differently people thought about their worlds in the Bronze Age for example. Just as it allows you to consider Byzantine belief as a real element of a past world. I do wonder, however, if it is possible, given your commitment to atheism, to place your beliefs and the beliefs of Byzantine people on the same ontological plane?

SOPHIE: This is precisely the challenge of the ontological turn in my opinion. We all have beliefs and biases, metaontologies if you like, that we carry with us and bring to our archaeological analyses, and truthfully, placing anyone else's beliefs on the same ontological plane as your own is difficult because it requires a deep engagement with what we ourselves think about reality at the same time as considering other people's beliefs. Saying that, I do think it is possible if we recognize the difference between placing belief (in this case Byzantine) on the same ontological plane as my own faith or lack of it, and "believing" in Byzantine theology that would suggest that I had converted to a Late Antique Orthodox Christianity. For me this comes down to the differences between belief, knowledge, and faith, as I discussed in Chapter 6.

I think that placing Byzantine religious practice and my own experiences on the same ontological plane is fundamentally about knowledge – what did Byzantine people know about the world, and how did this impact how they engaged with it?

LINDSAY: For me this discussion brings up a series of tensions around the underlying goal of placing people or beliefs on the same ontological plane. As an intellectual exercise and an analytical stance for archaeological work in North America, I gravitate toward the idea that we should try to use the ontologies of Indigenous peoples as interpretive frameworks for the material record. At the same time, I worry about whether this represents yet another imposition of a Western academic agenda onto Indigenous people and knowledge (see also Chapter 5; cf. Chapter 10). It may be the case that Indigenous beliefs have no place in archaeological analyses and are best left for Indigenous peoples to use as they see fit in the present. This is in some ways a dilemma specific to settler colonial contexts and ongoing considerations about how to best facilitate Indigenous sovereignty. That being said, I think the most important move that archaeologists can make is to acknowledge the validity of alternative belief systems and worldviews and to become aware of the ways in which western beliefs systems may differ from and articulate with them.

RACHEL: As discussed in Chapter 5, I think it is about treating them as equally real because they both have effects in the world. Once we treat them both as equally real and not as mistaken, we are in a better place to take them seriously.

LINDSAY: Although this is a bit of a contrarian position, in my mind the difference between belief and knowledge is not particularly relevant to archaeological work with Indigenous people. In my opinion, it does not matter if archaeologists believe that the origin stories or worldviews of Indigenous people are true. As many Indigenous folks I have talked with point out, Indigenous people hold these narratives and beliefs to be true and meaningful and they certainly don't need archaeologists, anthropologists, or historians to confirm or validate them. Taking this perspective into consideration, what would seem to matter is that archaeologists *treat* those stories and logics as equally real as their own stories and worldviews (e.g., atheism, Marxism, new materialism, posthumanism). It seems to me, that this is the most respectful way to engage with communities who have been historically marginalized and is an important prerequisite for scholars seeking to step outside of their own time–space–body–mind.

Conclusion

SOPHIE: In this chapter, we explored themes of human experience, the compatibility (or otherwise) of different theories, and the relationship between ourselves as researchers and the peoples and places we study. Phenomenology offers a relational and non-dualistic approach to the world and, specifically, to exploring the nature of human experience. For me, human experience is a key part of the world and one that should not be left out of our analyses, but it is also something in which non-humans play a fundamental role. I use theory as a tool kit to help me solve particular problems in my analyses, and it has been interesting to see the debate in this chapter about the specific nature of different thinkers and how we think differently about whether their ideas can be combined or not. In the next chapter, Rachel explores the theme of power, something often presumed to be absent from posthumanist approaches.

Note

1 In each case here, I have deliberately left in the hyphen in place between post and human-ism, anthropocentrism, and dualism to emphasize the intellectual move of stepping away from these positions, following Ferrando (2019).

8

POSTHUMANIST POWER

Rachel J. Crellin

Introduction

One of the things I study is the Bronze Age. The dominant narrative of the period suggests that the arrival of bronze led to the development of inequality and new power structures. Bronze is an alloy, most commonly formed of copper and tin. The distribution of both ores is restricted; in Europe, copper is more common, tin is rarer. Bronze is often effectively interpreted as a form of early capital and what followed in its wake was inequality between those who had access to bronze and those who did not. Those who had access became leaders; those who did not became followers: eventually the subjugated. With the subsequent development of swords and spearheads from the Middle Bronze Age onward, the power of those already well networked into trade routes is suggested to have increased: they now had weapons with which to defend their capital. Those with the metal were those with power, and they are always portrayed as men. In continental Europe, Kristian Kristiansen (2018:27; for similar arguments, see also 1998, 1999; Kristiansen and Larsen 2005) argues that sons who did not inherit their family farms separated from their families to become roaming bands of young warriors. These young warriors were essentially "swords for hire" to the highest bidders, used to defend trade routes and capital as they traveled across Europe "through 'civilized' and settled landscapes from Denmark to Italy" (Horn and Kristiansen 2018:2). Thus, a class system was born, at the top the warrior-chief,[1] below him, the warriors, below them everyone else. Warriors and chiefs were free to roam across Europe, fighting heroic battles (see Figure 8.1). People and objects moved along trade routes seeking access to "commodities" such as copper, tin, bronze, amber, and salt. As they did so, they came into contact with "Others" different from themselves. We are told

FIGURE 8.1 A Bronze Age warrior? From "Age du Bronze: costume de guerrier."

Source: Scanned by General Research Division, The New York Public Library. New York Public Library Digital Collections. Accessed April 2, 2020. http://digitalcollections.nypl.org/items/510d47e4-4938-a3d9-e040-e00a18064a99. Wikimedia commons.

"warfare and exchange are each other's *sine qua non*" (Horn 2018:58). Difference resulted in violence: "war is waged against the 'other,' people who are somehow different, whether in appearance, language or simply beliefs" (Harding 2018:20). Some authors even go as far as to suggest the existence of standing armies with professional soldiers under the control of ruling elites in the Bronze Age (Meller 2017). Warfare was glamorous, institutionalized, held a socially prestigious role, and was the concern of men. The narrative is deeply androcentric, masculinist, modernist, capitalist, and problematic.

For a long time, I have struggled with how to transform this narrative. We do see the emergence of swords in the Bronze Age, often referred to as the first weapons specifically designed to kill other humans. There was a transformation in attitudes to gender in this period: gendered bodies were represented differently in art and treated differently in the grave (Robb and Harris 2013, 2018). We have evidence of a large-scale battlefield from the Tollense Valley in Germany, where over 100 skeletons, some showing markers of trauma, have been recovered often in contexts where arrowheads of both flint and bronze, as well as spears and swords, have been found (Jantzen et al. 2011). Those who argue against this chiefly warrior model are described as "romantics," who want to pacify the past and are often told that they are denying the archaeological evidence (Kristiansen 2018:24, footnote I; Vandkilde 2018). Archaeologists such as Joanna Brück (2017:37, see also Brück 2005b) have argued that the chiefly warrior model "assumes that positions of social, political, and economic power were held solely by men, and that women were (like fine weaponry) the objects of elite exchange rather than social agents in their own right." Brück and David Fontijn (2013) have argued that the model of chiefly leadership is based on a series of theoretical presumptions that have their basis in Enlightenment thinking, not the Bronze Age archaeology of 4,000 years ago. They have argued that the dominant model presumes the existence of modernist individuals when a relational model of personhood is more appropriate; they have critiqued how the model makes bronze an early form of capital; furthermore, they have shown how the archaeological evidence itself can be understood differently (Brück and Fontijn 2013). In spite of this excellent critique, the model continues to dominate the literature (see, for example, Horn and Kristiansen 2018 and papers therein).

The dominant narrative of this period, where males emerged as warriors and leaders, is troubling to me. These warrior leaders stand above the rest of society. They are powerful: they possess power. The have the power to control the objects under their ownership, their swords and spears. They first dominate animals through hunting and then other humans in combat. They possess and wield their power to subjugate others. Women are excluded from the "civilized" world of heroic battle. We see them discussed as "foreign wives" traded between chiefdoms to support political power. In one case, the distribution of "foreign wives" is used to map out the chiefdoms within a confederacy (Kristiansen and Larsson 2005:fig 107). Women here are objects too, they are inactive, they lack power, they are subjugated. Warriors, and more so, warrior-chiefs were wealthy and they were therefore powerful. Power in this model is something possessed by individuals. Power is wielded by a subject over an object. It is repressive for the powerless. It is what sustains and creates leaders, it shapes the political.

I arrive at a conundrum: Do I want to deconstruct the warrior-chief model? Yes. Do I know what to put in its place? No. Do I want to acknowledge that women have been repressed and subjugated through history? Yes. Do I want the period I study to be a place where we simply see a mirror of the patriarchy I live in? No. I am writing about the Bronze Age past, but it is a Bronze Age past that exists in, and has impact on, the present. I do not want to write narratives where women emerge as always less-than, or where I naturalize their position as the second sex (cf. de Beauvoir 1997). In the warrior-chief model, I see the assemblage of the patriarchy. I see how the archaeological evidence is interpreted through a particular lens. I see the patriarchy's model of power: power is associated with wealth, power is masculine, power is violent, power creates the Other as negative and less-than, and power and leadership are knitted together.

In this chapter, I consider how we can think about power differently. Specifically, I take a posthumanist position and think about how power works in assemblages. The chapter begins by considering the critiques that have been directed at relational non-anthropocentric approaches: namely, de-valuing the human, being disconnected from issues of social justice, and failing to consider power. I outline how a posthumanist stance has social justice issues at its core. I then consider how we think about power in a world where dualistic separations of subject and object are no longer upheld.

Non-anthropocentric approaches – do they care about power?

This book partly emerged from a desire to engage with the current fluorescence of relational approaches in archaeology (see Chapter 1). These new approaches hold much in common, but they do not all share the exact same philosophical ground and as a result there are different ways that we can categorize them (compare, for instance, the different methods used by Ollie and Craig in Chapters 2 and 10 of this book). From my point of view, all of these approaches are united by their desire to seriously consider the non-human elements of the world, the relations we have with them, and the roles they play. However, only a subset of them argue for a radical reconceptualization of the place of humans within the world. Symmetrical archaeology (see Olsen 2007, 2010; Olsen et al. 2012; Shanks 2007; Webmoor 2007; Webmoor and Witmore 2008; Witmore 2007), new materialism (see Barad 2007; Bennett 2010; Braidotti 2011a, 2011b, 2013; Coole and Frost 2010; Grosz 1994), and the related assemblage approaches (see DeLanda 2006, 2016; Jervis 2018; Jones and Hamilakis 2017 and papers therein) share a desire to move beyond anthropocentrism. As this book, most specifically Chapters 4 and 10, demonstrates, these western philosophical approaches overlap, share common ground with, and borrow from, some Indigenous philosophies that also emphasize the relational nature of the world and the position of humans as one-of-many actors. Symmetrical archaeology actively calls for the ontological elevation of things onto the same plane as humans so that they may be considered to "symmetrically" make up the world. New materialism highlights the vitalist nature of all matter, whether it is human or non-human and, by taking matter itself as the starting point, this approach recasts humans as one-of-many through an explicitly posthumanist stance.

Non-anthropocentric approaches argue that we should no longer place humans at the "ontological apex" (Bennett 2010:ix) in our analyses, but instead recognize the key roles played by non-humans. This involves a decentering of the human and an active effort to elevate the role of non-human "Others." No longer should we see humans alone as the chief protagonists in history, instead we need to recognize the roles played by non-humans such as cars, pots, axes, swords, gods, lizards, and lakes (to name but a few). This is often framed in terms of a flat ontology (DeLanda 2002:51), a term that critiques the hierarchical ontology of the modern West where humans sit above animals, plants, and things, and suggests this hierarchy should be flattened so that all things, both human and non-human, are positioned on the same ontological plane (see also Cipolla in review b).

These approaches have understandably provoked a backlash. Ben Jervis (2018:12) characterizes the critiques as centering on the issue of whether a non-anthropocentric approach is a "risk to humanity." Calling for humans to be removed from the ontological apex has been seen as an affront to the study of the humanities itself; for some the response to a non-anthropocentric approach is to call out: "But I study humans!" In Europe some of those working with Bayesian analysis of radiocarbon dates to develop new histories of the Neolithic have argued that non-anthropocentric approaches are taking away agency from humans (see, for example, Draşovean et al. 2017; Ebersbach et al. 2017). Worse still, non-anthropocentric approaches are perceived to be doing this at the moment when Bayesian analysis is opening the door to talking in much more depth about human decision-making in the past (but see Crellin 2020:88–90, 177–8). John Barrett (2016) launched a ferocious critique of non-anthropocentric approaches, describing them as a "new antiquarianism" and suggesting that the interest in materials and things comes at the expense of humans. Similarly, Ian Hodder (2014:229), in response to an article by Christopher Witmore (2014), suggests that flat ontologies "distract attention from social inequality." Ruth Van Dyke (2015) has published a sustained critique of these approaches alongside a call to retain anthropocentrism. She states that "the elevation of things seems to come with what I would argue is a steep price tag – a loss of focus on people" (Van Dyke 2015:18). She goes on to suggest that abandoning anthropocentrism opens the door to treating people as objects. She argues that we have to retain our anthropocentrism in order that we can take ethical stances, care for marginalized humans, fight for social justice, and hold people responsible for evil actions (Van Dyke 2015). In a less critical piece, Julian Thomas (2015:1294) has suggested that whilst non-anthropocentric approaches have a clear utility, we should have serious reservations about "treating a historical event such as the Holocaust as an assemblage of disparate entities if it in any way reduced the scale of human responsibility." To summarize, non-anthropocentric approaches have been critiqued for appearing to abandon the human, removing human responsibility, and therefore for potentially no longer caring about social injustice and inequality. Van Dyke (2015:7) suggests retaining an anthropocentric focus allows her to "contribute to discussions about the negotiation of power within social relationships."

In these critiques, power is a clear undercurrent. The objection to non-anthropocentric approaches is that they stop us focusing upon the worst excesses of human power, that by focusing on the non-human we might forget the awful things that humans do to each other: inequality and social justice are power issues. In this orientation around human care, we can begin to see the problematic nature of our definition of power. Why should studies that elevate the non-human be any less concerned with power than anthropocentric approaches?

Part of the problem here is that the complex and varied philosophical ground surrounding non-anthropocentrism is being treated as homogeneous by both those offering important critiques and those utilizing such ideas (see Witmore 2014). Harris and Cipolla (2017:138) rightly identify two different waves of symmetrical archaeology. In the first wave (see, for example, Olsen 2007; Olsen et al. 2012; Shanks 2007; Webmoor 2007; Webmoor and Witmore 2008; Witmore 2007), symmetrical archaeologists were most heavily influenced by Bruno Latour (1993, 1999, 2005a) and the narratives that they produced focused on the symmetrical relationships between people and things. The generalized symmetry that they posit has been argued to prevent the analysis of power relations at work between actors and objects (Braidotti 2019b:42). In first-wave symmetrical archaeology, it is clear that humans still play an important role. More recently however, in what Harris and Cipolla (2017:138) term *second-wave symmetrical archaeology* (see, for example, Olsen 2010; Olsen and Pétursdóttir 2014; Olsen and Witmore 2015; Pétursdóttir 2012), they have been more heavily influenced by the object-oriented ontology (OOO) of Graham Harman (2011). This might seem like semantics; however, philosophically it is significant. In OOO, the emphasis becomes on things as the primary, and sometimes only focus of analysis: this is things at the expense of humans. Research in this vein has focused on subjects such as ruins. Þóra Pétursdóttir (2012), for example, has written evocatively about an abandoned Herring station in Eyri in northwest Iceland. Studying the crumbling ruin, deserted by people, allowed her the chance to focus on "how things exist, act and inflict on each other . . . outside the human realm" (Pétursdóttir 2012:578). In Pétursdóttir's (2012) study of the abandoned herring factory, there is, as she acknowledges, no discussion of the nature of global capitalism, industrialization, or the effect of the collapse of the herring factory on those who worked as part of the industry. Here it is easy to see Hodder (2014) and Van Dyke's (2015) criticisms as valid.

Taking a pragmatic approach to non-anthropocentrism, Thomas (2015:1294) comments that "although we might wish to reject anthropocentrism, archaeologists will probably continue to concern themselves with humanity, if only as a historically emergent phenomenon." Thomas (2015) has an important point here, second-wave symmetrical archaeology has not become the disciplinary norm and humans remain a focus. I reject anthropocentrism, but that does not mean that I do not study people; rather I study them as one-of-many, always changing, embedded, embodied, and relational. I reject the "arrogance" (Braidotti 2011b:139) of anthropocentrism and choose to see humans as deeply embedded and inseparable from non-humans: humans are one-of-many. I think here the semantic difference between a *post*-anthropocentric and a *non*-anthropocentric approach is perhaps illuminating. Rosi Braidotti (e.g., 2011b, 2013, 2019b; see also Ferrando 2019) in her posthumanist, matter realist, feminist philosophy often uses the term "post-anthropocentric." Non-anthropocentric, a term readily used in the symmetrical and assemblage literature, seems to conjure in the minds of archaeologists a rejection of the study of humanity that seems impossible and unethical. Perhaps post-anthropocentric is a better term defined not in the negative of "non" and avoiding the suggestion that we no longer study humans. Instead, post-anthropocentric appears as an "after," a moving forward, a new phase. It is in the work of posthumanists like Braidotti that we can find ways to address the critiques of those who question our desire to move beyond anthropocentrism.

Posthumanist approaches

Posthumanism and post-anthropocentrism converge around their critique of human exceptionalism. Posthumanist scholars take a feminist stance that argues that not only are humans not ontologically exceptional, but that humanist thinking has been actively damaging and exclusionary. Posthumanists argue that humanism operationalizes a specific definition of "human" that casts humans as the seat of agency and rationality, this definition acts to exclude some from the human category. Within humanism, a certain subset of humans have been upheld as the model of humanity and seat of agency – namely, white, western, educated, property-owning, heterosexual, able-bodied, young men – visually captured in the image of Vitruvian man (Braidotti 2013) (and perhaps also in Figure 8.1). All other forms of humanity have been unfavorably compared to this idealized image of a human and as a result have been Othered and naturalized (Braidotti 2013:15, 27–8). That which is not "Man" is shaped into an Other and defined negatively as less-than (hu)Man, closer to nature. This definition of the human is ahistorical and unchanging, based on exceptionalism and excludes the majority of humans.

Power acts as a key axis within this process of naturalizing and othering. Those that are excluded from the "human" category are presented as less powerful, rational, and active. Fungi, plants, viruses, and animals lack human rationality and agency; therefore, humans are more powerful than them. Similarly, women, non-Euro-Americans, Indigenous groups, differently able bodied, and LGBTQI+ identities are cast as less powerful and less rational than the idealized "Man." Identities here are formed negatively and in opposition to something else; the distance from the idealized Man is what counts. Binaries abound as woman is defined as not man, animal as not human, homosexual as not heterosexual, etc. What results is an ontological hierarchy of identities and the exclusion of a whole subset of people from the category human. Humanism upholds inequality and distributes power asymmetrically.

Posthumanist thinkers argue for the need to move beyond humanism to a more complex, historical, and changing understanding of what it means to be human. What replaces humanism for posthumanist thinkers is a relational, embedded, and embodied position. They share ground with those calling for non-anthropocentric approaches, as humans are seen as deeply entangled and inseparable from non-humans and from other humans: they can never be isolated. They act in confederations with other people, things, animals, plants, ideas, landscapes, etc. This is not about devaluing humans but about ontologically elevating a diverse cast of others. New materialism offers a way for posthumanists to rethink the world – all matter is placed on the same ontological plane and seen as immanent and capable of change (see, for example, Bennett 2010). Humans are just one form of matter, alongside teapots, rabbits, and moss, for example. The emphasis on the vibrant and shifting nature of matter means that a concern with process emerges: processes of change, processes of becoming, processes of identity and subject formation. Assemblage theory, drawn from the work of Gilles Deleuze and Félix Guattari (2004), offers a way to conceptualize this world of vibrant matter. Within assemblage thinking, humans are one-of many, no longer ontologically elevated above non-humans. Assemblages are ad hoc temporary gatherings of diverse matter, they are always changing and always in process (DeLanda 2002, 2006, 2016; Jervis 2018). They are materialist, but their tetravalent nature (Deleuze and Guattari 2004:556) means there is also space for the immaterial: thoughts, ideas, and symbols play important roles within assemblages. DeLanda (2002:51) posits a flat ontology in his formation of assemblage theory, but this is not a flat ontology that presumes that all components are the same, rather it just presumes that all matter is equally capable of effect and affect in the world in spite of the differences between the forms it takes.

Humans are clearly capable of being powerful components within assemblages. Braidotti (2019b:31) describes the posthuman subject as a "relational embodied and embedded, affective and accountable entity." Seeing humans as deeply entwined in relations with others and elevating the ontological status of matter (and thereby non-humans) is not about removing culpability or blame from the human. It is not the case that we should turn a blind eye to despotism and dictatorship, or that we are not accountable for our actions. Equally though, overcoming inequality and fighting complex social justice issues always have to be done from a position that recognizes this entanglement and inseparability of the assemblages that make up our world. If we want to overturn the assemblages of patriarchy, classism, or racism, simply espousing equality is not enough. To *deterritorialize*, in Deleuze and Guattari's (2004) phrase, the assemblages of patriarchy, for example, we have to deal with all kinds of relations, we have to change relations between employers and employees, we have to change the status of breast milk and menstrual blood, we have to think about childcare, we have to think about the structure of buildings, the form of the work day, attitudes toward food supply, and a whole host of other relationships that pay no heed to our human/non-human boundary. We absolutely can, and should, call out those who do wrong, but we also have to change whole assemblages of material, immaterial, human, and non-human relations to bring about real change.

Posthumanism is a critical approach that has issues of equality (and inequality) at its heart. Posthumanism is not about the abandonment of the human but rather about a radical rethinking of what the human is. It recasts humans as inseparable from the rest of the world, and it takes the "missing people" (Braidotti 2019b:49–51), excluded from the humanist definition of human, and places them at the center of what it does. As such, it is deeply concerned with issues of inequality and social justice. From my perspective, it is not therefore subject to the critiques raised by Hodder (2014) and Van Dyke (2015). In Braidotti's (2019b:43; see also Braidotti 2019c) outline of a theoretical framework for the critical humanities, power and power relations of exclusion and domination are key concerns.

Posthumanist power

The posthumanist stance is also anti-binary: it does away with subjects and objects (Ferrando 2019). The call for a flat ontology means that a far wider and more heterogeneous cast of components are elevated. Moreover, the posthumanist critique calls attention to how humanism has promoted a vision of power as not only reserved for human subjects but also something more readily associated with a certain subset of humans. The traditional model of power as possessed by human subjects and exercised over objects is clearly incompatible with a posthumanist, new materialist, assemblage approach.

The anti-humanist thinking of Michel Foucault (1979) famously discusses power as not merely repressive but as enabling. This understanding of power is not unfamiliar to archaeologists. For instance, Daniel Miller and Christopher Tilley (1984) drew on Foucault's thinking during the development of post-processualism as they explored power and ideology. Miller and Tilley (1984) suggested that power is exercised by all human beings and is the ability to change the actions of others. They drew upon Foucault's observation that power is not merely repressive and negative, what they term "power over," but can also be enabling and positive and is linked to the production of knowledge, what they term "power to" (Miller and Tilley 1984:7). Power is described not as an object to be possessed, but as a network that runs through people without a single origin. Miller and Tilley's (1984) work has been deeply influential in bringing Foucauldian thinking into archaeology, but as Thomas (2002) highlights, their characterization of power falls short in places – they reject Foucault's argument that wherever there is power, there will also be resistance and ultimately fall back on a negative definition of power stating that "all forms of power . . . can be reduced to either physical force (or its threat) or manipulation" (Miller and Tilley 1984:7).

Thomas (2002:37) points out that Foucault emphasizes the "historical particularity of power relations." Whilst power exists everywhere and at all times, it is not static; what matters is the specific, and always historical form that it takes. This is used as a stepping-stone by Thomas (2002) to argue that what we should draw from Foucault, as archaeologists, is the generalities of how power works because the specifics discussed in his work are just that: historical specifics from the Medieval and Early Modern world of Europe. They are, however, also useful to my project in the Bronze Age because when we look at the specifics of how power is often conceived of today – as something exercised negatively by someone who stands separate to, and above, those over whom *he* has power – we learn that we are not seeing the true form of power, but rather one historical instantiation of it. We should not therefore expect to see power take this specific form in other times and places. Thomas (2002:41–5) goes on to highlight how Neolithic (and Bronze Age) chiefdom models are predicated on an inappropriate "sovereignty" model of power.

Miller and Tilley (1984) certainly opened up archaeology to new ways of thinking about power, and Thomas (2002) is right to highlight the need to think about power much more carefully in archaeology. Thomas (2002:47) argues that power is "relational and continually in process . . . enabling, as well as constraining, and is constitutive of identity and understanding," but Thomas' definition of power is still one firmly wedded to the human. To develop a position on power that is capable of engaging completely with a post-anthropocentric and posthumanist position, we need to decouple power from human exceptionalism completely.

To do this, I draw upon Deleuze's (2006a) own thinking about Foucault and the interpretation of both that runs through the work of Braidotti (2011a, 2011b, 2013, 2019b). Foucault was a clear source of inspiration for Deleuze who wrote a study of Foucauldian thinking (Deleuze 2006a) as he mourned Foucault's death (Morar et al. 2014). He explored Foucault's thinking through an inevitably Deleuzian lens with clear links to his assemblage and nomadic thought. As Deleuze (2006a:60) states, discussing the work of Foucault:

> power is not essentially repressive (since it "incites, it induces, it seduces"); it is practiced before it is possessed (since it is possessed only in a determinable form, that of class, and a determined form, that of State); it passes through the hands of the mastered no less than through the hands of the masters (since it passes through every related force).
>
> *(Deleuze 2006a:60)*

Power is understood to be both *potestas*, that is the negative, repressive and entrapping aspects of power, but also *potentia*, the positive, affirmative, empowering aspects of power (Braidotti 2011b:4, 2019b:33). It is not that power is either entrapping or empowering, it is always both at once. Power is not a single entity, nor does it have a singular origin, nor a subject or object – it is relational, multiple, multilayered, and dynamic (Braidotti 2011b:4, 2019b:32, Deleuze 2006a:59–60). Deleuze (2006a:62) states that power does not "emanate from a central point or unique locus of sovereignty, but at each moment moves 'from one point to another' in a field of forces, marking inflections, resistances, twists and turns." Power is a flow, it is in process. This sense of non-hierarchical and twisting movement marries well with Deleuze and Guattari's (2004) image of the messy, unruly rhizomatic nature of assemblages of connections between different bodies. Power is in process just as assemblages are. Power is "not an attribute but a relation: the power-relation is the set of possible relations between forces" (Deleuze 2006a:24). Relational, new materialist, and posthumanist philosophers ask us to focus on how relations shape the emergence of people, plants, animals, insects, things, and landscapes: these relations themselves are shaped by power. Power has a crucial role in determining the properties and particular affects that a given component can have (Deleuze 2006a:63), and this is because power is a key aspect of the relations that exist between components: it shapes what is possible.

Drawing on Foucault, Deleuze (2006a:60) tells us that power has no form but rather "shows up as an affect" and is both the ability to affect and to be affected. We cannot locate power in the warrior with the sword standing over the dead body of the vanquished foe. Rather, it is flowing in all kinds of relations between warrior and sword, sword and blacksmith, warrior and foe, sword and foe. To study power, we need to make cartographies that map these flows of power through relations (Braidotti 2011b:4). We start with a flat ontology that presumes all components are equally capable of change, but the relations between different components, and the power that flows through those relations, shape what components are capable of within specific relations.

A new image of power is emerging here. It is not possessed or exercised. It is not limited to humans, nor to things or animals; rather, it flows through the messy relationships between them appearing as a rhizomatic tangle. As we saw in Chapter 2, relations define the components that emerge alongside them – power is a key aspect of this. Power has both positive, affirmative, empowering aspects *and* negative and repressive aspects; it is not either one of these but both at the same time.

Posthumanist assemblages and power

This image of power is not about creating a harmonious, free-flowing romantic image of the world where plants, animals, people, and things all just get along. This model of power helps us to better understand issues of social inequality and injustice as well. Power exists differently in various parts of assemblages; it becomes concentrated in some relations and is part of what allows these relations to stabilize and endure. In other parts of assemblages, it is less intense.

Within assemblage theory, two key concepts are *territorialization* and *deterritorialization*, the latter already mentioned. These two concepts link to how assemblages are always temporary, never fixed in time and space, and always changing. At any given moment, some components within an assemblage are acting to stabilize the assemblage, making its boundaries clearer and the components more homogeneous; this is termed territorialization (DeLanda 2006:12). At the same time, other components are acting to break the assemblage apart, to blur its boundaries, making its identity less clear and allowing some parts to fall away, this is termed deterritorialization (DeLanda 2006:12). DeLanda (2006:12) argues that at any given moment, there will be parts of the assemblage that are territorializing and others that are deterritorializing. This process of stabilization and destabilization is linked to power; power allows some relations to stabilize and others to breakdown. The temptation here is to see those stabilizing aspects of assemblages as examples of the negative and repressive aspects of power and those that are destabilizing as part of the affirmative and empowering aspects. I think this would be a mistake. Whether power is empowering or repressive is a matter of perspective; for example, resistance is empowering for one person and destructive for another. Power, as Braidoitti (2011a:4) argues, is always both potentia and potestas at once.

Deleuze and Guattari (2004:59) use the term stratified to capture how some relations become so entangled and so dense that they come to endure (for a discussion, see Chapter 2; Jervis 2018:41). We can think about the way the British monarchy has endured (though also changed) over centuries as an example of a stratified assemblage. The relations that surround and produce it are numerous, deeply entangled, and contain a concentration of power flows. Power does not rest with the monarchy but in the relations that surround it, in relations between flags, anthems, postage stamps, parliaments, bank notes, and newspaper front pages. The importance of the monarchy can change; newspapers print stories about scandals or extravagant spending, the flow of power shifts direction and intensity; this in turn elevates some components at the expense of others and thereby shifts public opinion, the relations between monarchy and the public change as people come to think differently of a member of the royal family.[2] Whilst the power in one part of the assemblage is changing elsewhere, other components remain stable: the flags still fly, the Queen's head is still on postage stamps and coins, and Buckingham Palace remains.

Considering the patriarchy as an example of an assemblage is a good way to think through our posthumanist stance on power. It is not the case that the patriarchy exists in the mind of some master manipulator who has designed it for his own convenience, nor is it concentrated in one single sovereign locus; rather, it is dispersed through millions of relations. The patriarchy is a complex assemblage; it is in things, animals, and plants as much as it is in people; it is not just ideas about the rightful place of men and women and the nature of sexual and gender difference, it is also in buildings, in work schedules, and in the order of names on publications. Power flows through relations in order to stratify them, and in the material world relations are often more stratified and stabilized. Consider, for example, two parents who believe in equal distribution of childcare, but when the changing table for a baby in a café is only in the female bathrooms, their patriarchy-smashing views come up against the stratified patriarchy assemblage reinforcing the idea that childcare is the role of the woman. The power in relations acts to code certain sorts of behavior; coding is the process through which relations come to be sorted and organized (for a discussion, see Chapter 2; Jervis 2018:38–9). Power also allows certain sorts of components to emerge. Power shapes the relations that young women exist within; it produces the particular form of newspapers, television shows, podcasts, and magazines; it creates individuals who become teachers or role models; and all of these relations have the capacity to effect young women to make them believe that any job is open to them or that leadership roles are only for men. These relations then actively shape the young woman affecting her capacity to develop a certain kind of identity to become entangled in certain kinds of relations. In a posthumanist assemblage approach, there is both *no reason* why men should inherently, naturally, and timelessly emerge as leaders and *every reason*, produced through thousands of relationships in a multitude of assemblages, why this is usually the case.

The power in these relationships is both potestas and potentia. Relations of power shape how men and women emerge. On the one hand, the potentia aspect of power empowers men to, for example, more easily join an army, be armed with weapons, shape a particular kind of body, and go to a battlefield to kill the enemy. On the other hand, the potestas aspect of power isolates that man from his family, restricts his behavior, and gives him posttraumatic stress disorder. Power always has this double aspect: empowering and enabling whilst also entrapping and restricting.

The image of power that emerges here is one that allows us to explain the nature of power, the concentration of it within certain assemblages (and areas within assemblages), and how some components emerge as particularly powerful as a result of their relationships. It is capable of explaining and describing the type of relationships that the humanist image of powerful men is predicated on. Importantly, however, it is *not* a timeless static image of power that says that it is necessarily that men emerge as powerful leaders; it allows us to map power differently because it is decoupled from human exceptionalism and from the subject–object binary. Rather, power flows through relationships, relationships that need not be between a powerful man and those who he subjugates. Other flows of power, and thereby other forms of leadership, are possible.

Returning to the Bronze Age

Having considered the theoretical framework necessary to understand power, I return to the Bronze Age with new tools to critique, deconstruct, and begin afresh. Critiques of the warrior-chief are not uncommon, yet the model continues to assert a hold on the period. There are many reasons for this, not least the entanglement of the argument with modernist and patriarchal thinking. This is compounded by the nature of the archaeological evidence from the period; it indicates real changes in conceptions of gender and more material evidence associated with violence. Furthermore, like all archaeological evidence, it invites multiple interpretations: Are warrior graves evidence of real warrior lives? Is rock art a depiction of lived reality? Are weapons symbolic or functional? I argue that power is also playing a key role here, the warrior-chief model is based on a very common (but problematic) understanding of power as linked to the subject–object binary and human (specifically male) exceptionalism.

The warrior-chief is the invention of a humanist ideal against which all other Bronze Age humans fail to compare: he is European, he owns property and capital, he is educated in the ways of the world, he is able-bodied enough to fight, and he has a wife or wives. He is rich and therefore he is powerful and therefore he is a leader. The warrior by comparison is the lesser version: he does not quite measure-up, his lack of property drives him toward violence as a means to gain capital. Other identities (when they are considered) are presented as secondary, inactive, and unimportant. It is clear that this model is as humanist as it is patriarchal. The idea that the chief possesses power as he possesses bronze, and the later warrior-chief possesses power that he uses weapons and violence to exercise, fails to appreciate the nature of power. Power does not have subjects and objects, it is not possessed; rather, it is a quality of relationships. When we continue to see power as something that has an origin and locus and can be possessed, we continue to uphold and promote a bad model of power and leadership and we act to make that model appear timeless.

Critique alone will not be enough to deconstruct the warrior-chief and his power – we need new narratives too. Therein lies the challenge at the heart of my dilemma from the opening of the paper; what new narratives do I want to replace it with? I think there are two key steps. First, we need to continue to critique, deconstruct, and then replace the warrior-chief model. Second, we need to focus our efforts on other identities in this period and other forms of power.

For posthumanist thinkers, identity is not a category that we place people in, but a process (Braidotti 2011a, 2011b; Puar 2012) and humans are always deeply entangled in multiple relationships. A recent paper by Derek Pitman and Roger Doonan (2018) highlighted how the warrior is presented as someone outside of society. They argue instead that we need to resituate them within society as people embedded in relations. In particular, Pitman and Doonan (2018:122–3) take an embodied approach and argue that in order to become a warrior, one needs to have weapons and to work with them, reshaping both the body and the objects in the process; one is not born a warrior but becomes one (cf. de Beauvoir 1997). Moreover, to become one takes relations. Imagine a single spear; to produce it one needs copper and tin, a mold, crucibles, knowledge about smelting and casting, wood for a shaft, and many more other things. You need relations with blacksmiths, miners, and traders. Perhaps you even need things to exchange with the blacksmiths and traders in return for your spearhead. Or you need to have all the skills, knowledge, and access to materials to make your own. The warrior has to be part of a whole series of relations entangling them with other people, places, materials, plants, and animals. Power flows through all these relations, it shapes who will work with them, who will not, what materials are available, what forms of objects are possible. That power is both potentia and potestas; the spearhead empowers the warrior with greater capacities for violence, but it also entraps them in assemblages of relations with others creating dependencies and debts. The spearhead might well empower them to kill another, but it also marks them apart, separating them from others, making them feel differently, perhaps negatively; it opens up some possibilities at the same time as cutting off others.

Fontijn (2005) has argued that warrior identity was not fixed but fluid; Fontijn and Harry Fokkens (2007) have argued that weapon deposition might have taken place at key moments of transition in the lives of warriors (e.g., death or becoming an elder). ChristianHorn (2011) has argued that hoards of weapons, common in the European Bronze Age, could well be weapons used in combat that had to be symbolically decommissioned and destroyed following battle. TobiasMörtz (2018) takes this further and argues that these practices could be part of the processes through which warriors could begin to lay aside violence and return to normal society. Identities are shaped through relations; they are processes, not categories, and power plays a key role in their construction. The archaeological evidence suggests one could become a warrior in the Bronze Age; this process of becoming is deeply entangled in wider assemblages of relationships: relationships shaped by power where power defines what is possible and what is not, power that is both empowering and entrapping at the same time.

I have begun to sketch the outline of a new understanding of the warrior as embedded and entangled, not as a locus of power but as part of a rhizome that power flows through. Much more work is needed. The second step in this process is investing effort in the other identities of the period, in those that have been painted as secondary to the chiefs and warriors. Deleuze and Guattari (2004) argue for the importance of minoritarian narratives, or narratives that are not dominant and mainstream (see also Braidotti 2011b:30–1). Becoming-minoritarian is a process, and to become-minoritarian in the Bronze Age we need to explore other identities and other ways of being in the world. We need to, for example, explore the processes of becoming-woman that emerges across the Bronze Age. We need to think about the formation of multiple different kinds of identities for women in the period, and, importantly, we need to think about how these are constructed through relations and the role that power plays in this. Excellent work on this topic has already been done by Brück (2005b, 2009) considering the identities of women in relation to the dead and the production of textiles. By mapping the role of power in these relations, we can begin to consider different assemblages of power relations, different forms of leadership, and the creation of different capacities, possibilities, and identities through them.

On this journey to bring alive minoritarian narratives from the Bronze Age, I take heart from the lessons of Braidotti (2011b:43) – she describes becoming-minoritarian as an open process, not something that we can ever complete. She argues that often the first step is to argue for a role reversal, in the case of exploring Bronze Age identities, this might be placing the woman in the position of the warrior or leader, but she argues this is never enough because it maintains a form of identity that is binary and oppositional. In this case, it would also potentially retain a damaging model of power. We have to keep working to move beyond this, to create new cartographies of power so that we can explore the process of becoming-woman in the Bronze Age.

Notes

1 Much of the Bronze Age literature continues to use the term "chief" to refer to leaders and uses the term "chiefdom" to describe the nature of political leadership and social structure in the period. Timothy Pauketat's (2007) book *Chiefdoms and Other Archaeological Delusions* eloquently critiques both concepts and highlights their problematic nature. Similarly, Brück and Fontijn (2013) have problematized and deconstructed the term in a European Bronze Age context. The term is retained here in order that I may critique it and to offer clarity in connection to the existing literature.

2 The shifting relationships between Prince Harry, Meghan Markle, and the royal family is a case in point.

9

DISCUSSING POSTHUMAN APPROACHES TO POWER

Marxism, politics, affect

Introduction

Posthumanist and new materialist theories place critical emphasis on relationality, material vibrancy, and the arbitrary nature of modern Western thought. Critics of these new ideas sometimes mischaracterize them as apolitical and ahuman, and whether we agree or not, it is certainly the case that many archaeologists experimenting with these new directions in theory have yet to seriously address the status of power and politics. In Chapter 8, Rachel argued for the continued importance of addressing power from a posthumanist and new materialist standpoint. She did so through a consideration of the Bronze Age. In this chapter, we continue to explore Rachel's argument via a series of dialogues about Marxism, politics, agency, and affect. Our comparison between various strains of Marxist thought with Rachel's approach serves to better define the similarities and distinctions between materialisms new and old. The issue of politics allows us to further emphasize the differences between posthumanism and ahumanism. Finally, our considerations of the differences between agency and affect help to better situate a new materialist/posthumanist understanding of relationality.

Materialisms old and new

CRAIG: Rachel, you raised some important points about power in the last chapter. I'm particularly interested in your turn to posthumanist feminist thinkers like Braidotti (2011a, 2011b, 2013, 2019b) to help you rethink the Bronze Age. Because archaeologists have spilled a significant amount of ink on the topic of power, I wonder if there is room for further critical comparison between the approach you've outlined and more "traditional" archaeological engagements with this theme.

In particular, I am thinking about archaeology's long-term connections with Marxism (e.g., Johnson 1996; Little and Shackel 2007; McGuire 1992). We could look back to Shanks and Tilley's (1982) chapter in *Structural and Symbolic Archaeologies* (Hodder 1982) and find an early relational approach to power, but one that turns to ideology using a Marxist-inspired frame. They (Shanks and Tilley 1982:131) drew upon Althusser's (e.g., 1977) work, defining ideology as:

> mode(s) of intervention in social relations, carried on through practice, which secures the *reproduction* rather than the *transformation* of the social formation in the presence of contradictions between structural principles at the level of structure, and of clashes of interests between actors and groups at the level of the system.

An important component of these "interventions," according to Marxist-leaning archaeologists, is the material world, including the artifacts we uncover and think through. In historical archaeology, Mark Leone (1988) employed a similar model to critique James Deetz's (1996) notion of the "Georgian Order." Leone pushed back against Deetz's structural model to show how the materials under focus played *active* parts in the world, helping to naturalize the growing inequalities of capitalist North America. This work also emphasized the notion of individuality in ideologies of capitalism, showing how beliefs in "atomic" individuals – conceived as falsely apart from the rest of the world and wholly responsible for their own fates (pulling themselves up by the bootstraps . . . or not) – helped to maintain and advance capitalist inequalities (see also Matthews 2010 for a discussion of ideology and individualism).

Of course, Marxism also offers a means of challenging capitalism through praxis. As Barbara Little (2007:14) notes, historical archaeologists often seek to make "history useful." In a synthesis chapter on Marxism in historical archaeology, Randall McGuire (2006:124) highlights three important goals of Marxism: (1) to *know* the world; (2) to *critique* the world; and (3) to *transform* the world.

So, in short, how does a general posthumanist feminist approach compare with these materialist theories –in terms of both knowing the past and changing the present?

RACHEL: You are correct to draw out these connections between my own thinking on power and Marxist approaches. Marxism, as a materialist philosophy, clearly shares ground with the emphasis on materials and the role of the non-human in my own work, which I draw more from my engagement with posthumanism and new materialism. I think there is also significant ground shared between myself and specifically Marxist archaeologists in the political approach that we take to our studies of the past. Like Randall McGuire (2006:124), I too desire to *critique* the world I live in and to *transform* it in the wake of that critique. The difference between our approaches is most evident in the first goal "to *know* the world" because I choose a different theoretical framework through which to come to know the past worlds I study and the present worlds I live within.

One of the key areas where I think we can see the continuing influence of Marx is in social evolutionary models of society that posit a series of stages through which societies move (e.g., Sahlins and Service 1960). One of my main research interests is in how archaeologists study and theorize change (see Crellin 2020); as a result of this, I find the Marxist model of societies moving through a series of gradual changes punctuated by moments of revolution to be unconvincing. My new materialist influences mean I see all material as vibrant and as a result I reject what I term *block-time* approaches where we have periods of stasis punctuated by moments of radical transformation (Crellin 2020:Chapter 1); instead, I see the world as in constant motion. In addition, my posthumanist thinking makes me consider how these types of models have been applied in damaging ways to classify different societies as "less civilized" and thereby less human. This is something that post-processual Marxist approaches in archaeology sought to directly address; for example, Miller and Tilley (1984:2) critique approaches where societies have to move through a "league table" that passes judgment on them.

LINDSAY: I'd like to jump in here and echo Rachel's comments regarding the problematic and lingering nature of social evolutionary models. Although archaeology as a discipline has formally denounced the racist underpinnings of nineteenth-century social evolution *a la* Lewis Henry Morgan and Herbert Spencer, it has been more difficult to abandon the theoretical concepts underlying a "block-time" approach as Rachel calls it. For example, archaeology textbooks overwhelmingly follow a linear format that begins with hunter-gatherers, proceeds through the Neolithic revolution and the development of writing, and concludes with state-level societies. This structure in many ways resembles Morgan's proposed progression of human societies from savagery into barbarism and finally "civilization." Indeed, despite post-processual interventions, it seems that most archaeological research continues to be framed through the discourse of "complexity." The resiliency of these ideas leads me to wonder if there is something inherent and inextricable about Western notions of temporality that limit efforts to move beyond "block-time" approaches. In other words, is this an ontological problem or merely a matter of disciplinary will?

RACHEL: I agree Lindsay, I think ideas of progress, development, and complexity are very often present in the narratives that we write about the past. Usually this is implicit rather than explicit. I know when I have spoken in research seminars about the issue of progressive narratives in our discipline, I usually get a response along the lines of "but we have moved past that" I do not necessarily think we always have. I also think the connection with temporality that you make is key. As Gavin Lucas (2005) has demonstrated, the fact that we think about time in the West as unilinear, universal, singular, and unidirectional has consequences for how we think about change. An alternative understanding of temporality is necessary to get away from this, so we definitely need an ontological shift. I think the disciplinary will, as you put it Lindsay, is secondary to the ontology but still a part of the problem – moving away from progressivist models means abandoning many of the "foundation myths" of the discipline and working out how to tell a different story to the public in particular – this is challenging.

In my work, I turn to ideas from new materialism that suggest time emerges from material change (or action if you prefer) and is multiple. I feel optimistic at present (there is an irony coming) that we can begin to really undo some of this problematic thinking because I think many of the progressive and teleological models are held up by the idea that "things are getting better" and that "humans are always making things better." Evidently, this is not true as we come to terms with the climate crisis and our attitudes toward others. Awareness is increasing of the horrific and damaging ways that westerners have classified people (from transphobic attitudes, to racism, to anti-migrant sentiment, to name but a few) and approached their relationships with non-humans. As a result, I think the idea of progress can be more readily critiqued now than in the past.

CRAIG: These are excellent points about the dangers associated with narratives of progress. How exactly do your critiques compare with the post-processual thinking that was inspired by Marxism?

RACHEL: The kind of thinking that was inspired by Neo-Marxism, like that of Miller and Tilley (1984) that emphasizes moving beyond progressive unilinear frameworks of change, holds more potential for me. That said, I take issue with how ideology is presented in Marxist approaches as a form of "false consciousness." I can see that these are really interesting ideas that can be productive, but I reject a position that suggests that some people and communities do not "correctly" understand their world and reality or that they are in some way dupes. I see this as the same form of argument that has been used repeatedly to suppress a range of people; for example, women don't have the ability to understand the complexity of the world, or Indigenous groups do not understand the reality and universality of science. Perhaps more importantly, I am not saying that we cannot be mistaken in our understanding of the world, rather I reject the concept of false consciousness because I do not think there is one version of understanding that is truly correct and accurate, and that all others are false.

CRAIG: Okay, I'm beginning to see some important distinctions between your new materialist approach and that of Neo-Marxist archaeologists. Yet I think more comparison to general dialectical models is still in order. For instance, McGuire explains how dialectical models address some of the dualisms we explore in this book. He writes (McGuire 2006:141),

> The dialectic helps archaeologists to escape many of the oppositions that frequent debates about archaeological theory: it also provides a method to study change. The oppositions include science versus humanism, objectivity versus subjectivity, the material versus the mental, and evolution versus history. The dialectic leads us to examine how these poles are interconnected rather than seeing them as irresolvable opposites. How does this model actually compare with posthumanist approaches that seek to challenge dualistic ways of knowing or being?

RACHEL: In terms of the nature of dialectics, this is where I part company most clearly with Marxist approaches. I agree with Timothy Webmoor and Christopher Witmore (2008), who argue elegantly that using dialectics never truly allows us to overcome binary oppositions. When you start from a position where there are two clearly defined and opposed categories in the beginning, you can never truly move beyond that. The dialectic is not a binary or dualism overcome. I also agree with Webmoor and Witmore (2008) when they argue that within these dialectics, the emphasis, all too often, falls on the human side; they consider, for example, Miller's (2005) dialectical theories of materialization and objectification in which people make things and things make people – whilst the two appear to construct each other equally, the emphasis in analysis usually ends up being on the human side of the dialectic as a result of our anthropocentrism.

I often associate (rightly or wrongly) Marxist inspired approaches with historical archaeology (e.g., Johnson 1996; Leone 1988), despite its early use by those studying the Neolithic and Iron Age (see, for example, Miller and Tilley 1984; Parker Pearson 1984; Shanks and Tilley 1982); in particular, I wonder whether it has become more easily applied to those studying capitalism and its effects. Craig, what do you, as someone who often studies the interaction between early capitalism and Indigenous communities, think of Marxist approaches to power and ideology?

CRAIG: I see Marxist approaches to power and ideology as a core and irreplaceable part of historical archaeology. Even though I choose alternative theoretical pathways in my own work for reasons discussed later, the importance of these ideas in archaeologies of colonialism and capitalism is undeniable. Although I do not use them directly, I certainly build upon and critique Marxist archaeologies by simply participating in discourses colored largely by these approaches. For me, three key contributions of this literature stand out. First, exemplified in Leone's (1988) critique of the "Georgian Order" (Deetz 1996) mentioned previously, Marxist approaches offered a much-needed challenge to structuralist models that relegated materials to passive and reflective elements of social life. Instead of explaining the emergence of individual table settings in eighteenth-century America as simply *reflecting* a normative shift to a more individual-centered worldview or mindset, Leone asked about how these emergent material conditions actively structured social relations, particularly those related to wealth inequalities. Second, and directly related to one of my critiques of "world-centered" ontological approaches in the next chapter, Marxist approaches recognize continuities and relations that cross-cut social and cultural "boundaries." For me this entails recognizing aspects of colonialism and capitalism that bound and continue to bind settler colonists with Indigenous and other peoples typically thought of as "subaltern." There is a realist element here that looks at human social relations and challenges Western worldviews, particularly conceptions of the individual; instead, Marxists point to the interconnections between so-called "individuals" (e.g., structural inequalities). Finally, as you've already noted, Marxist emphases on political action are incredibly important. It reminds us that we do not conduct archaeology in a vacuum and that it is absolutely crucial to carefully think through how our archaeologies affect the world around us, including our fellow humans.

RACHEL: It clearly provides a core aspect of historical archaeology, but I don't think of you as a Marxist archaeologist – so I guess there are some aspects of it that you do not find useful?

CRAIG: Correct, there are some limiting aspects of Marxism in my opinion. For the purposes of this discussion, I see three main issues. First, I've always found practice theory (e.g., Bourdieu 1977; Certeau 1984; Giddens 1984) a necessary supplement to Marxist approaches. Practice theory certainly takes into account intentional human actions designed to push back against social structures (i.e., praxis), but it also considers the roles that practical consciousness and unintended outcomes play in generating bodily dispositions (*habitus*, Bourdieu 1977) and shaping social and cultural reproduction in general. Here, Foucault's (1979) writings on power also come into play; for him, power was diffuse and distributed across much more than the dominant group (see Chapter 8); his work also considers the role that the material world, such as the panopticon, played in disciplining *all* bodies. Second, similar to you, I see most Marxist approaches as anthropocentric. Intentionally or not, many Marxist approaches seem to reify beliefs in a human-separate and human-centric world (see Mrozowski 1999 for a similar critique). For instance, commodities, use values, and exchange values – as defined by Marx (1990; see also Matthews 2010 for a useful discussion of these terms) – emphasize *human* values. The commodity is "an object outside of us, a thing that by its properties satisfies human wants of some sort or another" (Marx 1990:41). Much less or no attention is placed on the vibrancy of matter and how non-humans participate in, afford, and limit human histories. People have the lion's share of power in these models and they control or resist other people or groups of people primarily via intentional acts. Yes, this power is connected with – and flows through – the material world, but it is much more of a human-centered model. What about other types of power, such as non-human energy flows that make and sometimes break capitalist histories? I recently began exploring this possibility in my collaborative work with Amélie Allard, in which we look at the importance of rivers in making and breaking the fur trade in North America (Allard and Cipolla in press; Cipolla and Allard 2019). Third, these views seem to regard Western modernity as their default starting point; because, as you note, I work on more-than-Western-histories, I am open to exploring other alternatives. An excellent example of one such alternative is Anna Tsing's (2015) non-anthropocentric, assemblage-approach to late capitalism.

This whole discussion brings up the broader question of translation, which we address again later in the book (Chapter 11). For now, it is worth raising the question about theoretical "purity" and just how much we have to transform an idea before we think it's worth calling it something new. For example, practice theory certainly emerged in dialogue with – and in partial opposition to – both structuralism and materialism (e.g., Parker Pearson 1984; Shanks and Tilley 1982), but most contemporary archaeologists choose to identify it as a discrete theory with its own label. One could argue that any use of theory from disciplines outside of archaeology involves some degree of translation (and we could push this even further if we so chose). I would certainly say that the use of Eduardo Viveiros de Castro's (2013) perspectivism in archaeology (see Chapter 10), for example, represents an act of translation; it has become something "new," in my opinion, worthy of a different moniker.

What I derive from this discussion thus far is that we both strive to keep something that resembles general Marxist calls for praxis and political action. But we also seek ways around the anthropocentrism of Marxist approaches. For these reasons, we identify our respective theoretical stances as something other than Marxist. But are there any other major issues that set your approach apart from an "old materialism"? What about new materialist perspectives on the shifting boundaries of assemblages and their components? That strikes me as quite different from a materialist perspective.

RACHEL: Yes, I think you are right about that Craig. New materialist approaches identify assemblages (and the components they are made up of) as always shifting and in process, they have permeable boundaries and are not static (e.g., Barad 2007; DeLanda 2006, 2016). In such a world, there are no fixed subjects and objects, and no fixed commodities and consumers. Assemblages and the components they consist of can be both at once and shift between being these different descriptions. These are not the kinds of changes that take a revolution to bring them about but rather they are constant and ongoing in the world.

Power, politics, and archaeology

LINDSAY: Rachel, I want to move the discussion away from Marxist approaches and turn toward the issue of power more broadly. In reading through your discussion of posthumanist post-anthropocentric approaches to power, I found myself drawing parallels with some Indigenous understandings of power. I'm particularly thinking about the Numic-speaking worlds' concept of *puha*, which refers to an animating force that exists among all living things and flows along particular channels (Miller 1983:351). This is a non-anthropocentric view of power, in that humans, spirits, flora, fauna, and geographical features are all repositories of puha. It is also a non-hierarchical approach, in that both human and non-human actors can have different amounts of puha, but they do not have power over other entities as a result of these differences. With this framework in mind, I would agree with your argument that a non-human centered approach offers an important alternative to dualistic notions of power based on hierarchy and exploitation.

RACHEL: I had not come across the concept of *puha* before, but reading about it, there are indeed some striking similarities. I was particularly taken with the emphasis that is placed on flow and process. Jay Miller (1983:341) discusses the way that the Numic-speaking world is poorly described by nouns, he tells us that "verbs are usually much more important" because of the focus on process. Tim Ingold (2011:72) in his arguments for a more animated understanding of the world [in a broadly Deleuzian frame (cf. Ingold 2011:174)] talks about the names of animals being better understood as verbs rather than nouns; this is one of those moments where one worries about appropriating ideas (cf. Todd 2016). Similarly, the discussion of power as a kinetic rather than static concept chimes with my argument.

LINDSAY: I think you bring up a good point here about the slippery slope of appropriating ideas from different cultures. I suppose my goal in bringing up the concept of puha was primarily to increase the visibility of Indigenous concepts that have parallels in the Western canon and that may serve as more appropriate theoretical alternatives in certain culturally grounded contexts.

I like the notion of thinking about things in terms of verbs rather than nouns that you reference and see a lot of analytical utility in framing discussions of power in terms of flow. As you note in Chapter 8, these types of approaches to power require abandoning anthropocentricism. Building on your rebuttal to Van Dyke, Hodder, and Thomas, I would also challenge the notion that abandoning anthropocentrism leads to a neglect of social justice. It seems to me that archaeologists working on either side of the anthropocentric debate have analyzed power relations in the past while failing to address inequality in the present. Do you have any thoughts on why we haven't seen a larger shift within the discipline in how archaeologists approach questions of social justice in the past and present?

RACHEL: If I am honest I think some archaeologists just do not see social justice as part of their job and many archaeologists struggle to see how they can connect their own work on the past with social justice issues in the present (there are of course exceptions). Our work is never purely about the past: it exists in, and does things to, the present. It is always political.

I had been mulling over power in relation to posthumanist thinking for a while and was provoked to start writing and thinking about it more seriously on the morning following Trump's election. It struck me that the general conception of what power is, who can have it, and what it looks like is really problematic. I wanted to rethink power in a different frame. The Bronze Age themes I discuss in Chapter 8 – ideas of masculinity, violence, strength, wealth, success, and leadership – are all explicitly linked to this normative idea of power. When we talk about it in these terms in the Bronze Age, we are naturalizing it, we are making it appear ahistorical and eternal. Our students, and the public who visit museums and watch documentaries, get the impression that this model of power is normal and correct, and that it has existed always and everywhere. Seeking to write about power in different ways came from this place for me.

The obvious critique of my work is that my academic musing and philosophical thinking about power does little to actually change lives. I do not fully reject that critique, but I would say that teaching brings me hope here. Ollie and I teach archaeological theory at Leicester, and we have just developed a new course on power and difference. I love teaching theory because it is a course where you often get an excellent opportunity to change how students think about the world. If I can make a student realize that the idea that humans stand above and apart from the rest of the world is problematic, or if I can make them rethink gender and sexuality, or think about power not as something possessed by the mighty (and the male), then that is more important to me than them knowing about what exactly happened at 2200 BCE at Stonehenge. These are only small steps though.

LINDSAY: Along these lines it may be worthwhile here to return to Craig's discussion of the Marxist imperative to transform the world. To me this call to *transform* is an explicitly political one in that it refers to altering power dynamics and decision-making in the public sphere. As I make clear in Chapter 4, I believe that in many ways the Western world and the discipline of archaeology have become "apolitical." An apolitical attitude puts "group interests, private needs, and individualized activities above public interests" (Havelka 2016:13). In relation to Trump's election, I believe that this apolitical direction has led to declining voter turnout, the abandonment of bi-partisanship, and growing dissatisfaction with the career politician. Since the postcolonial and Marxist critiques of the early 1980s, archaeology also appears to have become largely apolitical. Social justice and inequality have become in-group matters (e.g., Indigenous archaeologists seeking to create new collaborative paradigms and foci) rather than disciplinary efforts. As Shannon Dawdy suggests in her 2009 article on Millennial archaeology, "most public archaeology should really be called public relations archaeology. Archaeology has been very useful lately, but primarily to itself" (Dawdy 2009:138).

While Dawdy goes further than I would in denouncing the utility of public archaeology, her statement speaks to a wider suspicion, and in some cases outright rejection, of the idea that archaeology should serve the "public(s) good." I view the apolitical bent of archaeology today as fueling theoretical debates about power while failing to spark parallel transformations in power relations. What, if any, role do you think apolitics play in limiting alternative conceptions of power? Do you have any thoughts on how one might break down the current barriers to larger disciplinary change created by apolitics and the proliferation of in-group interests (e.g., feminist interests, class interests, Indigenous interests, African-American interests)?

RACHEL: At the outset I want to say that all archaeology is always political, whether archaeologists like it or not. I agree though that there has been a real shift away from acknowledging this political aspect and specifically utilizing archaeology for political purposes, to address social justice issues, and for public good. In student essays on the power and politics of the past, they often react strongly against the (mis)use of archaeology for political purposes citing the classic example of the work of Gustaf Kossina in relation to Nazi Germany (Arnold 2006). This seems to lead to an outright rejection of the use of the past for politics from some of them; I wonder if this is how some archaeologists feel?

Like you, I agree with Dawdy's (2009:138) statement at least in part; I think the "outreach" work associated with many archaeological digs and research projects in Britain and Ireland is often viewed as public relations oriented rather than doing actual social good. I also think this has been partly embedded in this form by government policy in the UK – for example, the big research funders all require statements about "impact" as part of their application process. For a long time, the *modus operandi* for archaeologists to make "impact" in these terms has been to provide some volunteering opportunities, work with some school students, and produce some heritage resources. All of this is well and good, but often it is relatively pedestrian in terms of the actual effect the work has. On the other hand, on my own dig (where we do all those things), I see the immense value of working with local volunteers; I see people gaining work experience, fulfilling their passions and dreams, and gaining positive experiences from the chance to be part of a multigenerational team, doing physical work outside. I also see our school's program having an impact as schoolchildren get excited about the past and engage with math and science in unusual ways.

Away from this kind of work, which at times we could classify as apolitical as it is often public relations oriented, I want to bring up ancient DNA (hereafter aDNA) as an area where the problem of politics versus apolitics is coming to the fore in European archaeology (for a wider discussion, see Crellin and Harris 2020). The last five years have seen an explosion of aDNA research in Europe (Allentoft et al. 2015; Brace et al. 2019; Haak et al. 2015; Lipson et al. 2017; Mathieson et al. 2015; Mathieson et al. 2018; Olalde et al. 2018). Many archaeologists have been deeply uncomfortable with the form and tone of this work because the primary focus has been on migration and because it appears (to archaeologists at least) to be operating in a problematic culture historical framework (Brophy 2018; Carlin 2018:35; Crellin and Harris 2020; Furholt 2018; Hakenbeck 2019; Heyd 2017; Hofmann 2015; Frieman and Hofmann 2019; Vander Linden 2016). Much current DNA research makes me uncomfortable because it draws links between material culture, ethnic groups, and identities and because it constantly focuses on mass migration bringing about major landmark transitions in the past. As an example, Olalde et al. (2018) discuss the spread of "Steppe-ancestry"-related DNA across Europe at the beginning of the Bronze Age and argue for about 90% genetic "replacement" in Britain. Even in the left-leaning press in the UK, Olalde et al.'s (2018) article was reported with the headline "Did Dutch hordes kill off the early Britons who started Stonehenge?" (McKie 2017). At conferences, in editorials, and increasingly in publications we are seeing repeated calls for the political ramifications of this research to be considered (see particularly Hakenbeck 2019; Frieman and Hofmann 2019). Archaeologists are not denying the importance of migration, or that migration happened, but instead want it to be handled much more carefully, in a way that appreciates the complex, multiple, and nuanced nature of identity in a politically aware manner. They want this specifically because of the current global political climate in relation to migration. Geneticists seem to believe they are dealing in facts not politics – they appear to see their work as apolitical. Yet we know that right-wing groups engage with aDNA research and relate it to ancestry research today (Booth 2018; Richardson and Booth 2017); we also know that Europe is in the midst of a migration crisis and the rise of far-right populism. In Europe, the populist right has propagated a false view of migration as always negative and as leading to population replacement (the advertising campaigns surrounding Brexit provide key evidence here). Tom Booth (2019), an archaeologist who works with geneticists but has also explored the links between DNA testing and the right wing (Booth 2018; Richardson and Booth 2017), has argued that we should work to reclaim the phrase "population replacement" from the far-right and use it in its scientifically correct form. For me this misses the point, it is being used in an actively damaging and racist way by the far-right in Europe and archaeologists and scientists should not be providing fodder that can be appropriated to cause harm.

I have specific concerns and worries about the rise of aDNA research and lots of those views come from a place that fears that Europe is being used as an "uncontroversial testing ground" for aDNA work on historic migration and that eventually we will see this same type of work in places where it will be even more damaging than it has been in Europe. Kim TallBear's (2013) research on ancient DNA stands as a powerful warning on the risks and problems of this kind of research and as a key argument that this kind of science is not neutral or apolitical. We've seen one of the leading aDNA specialists,

David Reich (2018:163), say that he cannot understand why Indigenous peoples do not want to share their DNA with him as he sees DNA research as a "force for good"; but as Ann Horsburgh (2018) points out, Reich does not get to define what constitutes harm for Indigenous peoples. Looking at this debate, it should be clear to archaeologists that we cannot be apolitical about aDNA. The other thing that strikes me here is the locality of ethics and politics; I do not want archaeologists to talk about population replacement in the European past, but I would want us to talk about the population replacement and genocide that emerged in the Americas as a result of colonialism.

To bring it back to your original question. I do think we have seen the rise of apolitics in archaeology since the 1990s. I think that many archaeologists see their work as apolitical, neutral, and fact/data driven. In particular, I think archaeological science is often viewed this way (but see Jones 2001). This is a mistake because no data are neutral, and archaeology is always political. In a European context, we are beginning to see the rise of more explicitly political discussions once more in response to both aDNA studies and the rise of the far-right in Europe and America. In particular, a newspaper article recently showed images of neo-Nazis with flaming torches vowing to "take back" archaeological sites at Avebury, a Neolithic henge (Dixon 2019), and this seems to have had a galvanizing effect on archaeologists in Britain as they reacted in horror, on Twitter at least. Whether this will produce a new wave of more political archaeological research remains to be seen.

Relating power and affect

OLLIE: I'd like to take this in a slightly different direction. Rather than focusing on politics and power, I'd like to return to a topic from Chapter 2, affect, so we can explore this in relation to the discussion of power in Chapter 8. In Chapter 2, I described all relations as relations of affect. In Chapter 8, Rachel says that all relations have power in them and that "power has a crucial role in determining the properties and particular affects that a given component can have." Are power and affect synonyms here? Or are they describing different qualities of relations? Or are they different forms of relationship? As archaeologists, when is it useful to evoke the language of power, and when is it useful to talk about affect?

RACHEL: Let me start with the move from agency to affect. In terms of language, I think that, from a posthumanist perspective, affect is a much better term than agency. Agency is (unfortunately) still heavily linked to the concept of intention for many archaeologists. More problematically, I think that agency is a term that is deeply humanist: we more readily associate it with a certain kind of person, and it is this kind of person that humanism holds up as an ideal. The concept of affect, by comparison, makes it clear that we have the capacity to both affect and be affected, and it does not presume in advance who will have those capacities. By concentrating on affect, we open up a fresh space to talk about how different types of humans can affect and be affected (see Crellin and Harris in review). We also open up a space where we can more readily talk about non-humans being able to affect and be affected without running into all the problems that emerge when people *think* you are talking about object agency (though, of course, we never were talking about object agency because agency is a quality of relationships!).

LINDSAY: That's an interesting point Rachel, and I agree that the term affect offers one way of moving beyond the human. The definition of affect laid out in Chapter 2 describes it as a two-way street, in which bodies change the capacity of other bodies to act and in the process change themselves. This understanding of affect resonates to me with Indigenous conceptions of power, discussed earlier, which emphasize the relationship between different types of entities; we might think of this approach in terms of "power to" rather than "power over." Along these lines, I am curious Ollie how you think a new materialist focus on affect deals with hierarchy and how this might relate to the discussion of the intensive qualities of relations?

OLLIE: The relationship between affect and hierarchy is interesting to think about here. As Rachel set out in Chapter 8, new materialism often gets accused of ignoring power structures, or trying to flatten power differentials, it's one of the many ways in which the term "flat ontology" gets (mis) understood (cf. Cipolla in review b; Crellin and Harris in review). I think there might be really interesting ways to use new materialism to think about hierarchy, though by focusing on a term I introduced in Chapter 2: intensity. One of the important things about intensity is its irresistibility, it presses in on you whether you like it or not. This pressure can register as emotional, physical, or violent even, in human bodies at least. Thus, the capacity to focus intensive affects is in itself a form of power. When we write about hierarchy, the tools for how power is maintained are often overlooked, or subsumed within ideas of economic control, or secret ritual knowledge, or whatever. These explanations merely defer the critical question though: Outside of the state apparatus of modernity, why do people tolerate oppression? When we think of the intensity of affect, the way in which it puts pressure on bodies, changing what they can do and how they can operate, we can open up really interesting ideas about how it is that certain power structures are maintained.

RACHEL: That is a really interesting question Ollie – Why do we accept oppression? And an interesting way of thinking about it – that the intensity of affect plays a key role. Returning to your question about the relationship between affect and power, affect has a lot to recommend it from my perspective. In spite of that, I think that we need to retain the term power and work to reshape how it is understood. Power is a word with clear political leverage. I do not want to abandon the term because I think it is really important that we talk about, and write about, situations where people are affected by power, particularly when those affects are negative. It is important that we retain a language that allows us to talk about how migrants and refugees are affected by power at borders, or how power relations flow through weapons in the Bronze Age. I certainly think that not talking about power would do those who are repressed very little good.

OLLIE: I definitely agree with this. All of our terminology comes with baggage: with its own assemblage. The reasons you outlined previously are why I think we should largely stop talking about agency. For me, I think power is a useful way of talking about a particular set of affects, those involved in particular kinds of historically emergent relationships. So whilst we could discuss how clay and a potter interact in terms of power, in the relations between material and maker, it is more useful here, I suggest, to talk about affect. In this context using the term power makes it too easy to slip into a mode of associating power solely with the human being. In contrast, we could talk about the relations between enslaved people and owners in the Roman Empire in terms of affect, but this might lead us to downplay the political nature of the relationships that emerge. In effect, power becomes a critical adjective for describing particular kinds of affect, particular ways in which bodies can affect and be affected; it can lend our interpretations a specific texture in appropriate assemblages. Power thus offers us an opportunity to differentiate certain kinds of relations and insist they are recognized.

RACHEL: I completely agree Ollie, but I also think that we need to think further about how we use the term power. The risk here is that we use the term to talk primarily about relationships between humans and about relationships of exploitation and repression. This would miss the point that both Foucault (1979) and Deleuze (2006a) were trying to make. Power is not limited to humans and it is not merely repressive. So yes, we absolutely need to retain power to talk about specific kinds of relations, but we also need to make sure we are using it to talk about "power to" as well as "power over" and that we are using it to talk about non-humans as part of power structures too. Power is as much in resistance as it is in subjugation.

OLLIE: That's a really good point. I would think that we might want to talk about the power glaciers have, for example, to shape landscapes – an example of "power to." In our current world, we are witnessing the power changing climates will have to shape the world we live in.

RACHEL: Or the power of a virus to bring down economies, destroy businesses, reconfigure social relations, shift politics, and kill thousands of people.

OLLIE: Exactly. Power, like affect, has nothing necessarily to do with human beings. Indeed, it always involves non-humans, because even those assemblages that include humans involve non-humans too. The slave and owner example includes all kinds of non-humans from chains and ships to whips and weapons.

We can push this a bit further if we want to explore where power and affect come from, and how they emerge within the assemblages that Deleuze and Guattari (2004) write about. Deleuze (2007:124–5) emphasizes that rather than thinking about power as primary, we should instead think about desire as a pre-personal force that drives actions in particular ways. Desire is not prior to assemblages; Deleuze and Parnet (2002:71) remind us that desire only emerges in assemblages, but it is not after them either. Just as we saw with relations in Chapter 3, desire emerges in parallel with assemblages. However, understanding how desire flows through assemblages allows us to think about how the relations help to structure those flows of desire, guiding them in particular ways. To return to terms we defined in Chapter 3, the capacity to affect is virtual and emerges through the way the structures of an assemblage (its diagram or abstract machine) help to territorialize certain connections and thereby shape what is possible. The virtual is not a blank space; rather it emerges and is shaped through specific processes (Deleuze and Guattari 2004). Affects then are the potentials to affect and be affected that are emergent in this process, and powers – the power to do things, the power to be affected by things – emerge with them. This position requires us to rethink how we conceptualize and challenge power in the present, because its emergent qualities mean it is not located in ahistorical transcendent unities like "class" or "gender" but rather shifting and immanent. This means it can only be reshaped through experimentation, not revolution, and through work with both humans and non-humans. These experiments will always be risky, but they are necessary.

This is why the critique of a "flat ontology" as making everything the same is so problematic (Cipolla in review b). It is not the case that starting from a flat ontology means that we are suggesting there are no power structures, that anything is possible, and that everything, whether a dog, a coffee mug, or a president are all the same. The virtual space is shaped by power relations, relations of affect, which structure the capacities and potentials that a given element of an assemblage can have. So yes, a president is politically more powerful than a dog, but that is not universally and transcendentally true; it is a product of a particular set of historical processes, which emerge through the kinds of productive difference I discussed in Chapter 2.

Conclusion

RACHEL: Power is part of all relations and should be a central aspect of any relational approach to the past or the present. Talking about power is always going to be political – it involves suggesting what we think power is and how we think it works. A key aspect of the debate in this chapter has centered around the politics of archaeology – about the use of the past to bring about positive changes in the present. Taking a posthumanist and new materialist approach has real potential here because it asks us to consider all concepts as "in motion" and historically specific. This means that even if power and leadership are (rightly or wrongly) associated with masculinity, wealth, strength, and success in the present, we are driven to investigate both how this model of power arose and how it might have been different in different times and places in the past. This allows us to show that power is not a timeless universal but has always been subject to change. In the next chapter, Craig explores the relationship between the ontological turn and Indigenous paradigms, considering the politics and power in the relationship between the two.

10

IN SEARCH OF DIFFERENT PASTS

Craig N. Cipolla

Introduction

In 2004, Chantal Conneller broke new ground in an exceptionally early, and undercited,[1] archaeological engagement with ontological difference or novelty. She presented a set of questions about the site of Star Carr in the UK and a collection of deer antler frontlets recovered there (Figure 10.1). Archaeologists interpret these objects as headgear worn by Star Carr's Mesolithic occupants. Conneller (2004) noted that the frontlets had inspired only *two* basic archaeological interpretations: (1) they were part of functional disguises that people used when hunting deer, or (2) they were part of ritual disguises that people used when performing ceremony. Both interpretations operate on a similar premise – the main purpose of these masks was to conceal the wearer's human form. Conneller asked if these two options truly exhaust all possibilities. Were camouflage and ritual concealment the only explanations because they derived from a timeless and universal human condition that continues today? Alternatively, was this a symptom of the limited view and sensibilities of contemporary archaeologists who inadvertently project their own modern expectations when they attempt to "look back" in time? Conneller challenged us to think about the frontlets as more than just disguise; perhaps, she suggested, instead of concealing the human body, the frontlets actually helped to reveal a different *type of body* (2004:42) that resulted only from a relationship between humans and deer at the site. This line of thinking required defamiliarization with the archaeological materials and questioning of default Enlightenment sensibilities, including notions of what bodies are, how nature relates to culture, and how entities (e.g., human or deer) transform as they enter into new sets of relationships.

Illustrated masterfully in Conneller's rethinking of Star Carr, recent discussions of ontological difference challenge archaeologists to ask new types of questions

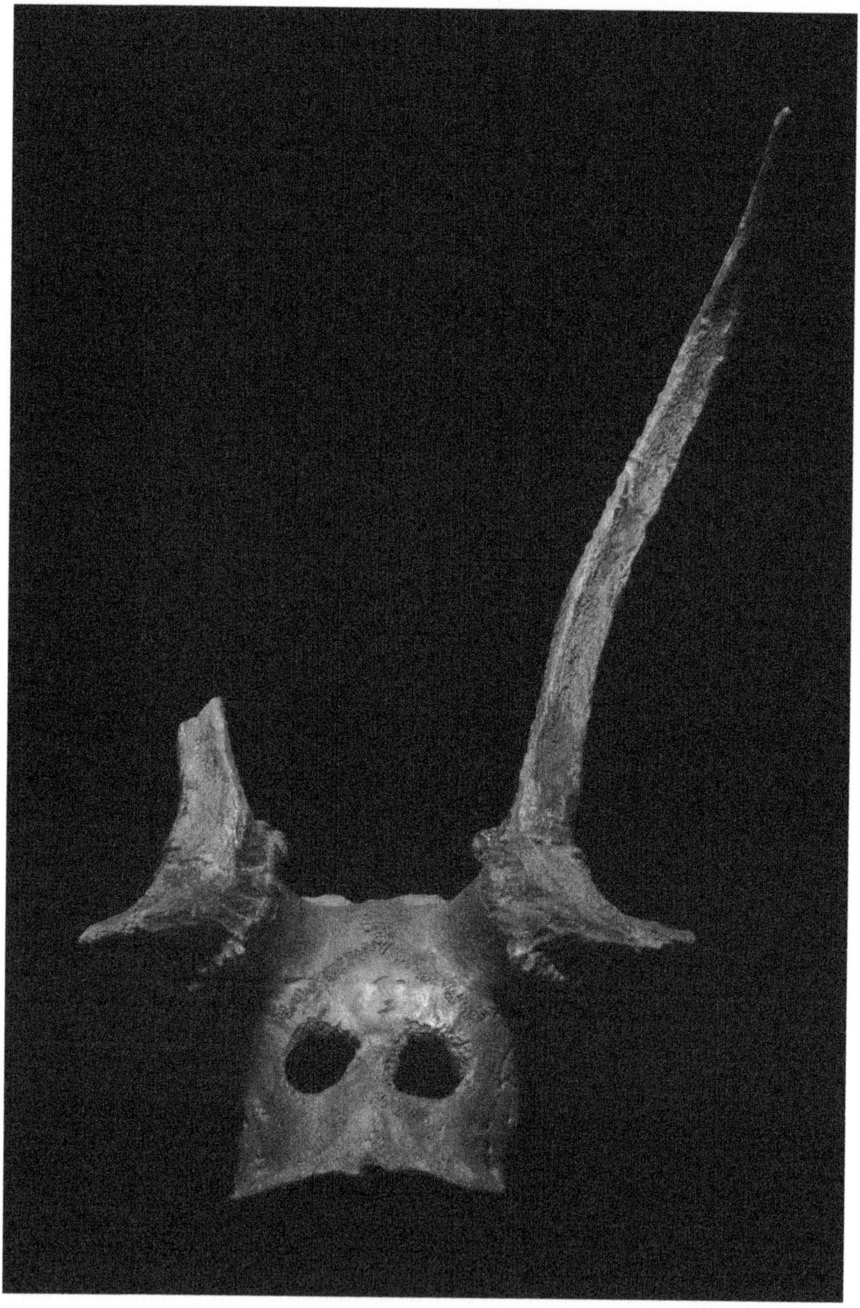

FIGURE 10.1 Deer antler frontlet from Star Carr.

Source: Reproduced by permission of University of Cambridge Museum of Archaeology & Anthropology (1953.61a).

and to become more attuned to the limitations and arbitrariness of their particular understandings of the world (Alberti 2014, 2016a, 2016b; Alberti and Marshall 2009; Alberti et al. 2011; Creese 2017a, 2017b; Harris and Robb 2012; Weismantel 2015; see also Descola 2013; Henare et al. 2007; Holbraad 2007; Holbraad and Pederson 2017; Kohn 2015; Viveiros de Castro 2003, 2007, 2015a, 2015b). Ontologically concerned archaeologists attempt to self-police and regulate the role of Western defaults in their work. They open up to Indigenous knowledge and theory, with some thinkers boldly stating that their approach allows them to take these sources of information more "seriously" (Alberti and Marshall 2009:344, see also Henare et al. 2007) than standard archaeological and anthropological approaches.

In this chapter, I explore how these recent discussions of difference translate into a general North American archaeological context (Cipolla 2017b, 2019; Cipolla et al. 2019; Harris and Cipolla 2017). The settler colonial contexts of North American archaeology, including the proliferation of Indigenous-led and collaborative research projects therein, serve as important testing grounds for these new approaches and ideas. As with Rachel's arguments in Chapter 8 and our discussion in Chapter 9, I highlight the importance of politics and colonial power differentials in the contours of such work. Echoing many of the concerns that Lindsay brought to light in Chapter 4, I ask critical questions about how archaeologists think through difference and about the political and ethical implications of different approaches. Questions remain as to if and how archaeologists can avoid the essentialization of difference and the translation of alterity into *sub*-alterity (Trouillot 2003). In order to further explore these questions, I compare recent ontologically concerned archaeologies with my experience as an outsider-participant in collaborative Indigenous archaeology projects and to my readings of Indigenous scholarship, particularly as found in the work of Sonya Atalay (2008), Vine Deloria Jr. (2003, 2012), Zoe Todd (2014, 2016, see also Davis and Todd 2017), and Gerald Vizenor (1999, 2008). The goal of this chapter is to assess the relevance of ontologically concerned archaeologies for North American contexts but also to place them in a critical postcolonial light that will hopefully better define the role that Western sensibilities (and power) play in these new ontological programs (cf. Bessire and Bond 2014; Heywood 2012; Keane 2013).

Between fear and contempt

Broadly speaking, archaeology inhabits a liminal space between Conneller's world – *the familiar* – and the world of Star Carr during the Mesolithic – *the foreign*. Archaeological pasts emerge from the relationship between archaeologists and materials (Fowler 2013; Lucas 2012). It is through this relationship that archaeologists like Conneller speculate about worlds and pasts possibly very different from their own. Ontologically focused arguments are correct in noting that important questions remain as to how we engage with "the foreign" – e.g., when we learn that deceased ancestors shape the world in which we live, or when we observe intentionally buried crystals that we think were once intended to protect the land (see Cipolla et al. 2019 for a discussion of the latter example). The disciplines of anthropology and archaeology boast deep histories of explaining away these differences in light of the observer's understanding of the world (Alberti and Marshall 2009; Holbraad and Pederson 2017). Like the standard archaeological interpretations of Star Carr challenged by Conneller, explanations based on uncritical uses of analogy or, worse yet, human universals, lead us to translate difference into the order of *our* world and *our* time. This is not to assume the existence of some means of completely avoiding acts of translation; it is, instead, a call for increased attention on the labor that translation contributes to the emergence of the past.

For Edward Said (1978), who wrote about western representations of Middle Eastern peoples, increased attention on how outside observers understand and represent difference was absolutely crucial. This entailed identifying how western observers actively shaped rather than passively observed the subaltern Other. Here, the "sub" in subaltern plays an important role. The contempt for the familiar discussed by Said relates to an underlying belief in human universals. Most culpable in the transformation of observed difference into something *less than* (and opposed to) the western observer's culture or world are evolutionary models like the ones discussed in Chapter 9. Undergirding many Western, Enlightenment-inherited worldviews, simplistic cultural evolutionary frameworks assert that all human collectives progress along a unilineal trajectory (e.g., White 1943). "In the beginning, all the world was America," wrote John Locke (1821) in his *Second Treatise of Government*. Therein Locke justified the colonization of the so-called "New World" through his description of the European ascent from nature to culture. *Terra nullius* was the mantra evoked at that time (see Cipolla 2013b; Gosden 2004); Westerners like Locke classified the Americas as empty land because they found no evidence of European-style modification and improvement, i.e., transformations of nature into culture. In such arguments, the non-western present transforms into the west's evolutionary past. In one fell swoop, western observers familiarized, appropriated, and demoted the foreign, designating it as a stepping-stone toward Western civilization, but also denying its difference or novelty. For instance, Said (1978:59) wrote of how the Other vacillated "between the West's contempt for what is familiar and its shivers of delight in – or fear of – novelty." As his work attests, fear and rejection of difference often lead down a well-worn colonial path.

Ontological turns

How can archaeology avoid the forms of fear and contempt that Said warned against? Enter the ontological turns. Philosophers use the term "ontology" to refer to *what is* – i.e., the mind-independent nature of the world – as opposed to how humans know the world, i.e., epistemology. Directly related to this realist philosophical orientation are anthropological and archaeological iterations of ontology that draw attention to how our materials reveal themselves to us in our work. As Holbraad and Pedersen (2017:5, emphasis added) recently phrased it:

> How do I enable my . . . material to reveal itself to me by *allowing it to dictate its own terms of engagement*, so to speak, guiding or compelling me to see things that I had not expected, or imagined, to be there?

Considered as part of a general dissatisfaction with the structural and post-structural emphases of early post-processual thinkers (e.g., Hodder 1982; cf. Olsen 2003, 2010), the rise of ontology in contemporary archaeological theory is unsurprising. It speaks to the growing anxieties that archaeologists feel regarding a highly familiar part of our world – the actual stuff, the artifacts and the materials we uncover, encounter, and think through in our daily work. As discussed in earlier chapters, this means moving beyond a strictly representational framework that reduces materials to static and mute bearers of arbitrary, culturally conventional meaning, to harmless signifiers, or to empty sign vehicles. As the general argument goes, beginning in the late 1970s and early 1980s, the emphases placed on symbolism in the archaeological "texts" or records we encountered allowed our collective attention to slip away from the work that the actual stuff of archaeology did and continues to do – how it shapes human histories and characterizes our world (Olsen 2003, 2010, 2012). Recent ontological considerations are, therefore, partially related to the posthuman critiques explored elsewhere in this book. But rather than finding one monolithic "ontological turn" in contemporary archaeological theory, in what follows I discuss four different lines of reasoning, respectively focused on worldviews, relations, objects, and worlds. Each comes with a unique but related set of orientations and goals worthy of critical attention. The rigidity of these types should not be overestimated; in practice, archaeological theorists mix and match these categories, sometimes with very little attention to the differences I emphasize in the following sections. I use the four lines of thought only as a heuristic device to discuss similarities, differences, and points in need of further clarification. Of particular interest for this discussion is how each of the types relates to a "metaontology," already mentioned in Chapters 1 and 5. For now, it is worth noting that the first three types involve metaontologies in one way or another while the fourth attempts to move away from any such framework.

Worldview-centered approaches

Of the four lines of thinking differentiated in this section, worldview-centered approaches are the most familiar for archaeologists and anthropologists. Their origins usually trace back to Hallowell's (1960) classic essay, "Ojibwa Ontology, Behavior, and Worldview," and the general approach resembles long-standing relativist discussions of culture. Practitioners using this approach attempt to reconstruct non-western worldviews (e.g., Betts et al. 2012; Brown and Emory

2008; Brown and Walker 2008). Maria Nieves Zedeño's work (2008, 2009) on Blackfoot and general Native American worldviews stands as an excellent example. Her writings on index objects and animacy focused on how certain types of objects act "as relational indicators or as indicators of animacy" and "occupy central positions in the *tribes' relational ontologies* because they can transform the properties and interactive capabilities of any other objects in their proximity, they can change the character of ordinary places and they can enhance human power" (Zedeño 2009:411, emphasis added). Zedeño derived this information from contemporary Blackfoot People and applied it critically to archaeological typologies that could potentially miss the importance of index objects *for* Blackfoot People. Zedeño thus critiques and adjusts archaeological epistemologies in relation to Indigenous worldviews. These adjustments are perhaps the main way in which worldview-centered inquiries distinguish themselves from standard archaeological and anthropological studies of culture. Hallowell (1960) made a similar move long ago, arguing that anthropologists must alter their typically Western understandings of personhood in order to avoid glossing over and doing violence to actual Ojibwa ways of understanding the world (see also Chapter 4). In both of these cases, relativist uses of the term "ontology" depart slightly from the term's traditional modes of use in philosophy. In these cases, ontology is not simply *what is* but rather *what is according to a particular (normative) cultural perspective.* From there, the analyst might create a hybridized epistemology derived from at least two worldviews: that of the archaeologist and that of the Indigenous collaborator or interlocutor.

These approaches carefully consider Indigenous knowledge and, in doing so, allow researchers the unique opportunity to see the cracks and arbitrary defaults in their own worldviews and disciplinary lenses. Similar to Conneller's (2004) study of deer frontlets, they do so in order to generate new questions and angles of articulation with archaeological materials. But, at the same time, they also run the risk of maintaining certain Western dualisms associated with representationalism, taking attention away from the materials themselves. In other words, these approaches focus on what things represented and did from one specific cultural perspective rather than – as discussed in previous chapters – how things relate and behave beyond specific cultural perspectives. Applicability is also a problem. Archaeologists working in some parts of the globe, particularly those working on deeper histories (see discussions in Chapter 5), do not have access to Indigenous elders and knowledge keepers. In this sense, they have limited means of challenging their own worldviews and disciplinary lenses outside of the archaeological materials that they think through. For these archaeologists, a worldview-centered approach loses the luster it has in contexts such as Zedeño's study of index objects. Finally, the fourth of our approaches (worlds-centered) will warn against the dangers of only partial acceptance of Indigenous perspectives. For example, even though a researcher partially accepts Indigenous perspectives as part of their interpretations, she does not typically see animism as a "real" force characterizing her own world. In other words, animism is accepted here as a particular view or epistemology rather than as an ontology. In these models, practitioners fit localized worldviews into the metaontology of Western science.

Relations-centered approaches

Aligned with "symmetrical archaeology," "new materialisms," and "relational ontologies" discussed throughout this book, the second set of approaches is more recent than the worldview-centered approaches just summarized. Although their history traces back to structuralism and its concomitant impacts in archaeological theory beginning with the post-processual critiques (e.g., Hodder 1982), practitioners only formalized these approaches in the new millennium after considering issues of materiality and object agency. One could argue that these approaches have yet to reach maturity, particularly in North American anthropological archaeology (Cipolla 2018). Practitioners taking this approach focus on the relationality of the world (Conneller 2004, 2011; Crellin 2020; Harris 2018a; Watts 2013b; see also Barad 2007; Bennett 2010; DeLanda 2006, 2016; Deleuze and Guattari 2004; Ingold 2007, 2013; Latour 1993, 2005a); here, relationality serves as a new metaontology meant to improve our understandings of the world and to shake off Enlightenment sensibilities. Timothy Pauketat's work on cosmology stands out as an important contribution to the North American literature. He asserts:

> [m]any now agree that the power to alter relationships and to shape history is clearly not human alone. . . . Indeed agentic relationships may be between two atoms in a molecule (molecular history), between the falling rain and a seedling (natural history), between armies meeting on the battlefield (military history), or between a devout churchgoer and the sunlight shining through the clearstory window (religious history).
>
> *(Pauketat 2012:28–9)*

In contrast to the earlier quotation from Zedeño, this argument gravitates further toward realism. According to this approach, agency emerges from relationships (cf. Chapter 2). This is a speculative proposition for how the world works regardless of any specific cultural understanding of it. These approaches emerged in opposition to the Enlightenment-inspired humanism that characterizes Western worldviews (cf. Chapter 8). Archaeologists like Pauketat argue that we must rethink the human and, in so doing, attempt to identify and mitigate the covert push and pull of Western dualisms in our interpretations. With these approaches, researchers give non-human things their due, recognizing human dependence on – and entanglement with – the non-human world. Compared to worldview-centered frameworks, these approaches fall much closer to philosophical discussions of ontology by speculating on the mind-independent status of the world and, from there, considering human histories and perspectives on it. Altogether, these approaches work toward recognizing the important roles that materials and things play in human history, opening up new questions on the vibrancy of matter and on human contingency.

Compared with worldview-centered approaches, one could argue that these new foci on relations take all human (including Indigenous) knowledge "less" seriously than they do their own propositions about how the world works. Practitioners using this approach must still develop stronger arguments for how local human perspectives on the world fit within this realist framework.[2] As noted elsewhere (Chapter 2; Harris and Cipolla 2017:198–212), relational approaches run the risk of homogenizing different histories in favor of a universal relationality. Andrew Jones (2005) called attention to this problem by asking about the impacts that anthropology in places like Melanesia (e.g., Strathern 1988) has on archaeological understandings of European pasts. He asked if drawing analogies with Strathern's work was leading archaeologists to increasingly "find" Melanesian personhood and social relations. As noted by Conneller (2004:44), we must ask similar questions about the potentially global impacts of Eduardo Viveiros de Castro's writings on Amerindian ontologies. All of this is to say that relational approaches must remain attuned to the connection between the universal and the local. These theories do, however, offer valuable sources of inspiration for those archaeologists that do not have access to Indigenous informants, collaborators, or perspectives in general. Relations-centered approaches generate new questions and new orientations to old archaeological problems.

Object-centered approaches

Object-centered approaches emerged from the relational turns just described. They pose new questions on how objects exist beyond their relations. For instance, Olsen and Witmore argued that "[t]hings do hold something in reserve, something that cannot be explained by such relational involvement or by the rationale of the in-order-to. Other distinctions exist" (Olsen and Witmore 2015:190). I find it useful to consider this shift from relations to objects as part of a "second wave" of symmetrical archaeology (Crellin 2020; Harris and Cipolla 2017) in that it represents a break with the initial call for symmetry (Webmoor and Witmore 2008; Witmore 2007).

The key thinker behind these new ideas is philosopher Graham Harman (2009, 2016a, 2018), who builds upon and critiques Latour's Actor-Network Theory (ANT) while rejecting new materialisms or assemblage theory altogether (see Harman 2016a). He acknowledges the importance of Latour's non-anthropocentric framework, but finds fault in his myopic focus on relations. According to Harman, the network draws attention away from the objects themselves. For him, all objects – defined broadly – hold something in reserve. As we saw in Chapter 2, according to him, the history of philosophy presents only two general ways of explaining objects (Harman 2016a:7–13, 2018:41–52). The first is through "undermining," or by explaining objects in terms of their composition (e.g., the atoms in a wooden table). The second is through "overmining," or by explaining objects in terms of what they do in relation to other objects (e.g., in relation to a floor, chairs, flatware, humans, etc. the table could become part of a dining assemblage). Harman argues that these two approaches fail to provide a satisfactory model for change. According to him, we need a third model that recognizes how objects hold something back (i.e., they are not exhausted by overmining or undermining – together referred to as "duomining"). We can only speculate on this extra "something," but for Harman it is the key to explaining how things change (see discussions of this issue in Chapter 3).

As with the relations-centered approaches set out earlier, object-centered approaches embrace realism and frame all human knowledge of the world as partial and skewed. These approaches do, however, frame their object-oriented view of the world as more accurate than other approaches. Importantly, for the present discussion, object-oriented approaches maintain a hard distinction between epistemology (what we know) and ontology (what there is); as discussed later in this chapter, this view contrasts sharply with certain Indigenous ontologies that fuse knowing and being. Even more problematic than this, however, is the unique fashion by which second-wave symmetrical archaeology samples the work of Harman, arguing that such an approach leaves little room for theorizing history (which would be relational and representational). This does not match up exactly with my reading of Harman's work. For example, he uses object-oriented ontologies to rethink historical phenomena like the Dutch East Indian Company and the American Civil War (see Harman 2016a, 2018). Regardless, symmetrical archaeologists argue that using objects to only think about history is problematic, a substantial and potentially paradigm-changing critique of our discipline.

Worlds-centered approaches

The final set of approaches reviewed here is the most radical. It draws inspiration from the perspectivism of Viveiros de Castro (2003, 2007, 2015a, 2015b) and aspires to move away from the metaontological frameworks that undergird worldview-centered, relations-centered, and object-centered approaches (Alberti 2016a; Alberti and Marshall 2009:348–9). This means attempting to do more than simply establish equal footing between Western and Indigenous ontologies; it entails accepting Indigenous ontological propositions as truths and attempting to move beyond Western ontological propositions that stand in contradiction. The pioneers of this approach in archaeology, Benjamin Alberti and Yvonne Marshall (2009), sought to explore the possibility for worlds very different from their own. They explained:

> [t]o propose a relational ontology based on matter's inherent dynamism solves the problem of needing an animating human hand to enable agency and action, but it does not necessarily place us on a path to ontological alterity. . . . This requires a further step which depends upon taking

> seriously the "cross reality" challenges which emerge from anthropological and archaeological accounts of other worlds.
>
> *(Alberti and Marshall 2009:349)*

Thus, rather than see the world as characterized by a universal reality (relational or otherwise), Alberti and Marshall sought to elevate the importance of local knowledge and sensibilities in our engagements with archaeological materials (see also Holbraad 2007).

As already noted, these thinkers argue that their approach allows them to take Indigenous knowledge seriously, transforming it into archaeological theory (Alberti and Marshall 2009:344; Henare et al. 2007:10; see discussions in Chapter 5). In making such claims, however, it becomes imperative to demonstrate that these approaches are more than archaeological business-as-usual, i.e., where a western metaontology frames the interpretations and narratives that result from this type of exploratory work. A major challenge for these forms of ontologically informed archaeology lies in the data. The archaeologists attempting this work seek to better understand Indigenous worlds through their own engagement with artifacts. As I recently argued, the results closely resemble those of general relational approaches in which everything is unstable and in a constant state of becoming (Cipolla 2019). In other words, despite their insistence on the importance of *the local*, worlds-centered approaches describe strikingly similar worlds regardless of the time period or place theorized. To me, this suggests that attempts to move beyond a metaontology in archaeology have not yet succeeded. An obvious means of exploring these propositions further lies with Indigenous archaeologists and with collaborative Indigenous archaeology projects (Cipolla et al. 2019) that actually involve Indigenous people and Indigenous knowledge and do not depend upon western translations of Indigenous perspectives into archaeological theory (see Chapter 5).

Summary: four turns

The four types of ontologically concerned archaeology caricatured here demonstrate variable framings of Indigenous and Western knowledges. Some seem to result in dualistic and asymmetrical treatments of the two. Worldview-centered approaches maintain a binary between these forms of knowledge, ultimately keeping an explicitly Western metaontology, but also striving for hybridized models that are ultimately animated by Western perspectives. Relations-centered and object-centered approaches move away from the dualism between Western and Indigenous knowledge (framing all as general human knowledge). They explicitly maintain a Western metaontology, albeit improved with new relational and thing-centered theories. Overall, however, relational and thing-centered ontologies still struggle with recognizing the local in relation to the universal. Finally, worlds-centered approaches maintain a binary between the West and the rest (i.e., in terms of knowledge "types") and attempt to circumnavigate the former in search of the latter; implicitly they appear to maintain a Western metaontology cloaked as a less-Western approach than the first three lines of thought (Figure 10.2) (Cipolla 2019).

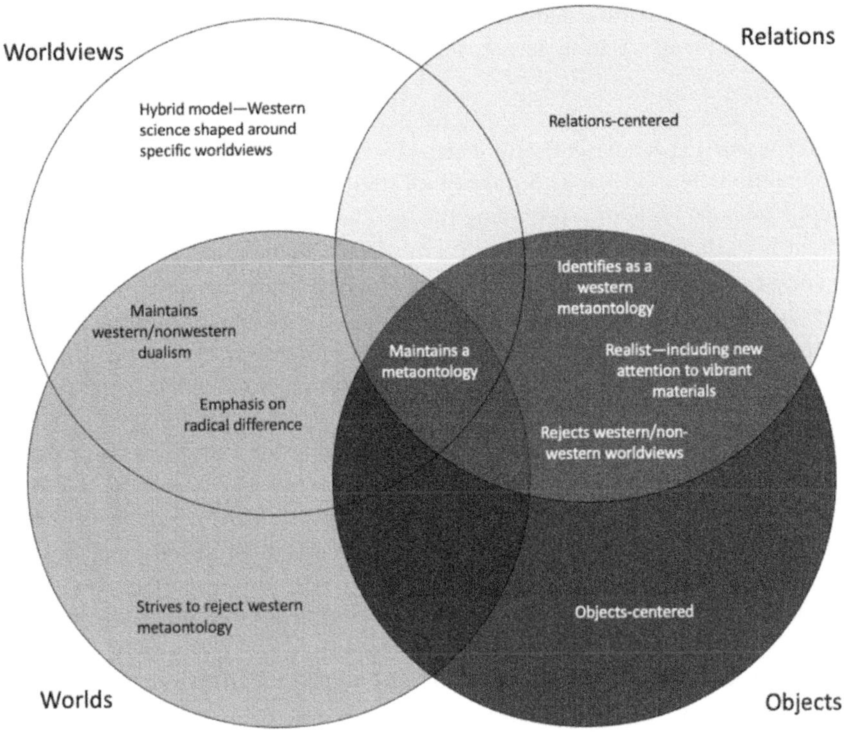

FIGURE 10.2 Diagrammatic representation of the four ontological "turns": worldviews, relations, objects, and worlds.

Recognizing colonial relations

Having now reviewed the key thinkers and theories typically used to explore ontological difference in archaeology and anthropology, something is clearly amiss. It seems odd for a chapter devoted to alterity to mainly cite Euro-descended male scholars such as myself. Métis anthropologist Zoe Todd recently brought this crucial issue to the fore, first in a viral blog post, and next in her (2016) article, "An Indigenous Feminist's Take on the Ontological Turn: 'Ontology' is Just Another Word for Colonialism." The article made an important point about vastly asymmetrical citational practices in contemporary anthropology (this also applies to archaeology, of course). But Todd's article has much deeper implications. She pointed out the similarities between some of the ontological approaches outlined earlier (though she does not use my categories) and Indigenous perspectives on the world; from there she emphasizes ongoing colonial power asymmetries and practices hidden beneath these new arguments:

> [I]t is important to think, deeply, about how the Ontological Turn – with its breathless 'realisations' that animals, the climate, water, 'atmospheres' and non-human presences like ancestors and spirits are *sentient* and *possess*

> *agency*, that 'nature' and 'culture', 'human' and 'animal' may not be so separate after all – is itself perpetuating the exploitation of Indigenous peoples.
> *(Todd 2016:16, original emphasis)*

Todd warned that ontologically engaged scholars run the risk of (sometimes unintentionally) cherry-picking aspects of Indigenous knowledge for purely academic pursuits without recognizing the broader context. Practitioners must ask about how they gained access to this knowledge. More importantly, they must recognize that Indigenous ontologies and epistemologies represent "legal orders through which Indigenous peoples throughout the world are fighting for self-determination, sovereignty" (Todd 2016:18).

Ontological cherry-picking tends to overlook certain connections between researcher and world; what about the similarities, continuities, and inequalities that exist between observer (cherry-picker) and observed? For instance, in a North American context, an outside researcher interested in ontological difference might show great interest in notions of animism (this helps them publish papers) but might disregard Indigenous taboos against disturbing the dead or disturbing ceremonial sites/objects with archaeology (this stops them from collecting certain types of data). When it comes to issues of sovereignty in particular, it is important to remember that difference from the West served as a very powerful colonial tool over the last 500 years (see Locke's statement on America discussed earlier; see also Chapter 8). My point, similar to that of Todd, is that the ontological turns sometimes run risks of overlooking similarities, continuities, and inequalities in their academic quest to come to grips with ontological difference; they are similarly vulnerable to glossing over the practical outcomes of their ontological claims and their implications for the future.

Increased critical attention to the asymmetry of our bibliographies is an important starting point, but it is only a means to an end. There is a fine line, as emphasized by Todd (2016:9), between properly acknowledging Indigenous expertise and thought in our work and misrepresenting and/or using it in an exploitative manner. In this sense, it becomes important to take Todd's critique as more than an invitation to add a few new names to our bibliographies. I read it as a call to trace how our sources (usually western males) compare with Indigenous knowledges and to invest time in trying to understand how these Indigenous sources differ from the sources we readily cite; this is something I recently attempted with my colleagues concerning theory in and of the Mohegan archaeology project (Cipolla et al. 2019). As a Euro-descended settler colonist in North America – one who practices North American archaeology no less – the only way to approach these problems is by explicitly acknowledging the colonial relations of which they are part. This means attempting to push Western knowledge off center stage while adding new sources of knowledge. But it also means recognizing that I, as a scholar, do not have all the answers and cannot understand ontological difference free from the weight of colonialism or from my Euro-descended settler colonist senses and knowledge.

Shared ontological spaces

The work of activist, historian, and author, Vine Deloria Jr., of the Standing Rock Sioux stands as another integral critique of Western mistreatment, misunderstanding, and misrepresentation of Indigenous North Americans (Deloria 2003, 2012). Deloria's writings make vital contributions to ontological questions in anthropology and archaeology (see Fowles 2013:252–4) and to general efforts to identify and challenge Eurocentrism inherent in our methodologies. In *God is Red* (2003), for instance, he outlined important differences between Western and Indigenous North American relations to – and understandings of – the world, placing particular emphasis on religion.[3] Deloria pointed to the tensions that arise from a Western insistence upon the separation of epistemology (what we know) and ontology (what there is) versus Indigenous North American fusion of these two categories (perception and knowledge coming closer together). For instance, in discussing the idea of seeing a ghost, Deloria (2012:5) argued:

> The Indian confronts the reality of the experience, and while he or she may not make immediate sense of it, it is not rejected as an invalid experience. . . . For the non-Indian the teachings of a lifetime come thundering down. . . . Reality, in a certain sense, is what you allow your mind to accept, not what you experience.

To put this into the contexts of contemporary archaeological theory, this example lays bare the differences between a flat ontology (the reality of experience without making "sense" of it) and a dualistic, Western ontology (where common sense tells us what is possible at all times).

For the purposes of the present argument, I focus on one of Deloria's (2012) less well-known publications, *The Metaphysics of Modern Existence*. This work stands apart from his other books; instead of focusing on the differences and conflicts between Western and Indigenous epistemologies and ontologies, it ambitiously drew on multiple sources – both Indigenous and Western – in search of a new hybrid vision of reality (2012:6). The new vision that Deloria presented transcended divides between Indigenous/non-Indigenous, science/religion while continuing to expose the cracks in Western defaults. For Deloria, of course, this new orientation to reality involved opening up to Indigenous knowledge: "I . . . firmly believe that the newly emerging view of the world will support and illuminate Indian traditions and that Indian traditions will prove extremely useful and accurate when cast in a new and more respectful light" (Deloria 2012:8). Here we find an early precursor to Todd's warning along with an argument that clearly took Indigenous knowledge seriously but did much more than isolate and essentialize ontological difference. Deloria called for a synthetic view that recognized continuities and convergences without erasing the distinctions. The new vision that Deloria described resembles the relations-centered ontological approaches discussed earlier. This bolsters Todd's already strong argument that western anthropologists are in many ways reinventing Indigenous-made wheels. For example, Deloria (2012:60–2) provided an early and – as far as I can tell – completely uncited discussion of the wave-particle problem along with a description of the world that closely resembles that of Karen Barad's (2007) "intra-action." As discussed in Chapter 7, Barad developed a relational ontology – what she refers to as "agential realism" – inspired by Niels Bohr's argument that an observed object and the agencies of observation are connected and emerge together; Deloria (2012:60–2) explored similar questions regarding Bohr's work, ultimately arguing against Western beliefs that humans "exist over and apart from the physical world" (ibid. 181).

Similar to Deloria's broad goals in *The Metaphysics of Modern Existence*, archaeologists practicing collaborative Indigenous archaeology and community-based participatory archaeology focus on how these diverse forms of archaeology bring different knowledges together in a shared ontological space. Following Susan Dion (2009), Sonya Atalay (2008, 2012) describes this shared space in terms of knowledge braiding. For her, this concept shows "the potential for knowledge to be valued, reworked, and combined in community-based archaeology" (Atalay 2012:207), but this is far from the specter of hyperrelativism that has haunted archaeology since the late 1970s.

> Rather than a multivocal model in which a cacophony of voices can emanate from numerous, unspecified locations, and focused in no specific direction, a model of "braiding knowledge" brings distinct forms of knowledge together. Research partners engage in situated weaving to create complex histories that are grounded in specific locations.
>
> *(ibid)*

The Mohegan Archaeological Field School, a collaborative research and teaching project I am involved with, takes a similar "braiding" approach (Cipolla and Quinn 2016; Cipolla et al. 2019). Although collaborative Indigenous archaeologies rarely discuss theory in print (McNiven 2016), I suspect that more attention to theory in collaborative Indigenous archaeology would shed valuable light on some of the theoretical questions explored in this book. In this spirit, we at the Mohegan Archaeological Field School recently shifted our focus to how collaboration "remakes" archaeology (Cipolla 2017b). We explore how this relates to recent ontological turns in a co-authored article (Cipolla et al. 2019). Co-authorship allowed us to address the similarities and differences between authors' respective understandings of (1) how we know the past; (2) how we define archaeological data in light of our critiques of false divides between nature/culture, at least as it pertains to Mohegan worldviews *and* certain relational-realist archaeological perspectives like relations-focused approaches outlined earlier; (3) how we understand humans and their relation to the world; and (4) how we view aspects of our shared histories, including the history of settler colonialism in North America. Important for the present argument, we took a one-world (meta-ontological) approach in the article that recognized continuities and distinctions between participants and authors. Such a project would fail if I attempted to take on the views of my collaborators and co-authors or, regarding Todd's critique, if I attempted to downplay the actual sources of my knowledge. The inverse is also true for my collaborators and co-authors; the project would fail if they attempted to simply take on my perspective of the world. In fact, collaborative Indigenous archaeology only works when you have a shared world that respects similarities and differences; here respect denotes recognizing alterity but attempting to avoid subalterity (as referred to in my previous discussion of Said's work).

The writings of Gerald Vizenor also prove important here. Academics know Vizenor, a member of the White Earth Reservation, Minnesota Chippewa, best for his influential contributions to American Indian Studies. His use and development of the term "survivance" stands out as a key concept for any scholarship concerning North American Indigenous history, including archaeology (e.g., Acebo and Martinez 2018; Allard 2018; Gonzalez et al. 2018; Silliman 2014). Survivance is an anti-essentialist and non-dualistic critique of how (mainly western) writers understand and represent Indigenous history. A combination of "survival" and "resistance," the term refers to the continued, dynamic, and active presence of Indigenous peoples (not just survival); this contrasts sharply with Western representations of Indigeneity. A self-identified postmodernist, Vizenor combatted misunderstandings and misrepresentations of Indigeneity through his notion of "postindian warriors." For him, "postindian warriors of postmodern simulations would undermine and surmount, with imagination and the performance of new stories, the manifest manners of scriptural simulations and 'authentic' representations of the tribes in the literature of dominance" (Vizenor 1999:17). Vizenor's survivance thus operates on a critical and active combination of similarity and difference.

Vizenor's attention to the western translation (and mischaracterization) of "real" Indigenous history looms large here. The question remains as to whether or not western archaeologists can ever escape the colonial sensibilities that they inherit from their world. What I read in the work of Vizenor is a message that all academics can and should attempt to decolonize, both on their own and in collaboration with diverse stakeholders. This entails opening up to dynamic Indigenous histories that push back against static, essentialist tropes. But there lurks an ever-present risk that colonial sensibilities will creep back in as soon as we let our guard down and decide we have finally liberated ourselves from the tyranny of this view or that we finally know how to take Indigenous perspectives seriously. We can absolutely strive to decolonize, to be settler allies, to learn from Vizenor's notion of the postindian warrior, but we are always susceptible to creeping colonialisms. When viewed from this perspective, the worlds-centered approaches in archaeology that I have encountered run the biggest risk of slipping back into old ways of doing and thinking camoflaged behind a new terminological guise.

Conclusions

The ontological turns discussed in this chapter *could be* important steps in reducing Eurocentrism in the discipline and thinking differently; for me, this means identifying and challenging the taken-for-granted, ethnocentric defaults of archaeology – a core theme of this book. In some cases, this could mean opening up the discipline to a wider segment of contemporary global society by asking difficult questions and approaching our work in "non-traditional" ways. This argument connects directly to the types of political pathways charted by Lindsay (Chapter 4) and Rachel (Chapter 8). This chapter demonstrates that it is crucial to continue asking new questions about how we understand different pasts – and I think that this is something with which Said would agree. As I have highlighted, however, it is also important to guard against creeping colonialism – against the essentialization of difference and the "sub" in subalterity. One very practical way to do this is to work and write with different archaeologists; for me, this comes in the form of collaborative projects like the one at Mohegan and like this very book. Following Todd, we must read more than western philosophers when attempting to achieve this goal and we must recognize the broader context from which Indigenous knowledge originates. There are potentially powerful synergies between these more practical goals and the theoretical frameworks of the ontological turns described in this chapter.

Yet, in my view, arguments against metaontologies forwarded by worlds-centered archaeologists simply do not work in these settings. On the one hand, quests for orientations to our work that forego a metaontology initiate adventures in worlding. On the other hand, they leave the gate open to colonialism. They do so by taking attention away from our own sensibilities and situatedness and how they guide us to sample and frame the archaeological problems and patterns we hope to solve; in this way, my argument connects back to feminist arguments for situated knowledge (Haraway 1988; Wylie 1997), a point we discuss further in the next chapter. As already noted, worlds-centered approaches (e.g., Alberti and Marshall 2009; Holbraad 2007; Marshall 2008) reach similar conclusions as relations-centered approaches. I read this as an important indicator that even though they shun the notion of a metaontology, worlds-centered approaches continue to conduct their work using one, usually something resembling assemblage theory (cf. Chapters 2 and 8; Cipolla 2019). In other words, they say one thing and end up doing another. To use Todd's phrasing, perhaps the fourth approach reviewed earlier is just another *world* in which colonialism is allowed to continue, unchecked beneath new terminology.[4] I argue that the ontological turns in North America live their best lives in dialogue with Indigenous peoples; for me, this comes in the form of collaborative Indigenous archaeology that braids knowledge (Atalay 2008, 2012) and recognizes collaboration as an assemblage that is greater than the sum of its parts.

Although 16 years have passed since Conneller (2004) published her article on deer frontlets at Star Carr, not much has changed in archaeology's collective quest to understand ontological alterity. There are two reasons for this. First, Conneller is an underrecognized trailblazer in global archaeological theory. Second, and much more relevant for this chapter, are the importance of recent relational approaches in our archaeological research and writing. Conneller drew upon both assemblage theory and Viveiros de Castro's perspectivism to recognize the limitations of archaeological perspectives on Star Carr at the time. She asked new questions that pushed us out of our comfort zone, but she did so in a way that recognized the limitations of archaeological views, which are inherently meta-ontological. This is because we are part of the world that we aim to understand (cf. discussions of phenomenology in Chapters 6 and 7). Following thinkers like Deloria and Barad, we need to keep our focus on how we are part of the pasts that we write and the differences that we find.

Notes

1 Undercited from a specific North American archaeological perspective; this article is well-cited in the UK.

2 One solution lies in approaches that combine worldview- and relations-centered lines of inquiry such as the work of John Creese (2017a, 2017b); Ollie (Harris 2018a) recently referred to such approaches as "more-than-representational."

3 Archaeologist Severin Fowles (2013) recently took great strides in incorporating this important work into his interpretations of Pueblo histories and spiritualities.

4 For example, anthropologist Paul Nadasdy (2007) demonstrated that we can still explore alterity in politically engaged research (i.e., a one-world or metaontological orientation that recognizes inequalities and continuities that bind Indigenous and non-Indigenous worlds together); he convincingly argued for the potential political impacts that anthropology might have when/if it disregards Indigenous ontologies. He focused on the importance of taking seriously Indigenous views of hunting as reciprocal exchange in which animals willfully surrender their bodies and lives to hunters. Yet his focus remained on what this different view means for the world shared by anthropologists and Indigenous hunters. Could western views be wrong? Could western disregard for this view have political impacts on First Nations in northern Canada? This is a case of exploring multiple views of the same world.

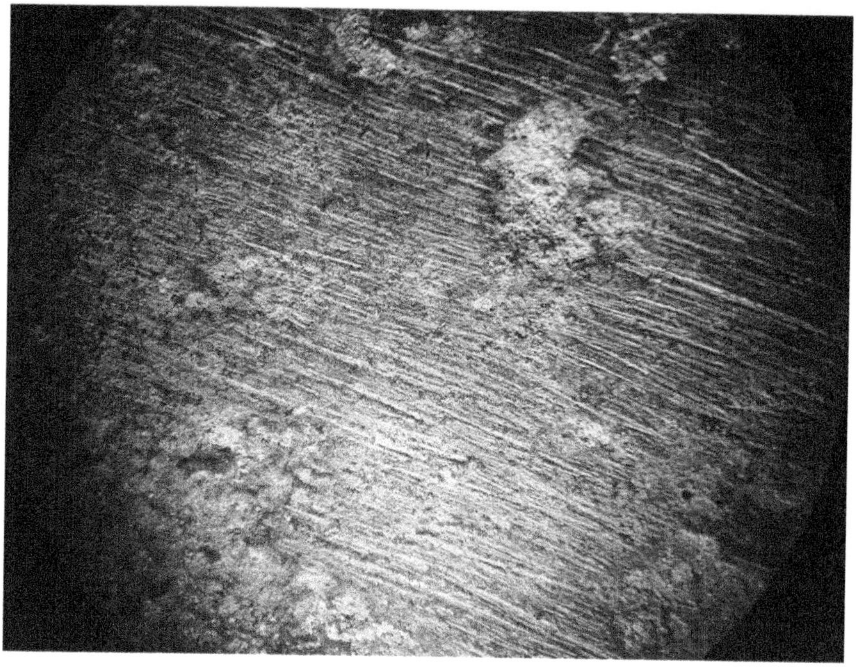

11

DISCUSSING DIFFERENT PASTS

Categories, interdisciplinarity, and metaontologies

Introduction

In this discussion the authors build on Chapter 10 by focusing on the roles of Indigenous thinking in emerging relational approaches; this exploration leads to a debate on how different, or not, Indigenous and relational approaches are, considering where they overlap, and what this overlap might do for theory. The chapter begins by examining how the different approaches that are often lumped together under labels such as "relational archaeology" or the "ontological turn" actually differ from each other in substantial and important ways. Considering the relationship between Indigenous thinking and relational archaeologies leads to a discussion of disciplinarity and transdisciplinarity as we dwell on the challenges of reading beyond our own subject and the gains to be made from doing so. The discussion opens up to consider issues of decolonization and collaboration between Indigenous and non-Indigenous colleagues and thinkers. From here we return to the issue of metaontology that we already touched upon in Chapters 5 and 7.

Categorizing theory

RACHEL: Craig, one of the (many) things I find interesting about your chapter is how you categorize ontologically engaged archaeologies. Both you and Ollie offer a discussion and comparison of current theoretical approaches and there is some overlap and some key differences between how you both do this. You categorize the approaches as:

- Worldview-centered
- Relations-centered

- Object-centered
- Worlds-centered

Whereas, in Chapter 2, Ollie uses the following categories:

- Relations as epistemology
- Relations as methodology
- Relations as metaphysics

Can you both talk a bit about why you did this and what the differences between your approaches are? I want to bring this out because this is a recurring problem in the literature surrounding relational approaches where a range of authors have categorized different approaches in a variety of ways and under different labels. Some of this grouping, which is of course necessary to explain and describe theory, has then gone on to create, in my view anyway, more confusion. An example of this is Christopher Witmore's (2014) paper *Archaeology and the New Materialisms* (discussed in Chapter 7). Witmore is, of course, most famously associated with symmetrical archaeology (e.g., Olsen et al. 2012) and whilst the paper moves some way beyond this approach, it retains clear aspects of symmetrical archaeology (see Chapter 7). I do not see symmetrical archaeology and the new materialisms as all that similar; for example, they take very different positions on the nature of matter. Yet at conferences and in press, I've seen people suggesting they are one and the same thing.

CRAIG: I see your point, Rachel, and I agree that archaeologists tend to typify and lump together these various new ideas in confusing ways. This makes it all the more important in this book to be explicit about why we seek to categorize and how our respective categories overlap or clash. Before getting into that though, I see an important distinction between the example of classification you offer and the categories presented in Chapters 2 and 10. Witmore (2014) lumps together a number of different approaches under a single heading, whereas Ollie and I present ways of teasing apart lines of thought or ways of using theories that might be lumped together as "relational archaeologies" in Ollie's case and "the ontological turn" in mine. So, in short, I think we are working in a different direction than the example you give. We are splitting categories, which I think is a good thing for these particular theories at this time.

In Chapter 10, I set out to trace what I see as some rather distinct lines of thought currently associated with the ontological turn, or according to me, the ontological turn*s*. As with posthumanism, archaeologists increasingly use the term "ontology," but rarely explain this choice and/or provide clear definitions. Alberti (2016a) helped remedy this issue by distinguishing between what I refer to as relations-centered approaches – which map onto what Ollie refers to as relations as metaphysics – and worlds-centered approaches. In addition to these, I distinguish two other lines of thought.

The first, worldview-centered, aligns well with what Ollie calls relations as epistemology and stands out as culturally relativist, therefore resembling many traditional anthropological discussions of culture in general. Importantly for this discussion, this approach is distinct from any realist-oriented theories because it privileges specific worldviews or epistemologies. The other line of thought I set out, object-centered, helps to distinguish between two forms of realist thinking – one focused on relations, the other on objects. One of the reasons I felt it was necessary to draw this distinction is because symmetrical archaeologies, including the article you mention by Witmore (2014), increasingly conflate these two approaches; we note this elsewhere in the book with our discussions of first- and second-wave symmetrical archaeologies (see also Crellin 2020; Harris and Cipolla 2017).

OLLIE: I definitely agree that my category of relations as epistemology maps onto Craig's worldview-centered approach, and that his category of relations-centered matches my category of relations as metaphysics. We use different terms for these, in part, because we are trying to understand different things – in my case it is the status of relations specifically that I wanted to elucidate. This is also why I have a section on relations as methodology, to recognize that there is another set of relational approaches that are less about how the world is, or what people thought, and more about techniques we can use to analyze the past. My interest in relations specifically, rather than ontological approaches, is also why I didn't include a category for the object-centered approaches Craig identifies. For me these approaches, which in philosophy can be grouped together as object-oriented ontologies (OOO), are fundamentally different to ones oriented toward relations, because they explicitly argue that we need to emphasize objects cut off from their relations (e.g., Harman 2018; Olsen 2010:155–6) – we saw this in our dialogue in Chapter 3, and Craig discussed this at length in the previous chapter.

Of course, the similarities and differences between various approaches are often a matter of perspective. Both first- and second-wave symmetrical archaeology have more in common with new materialism than they do with logical positivism, for example, and the philosophers Manuel DeLanda and Graham Harman (2017) have recently debated what their positions share (a commitment to realism) and where they differ, with plenty of the former as well as the latter (see also Chapter 7). So in a sense there will always be multiple ways of gathering ideas together, the critical issue is what your aims are when you do that. Does it help to make the differences clear between one group of ideas or another, or does it simply muddy the waters? Craig and I gather things slightly differently because we are trying to answer different questions. These different gatherings are not in themselves "right" or "wrong," because any gathering, any assemblage, is always only a temporarily bounded collectivity. There are histories that link different ideas together, histories we can map (e.g., Harris and Cipolla 2017), but the history of archaeological thought is live, it is always in the making, and like the past itself it can be put together in multiple (though by no means infinite) ways. Thus, the issue is not whether gathering approaches together in specific ways is true or false, right or wrong. The issue is what does gathering approaches together in specific ways *do*? Is it useful? I think the ways in which Craig and I have gathered approaches here are useful – they have certainly been helpful to me.

On interdisciplinarity

LINDSAY: In general, I agree with the larger argument made here by Craig and Ollie regarding the need to assess whether categorizing different theoretical approaches is an intellectually "useful" exercise. While in some ways, these categorizations are simply interesting thought experiments, they can help us draw important parallels between different ways of thinking, particularly those that lie outside of the Western canon. As you point out, Craig, intellectual "braiding" through co-authorship and collaborative research avoids asking western intellectuals to translate Indigenous perspectives into archaeological theory. I particularly liked that you brought up Zoe Todd's (2016) critique of citational practice; specifically, the importance of acknowledging how many of the theoretical interventions within the ontological turn also have Indigenous sources and for more references to non-western theorists in our work. I think that part of the reason why this hasn't been done more already is that a clear division exists between Anthropology and the various ethnic studies disciplines that tend to house said non-western thinkers.

I am continually struck by the intellectual gulf that exists between American Indian Studies (AIS), for example, and archaeologists working with Indigenous communities in North America. Since the 1980s, there have been several parallel intellectual developments within both fields, including the embrace of postmodernism, the critique of Western ontological and epistemological systems, and an emphasis on collaborative participatory based-research. And yet, archaeologists rarely cite or engage with AIS literature (a pattern demonstrated by the sparse references to Vine Deloria in college syllabi or in anthropological articles about Native Americans) and AIS scholars continue to baulk at the idea that North American archaeologists have anything to offer scholars working on Indigenous issues in the more recent past and present. I think that bridging the citational gulf between AIS and Anthropology will help prevent what Craig has aptly called reinventing Indigenous-made wheels.

CRAIG: Lindsay, your point about disciplinary divides is one that I hadn't previously considered. I think it is incredibly important that we read and discuss well beyond our disciplinary boundaries (cf. Deloria 1997). This general issue raised two related points for me. First, I feel that the low regard that certain other disciplines have for archaeology relates directly to some of the key themes of this book – e.g., language, text, and human experience are not everything and non-human things and our relations to them have much to teach us. Second, I noted that some of the arguments referenced in Chapter 8 (e.g., Braidotti 2019b, 2019c) suggest that posthuman critiques are leading to increasingly transdisciplinary research (see also Tallbear 2014). This makes me feel slightly guilty because I still have a tendency to regard certain non-anthropocentric arguments in archaeology as interesting but not *really* "archaeological." I've also been critical of symmetrical archaeology in general for its rejection of history – an element of archaeology that I find important. I wonder if this type of gatekeeping is slowing certain transdisciplinary efforts. On the one hand, I agree that cross-disciplinary discussion is important, but, on the other hand, I still feel that archaeology has an identity that certain transformations will challenge – and, to be honest, I'm probably not fully prepared for those challenges. This is something we will return to in Chapter 12.

Regarding your comment about thought experiments, I think it is worth noting that I see most forms of archaeology – even the staunchest Marxist archaeology – as indulgent to one degree or another. Most, if not all, archaeology involves a certain level of privilege and if we overlook it, we open things up to all forms of creeping colonialism. Don't get me wrong, I see our discipline as important, but I also see many other, more efficient, avenues for changing the world than doing (or thinking critically about) archaeology. I, of course, take issue with the problematic and exclusionary structures of academia and the wider world, but I don't see archaeology as dealing with these problems as directly as other forms of activism. Having recognized this, I still don't think this excludes any of us from trying to "decolonize" our discipline. My motivation for creating categories of ontological argument in archaeology and anthropology is that they don't quite match up with my experience working with Indigenous communities, including some of my collaborators who are professional archaeologists. I see certain ontological claims and projects as not actually delivering with their promise to "take Indigenous knowledge seriously." On the contrary, I see business as usual with some new terminology thrown in. In this sense, I thought further critical analysis of these ideas was in order. Decolonizing theory (and writing about it) is, of course, only one part of this larger decolonial project; the actual practice of collaborative archaeology is the main part. So, when I write about the ontological turns and dissect certain arguments, I really see these efforts as putting to paper what I've already learned, thought about, or done through various collaborative projects. This makes me wonder how you situate archaeology within broader activist efforts. Do you see a way to use archaeology to solve some of the bigger problems in the world? Or is this a matter of time better spent doing collaborative archaeology and working with communities rather than writing about theory? I see the two (doing and thinking) as closely connected because many of the things I write not only come from my collaborative experiences but also influence how I approach future collaborations (and their connections with academia).

LINDSAY: I agree that doing and thinking as you say are worthwhile enterprises with separate and valuable impacts. Indeed, much of the Indigenous archaeology literature to date has focused on building both ethical methodological tool kits and new approaches to the interpretation of the past. My main aim here is to broaden this already robust body of work by thinking about how larger social structures perpetuate epistemological injustice by constraining the formation of a more Indigenized archaeological discipline. While I am a huge proponent of integrating Indigenous voices into anthropological scholarship, it is also important to recognize how dominant systems of knowledge production shape the ways in which collaborative knowledge is evaluated, validated, and incorporated. Although the academy has increasingly taken up a liberal "feel good" mantle of diversity, public outreach, and collaboration, in many ways the underlying structures of academic research (publication as well as tenure and promotion) have remained unchanged. As a result, scholars, particularly from historically disenfranchised backgrounds, are left between a rock and a hard place. They must weigh the costs and benefits of embracing a new wave of incorporative practices and maintaining their positions within an institutional structure that does not always practice what it preaches.

Your chapter makes me think more deeply about our aspirations to "decolonize" the discipline. And I am left wondering whether archaeologists can ever escape from our "colonial sensibility"? In some ways perhaps yes, but in other ways no. Colonialism is not just a mindset but an omnipresent social, political, and economic reality. While deconstructing Eurocentric defaults and taking Indigenous knowledge seriously may chip away at the colonial edifice, it does not fundamentally challenge the larger structure.

CRAIG: I personally see the call to decolonize as a never-ending project. Perhaps that is what motivated some of my critique in Chapter 10; it sometimes feels to me like scholars speak of decolonizing our thoughts and practices as if we've reached the final goal. As you noted earlier, this is anything but the case. I suppose I see flexibility and humility as two of the most important parts of decolonizing archaeology and engaging with different pasts. What do you think?

LINDSAY: In addition to flexibility and humility, I would probably add that we should be willing to abandon our deeply held beliefs about how the world works. I think that this is an important prerequisite to creating the mental space needed to imagine alternative systems of knowledge production and consumption (see discussion in Chapter 7). It may also be worthwhile to do away with the strict dichotomy between Indigenous and Western theoretical frameworks upon which much of the ontological turns are based. This dualism perpetuates the mythology of an essentialized Indigenous Other referred to by Edward Said (1978) and presents an all too easy solution to deconstructing anthropological thought (one simply needs to abandon Western theory for Indigenous knowledge).

It is also worth pointing out that while western academics may struggle to extricate themselves from colonial power structures and epistemologies,

Indigenous peoples are also embroiled in this same struggle. As Maria Ferrera (2016:239) has noted in her work with Filipino-Americans, Indigenous groups living in North America have a "colonial mentality" – a mental framework shaped by Western culture, values, and systems of knowledge. This colonial mentality inferiorizes Indigenous cultural values, practices, and epistemologies. So, when we talk about incorporating Indigenous knowledge into archaeological theory, we must also attend to the ways in which 500 years (and counting) of colonialism have shaped this knowledge. Indigenous epistemologies and ontologies are not primordial theories but rather dynamic relational systems. In this sense, Indigenous knowledge in and of itself is not a panacea for creeping colonialism in the academy but rather something that may also be in need of "decolonizing."

CRAIG: I completely agree with you about the dangers of setting up strict dichotomies between Indigenous and Western frameworks; this was one of my key motivations for writing Chapter 10. I also recently wrote about this issue with James Quinn and Jay Levy (Cipolla et al. 2019); one of the main goals of our writing project was to look critically at the different ways we relate to the collaborative archaeology that we practice – including, of course, Mohegan-colonial history and heritage. We certainly found areas of difference between us – but not ones that could be cleanly classified as Western versus Indigenous – along with many similarities that might be brushed under the rug with the "world-centered" approaches discussed in my chapter. As you note, such an approach runs the risk of essentialism. These dangers are what Robert McGhee (2008) infamously warned the archaeological world against when he claimed that most forms of collaborative Indigenous archaeology might be guilty of what he called "aboriginalism." Considering my personal experience with collaborative research and my broader readings on other projects across the globe, I think he was wrong about how most collaborative research projects work (see discussion of McGhee in Cipolla and Quinn 2016). But I do think his concerns could become realized in uncritical adoptions of ontological arguments, particularly in archaeology where some don't collaborate, or even speak with, communities – again, this was part of my motivation for critically dissecting those "ontological" arguments.

I also see your points about the challenges that come with recognizing Indigenous knowledge as a moving target rather than a primordial essence. I agree that we need models that see Indigenous knowledge as a set of dynamic and vibrant systems that preexisted, but also lived through, early colonialism and continue on today, often in settler colonial contexts. This idea raised some questions for me regarding Todd's (2016) work and her broader critiques of academia and anthropology. In some applications, I worry that her arguments might be appropriated and translated into a dualistic set of essences similar to those that you described earlier. I want to avoid any type of thinking that associates *all* of western thought with dualistic frameworks and *all* Indigenous thought with relational frameworks. Although I don't think that this was her point, I worry that some readers of Todd will begin to see all relational theory – Actor-Network Theory (ANT), assemblage theory, etc. – as flawed replications of some monolithic Indigenous way of being and seeing (see also Chapter 5). Following Todd, I think we need to note the significant overlaps, to carefully trace historical connections, and to increase the breadth of our citational practices. But we also need room to recognize difference. For instance, contrary to Todd, I don't think that aspects of Bruno Latour's ANT are only part of a flawed Western replica of *Silla*; there are differences that must be recognized and this is what we attempted to do in our discussions of Mohegan archaeology (Cipolla et al. 2019).

On the location of metaontologies

RACHEL: This is a really interesting discussion about the relationship between Indigenous and western thought. Dwelling on the overlaps between these ways of thinking, rather than dichotomizing them, appears to offer a route forward to braid them together respectfully in a way that produces space for collaboration. I have often been a little troubled by how Indigenous thinking is lumped together under one label because I worry that rich differences and diverse ways of thinking are being flattened – but throughout the discussion (and this book more broadly) it is clear that there is not just one Indigenous way of knowing the world (see Chapter 4 for example). There is a parallel here with the opening discussion relating to relational approaches. Like Craig and Ollie, I much prefer to split rather than lump when it comes to describing relational approaches as I think there are very important and fundamental differences within that label. This leads me to bring up the slightly vexed question of metaontology again (see, for example, Alberti 2016a, 2016b; Cipolla 2019; discussion in Chapter 5). It is clear from the discussion in Chapter 5, especially from what Lindsay says, that dwelling on our metaontologies in a non-hierarchical way and considering the differences between them is fundamental. Lindsay talks about metaontologie*s* – they are multiple. Craig, do you agree that they are multiple? Do you think we can exist within more than one at once?

CRAIG: I largely agree with the first part of Lindsay's argument about a non-hierarchical or flat approach to multiple ontologies and epistemologies. As a privileged person who works with Indigenous Peoples, I always hasten to add that this is an *aspirational ideal* for me. I label it aspirational because, first, I think it is difficult to completely avoid letting my own understanding of – and place in – the world color my engagement with difference. Second, it is not only up to me to decide if decolonization is successful or not; it is also up to my collaborators and to other Indigenous Peoples who connect with the archaeology.

Generally speaking, I try to resist assuming that I *fully* understand radical difference because this might contribute to a rather traditional problem of academic privilege and assumed supremacy (cf. Deloria 1997). This concern parallels many of the problems that Eduardo Viveiros de Castro (e.g., 1992, 2015a, 2015b) found with traditional anthropological approaches to difference. This does not preclude engaging with difference, it just assumes that I always maintain aspects of my own imperfect Western metaontology. Evoking Gayatri Spivak (1988) for a moment, I don't feel comfortable *speaking for* the subaltern. I think this is a good thing. For example, recognizing the persistence of differences between participants in collaborative archaeology should be seen as a strength rather than a liability; this is because, for me, collaborative archaeology is similar to an assemblage – greater than the sum of its parts.

RACHEL: I agree, a diversity of thinking leads to something far richer than what emerges when we all simply agree and think the same. Earlier we talked about focusing on overlaps and what we share as a way toward collaboration. But the next step is to focus on the gaps, it is where there are differences between our understandings that the most productive conversations often occur; this book is based on that premise.

CRAIG: Exactly. Speaking of different perspectives or gaps, when it comes to the second part of Lindsay's statement, I disagree that archaeologists can deal with *multiple metaontologies*. Yet I can't help but feel that this disagreement is largely terminological rather than ontological. Before going any further, it's worth considering how the notion of "metaontology" appears in the literature. As far as I can tell, Alberti and Yvonne Marshall (2009:348–9) were the first archaeologists to discuss this idea as it relates to perspectivist-inspired archaeologies (what I refer to as "worlds-centered" approaches in Chapter 10). They use this idea in their discussion of relational approaches and their limitations, specifically as it relates to the work of Karen Barad (2007), Tim Ingold (2011), and what we call "first-wave" symmetrical archaeologists. The problem that Alberti and Marshall have with metaontologies is their *claim of universality* and how this claim potentially obliterates or softens radical difference. They are concerned with the tension between "global" relational ontologies and the singularity of peoples' ontological claims (Alberti and Marshall 2009:349; see also Chapter 10 for a direct quotation). In 2016, Alberti addressed this problem further in his review of archaeologies of ontology. He warned against a new metaontological orthodoxy (relational approaches) that might become "impervious to the words and deeds of small-scale societies, whose own metaphysics are often presented in a complex narrative form that . . . continues to seem quaint and inaccessible to systematization" (Alberti 2016a:172). According to these uses of the term, metaontologies make universal claims regardless of what, where, when, and whom those claims concern. The recent resurgence of realist philosophy (e.g., DeLanda and Harman 2017; see also Bhaskar 2008) and its influence in archaeology are excellent examples of how metaontologies work – there is a speculative, mind-independence of the worlds that they help to conceive. But there is another important component of metaontologies according to thinkers like Alberti – they aren't just theories about how the world is in all times and places, they are also applied in an imperialist or even colonialist manner because they are frameworks within which we identify and engage with difference. In other words, the observer/analyst is "making sense of" other peoples and other pasts – privileging the researcher's perspective as "better" (or "more accurate") than that of the observed.

My primary concern with all of this is that I am not confident enough to assume that I can derive a theoretical approach that allows me to step outside of my own metaontology – and I would argue that all archaeologists have a metaontology regardless of their allegiance to realist theories.

RACHEL: I agree that all archaeologists (and anthropologists) have a metaontology. I think we are brought up with particular understandings of the world that produce our ontologies. Engaging with archaeological theory and philosophy has shown me the shape of my own metaontology. I did not really understand that I had a metaontology until I was introduced to alternative ways of understanding the world. I loved archaeological theory as a student (and still do today) because of its ability to shake my understandings of the world to their core. Of course, it was part of my privilege that up to that point in my education I had never really questioned how I understood the world, I imagine the experience of growing up in a very different culture from that of your parents and/or home, or being Indigenous within a settler colonial world means that the experience of that ontological difference probably comes earlier and is often damaging. Over time I came to see how problematic my own metaontology was, how, for example, anthropocentrism in the West paves the way for our destructive attitude toward the planet. Through the study of theory, I have begun to reshape and redefine my metaontology. This has been rooted in a desire to do better – to have fewer damaging relations with the humans and non-humans around me. So I would argue that I have shifted my metaontology – as I have found myself really engaging with theories of relationality or posthumanism they have come to reshape how I see everything: I try my best (and often fail) to live my philosophy. I now start from a position where I understand the world in relation to my metaontology, always striving and aspiring, like you Craig, to do that in a non-hierarchical way, but that metaontology is not one governed by binaries and anthropocentrism but is instead rooted in posthumanism.

LINDSAY: I'd like to jump in quickly here and explain a little bit about why I pluralized the term "metaontology." When you talk with Indigenous people about their experiences living within a settler colonial society, many will tell you about the challenges that come within "living in two worlds." I understand this sentiment literally; it is referring to the fact that Indigenous individuals (and other people of color for that matter) are required to hold two distinct and often competing modes of understanding and interacting with the world simultaneously. For many Indigenous people, stepping out of one's metaontology is imperative for getting along in the world rather than a hypothetical scenario.

RACHEL: Craig, do you think the process is one of changing an existing ontology? Or adopting a new metaontology?

CRAIG: Hmm, that is a difficult question. Lindsay makes a great point; once again, one that I had not previously considered. To begin, it's important to emphasize that, like you Rachel, I view all of these types of ontology as *in motion*, i.e., not as essences. I suppose the theoretical reflection you discuss could transform at both scales. For example, in your ontology as an archaeologist, you might explicitly cite these sources and use them when conversing with other archaeologists – potentially reshaping the discipline as you do so. But I like to think that these ideas also reshape our metaontologies in that they affect how you engage with reality in ways that you aren't fully aware. I certainly think this has been the case with me since I began working on repatriation projects. I believe that those experiences – encounters with difference – have reshaped my metaontology in countless ways, some of which I'm sure I don't understand. The difference I am detecting between my view and Lindsay's is that I think of the metaontology as the thing that binds those "two worlds" together; it isn't the same as either of those worlds because it includes knowledge of *both* even though a person might only engage and express one at a time, depending on the social context.

RACHEL: I wonder if your point about ontologies in motion is the key one. Our ontologies shift through our experiences and really, it is a question of when we identify them as something different rather than simply as "in process" versions of an original. I think your other point, that our experiences reshape our metaontologies in ways we do not necessarily understand, is also important: they are always in motion but we are not always certain of how they are changing.

CRAIG: To take this a step further, I also assume that all people have metaontologies – speculations on how the world works in all times and places (including when they consider other ontologies and worldviews that are not their own) – but not everyone actually goes out and uses those metaontologies to make sense of difference on the scale that anthropologists and archaeologists do; or, to Lindsay's point, in the ways that precarious peoples living through settler colonialism are often forced to do. In short, I feel that archaeologists can't avoid privileging their own metaontology, thus making all other ontologies we encounter fit within our own (and, yes, this means that I don't think that Viveiros de Castro *actually believes* that jaguars are really humans in disguise).

RACHEL: Can you have a metaontology you are not aware of though? For those who are not archaeologists and anthropologists, or Indigenous people forced to live in settler colonist worlds, they might never have that moment of encounter with radical difference where they see an alternative world (though I would add here that I think part of our job as archaeologists and anthropologists is to try and let more people encounter difference in a non-hierarchical and respectful way). Without that encounter, do they have a metaontology? Or do they have an ontology?

CRAIG: I assume everyone has a metaontology even if they aren't aware of it. I see it as the largest scale at which you make sense of the universe, including the familiar and the foreign. This, of course, doesn't imply that everyone applies it in a colonialist manner.

RACHEL: I tend to think about the meta- in metaontology as being about the act of comparison. So, we have an ontology, and the engagement with difference is about seeing another ontology. This engagement then acts to transform your own ontology into a metaontology. As archaeologists or anthropologists, we all have a metaontology that shapes how we engage with the world and the difference we find within it; I agree that I do not think we can escape that metaontology, but that it is itself always in process and changing rather than a fossilized eternal truth.

CRAIG: I think that is a useful distinction, Rachel. To reiterate, I *do* think that we should strive to approach these differences in a non-hierarchical manner and I agree that Viveiros de Castro and his followers offer insights into how to attempt this feat – usually by questioning our own ontologies and speculating on the possibility that they are flawed in some way. In the end, however, I assert that we will never fully escape our own metaontology (singular, not plural). Incidentally, this is not to say that I disagree with the idea of *multiple ontologies* (cf. Harris and Robb 2012). But "metaontology" for me suggests the broadest scale at which we speculate about reality (including our understanding of views and ontologies that are not our own) and it is something that we just can't shake off or suppress completely. Claims that we are able to do this qualify us as extraordinary beings – *masters of reality*, if you will. This is not a claim that I am willing to make because I still believe in the importance of relativism that strives toward non-hierarchical (non-Eurocentric) approaches to multiple ontologies and epistemologies.

OLLIE: Indeed, I think the point John Robb and I were making in that paper you cite Craig (Harris and Robb 2012), that all people have multiple ontologies, is in itself a metaontological claim, although we didn't use that term at the time. I have to say I agree with Rachel. Unless we reserve the term meta-ontology to refer to "how we explicitly reflect on the question of ontology" rather than "speculations about the world," we run the risk of simply replacing ontology with metaontology, inviting us to coin meta-metaontologies and so on. So for me, metaontologies emerge through specific moments of difference, where you explicitly compare different ontologies, and have to adopt a position that facilitates that comparison.

CRAIG: I don't think I disagree with either of you; I suppose the point of contention here is that I was assuming that when we speculate on reality in a broad sense, that reality often does include points of difference, even from within our own local worlds.

This raises a bigger set of questions about how different disciplines reshape theory. I am quite interested in the differences between what I refer to as "worlds-centered" or perspectival approaches in anthropology versus archaeology. Ethnographers' interests (usually the present) and methodologies (speaking with people) are different from those of archaeologists, who usually have some interest in the past and who may or may not speak with descendant communities in the present. How do these different approaches recognize, confront, and engage with difference? Anthropologists usually do so in relation to Western sensibilities – that idea of experience sounds different *to me* – and once they lock on to an example of alterity, they explore it further through various forms of dwelling in that social context (e.g., dialogue, observation, other types of participation). This is very different from Alberti and Marshall's (2009) body pots; in that case, alterity emerged through the relationship between the archaeologist and their materials – I just worry that the archaeologist's role in this emergence is sometimes portrayed as diminished if not altogether absent. And here again, is where colonial sensibilities might be allowed to slip in.

OLLIE: To focus on one part of this, it is interesting to think a little more about Craig's provocative statement that Viveiros de Castro doesn't actually believe that jaguars are really humans in disguise – I'm sure that is true. But it is true for all sorts of complicated reasons. First, the claim being made by Amazonian people, according to Viveiros de Castro, isn't really that jaguars are disguised as humans, it is that the bodies are variable, depending on your perspective; this is an opening out to the world, its relational, it isn't about hiding an inner essence – so the whole issue of *disguise* works very differently here (Ingold 2000). Second, whether or not Viveiros de Castro really believes something isn't necessarily central. The issue is that when engaging in these forms of ontological difference, he is willing to suspend his skepticism in the light of the statements other people make. When trying to translate the specific claim that a shaman can become a jaguar, or vice versa, Viveiros de Castro is faced with two choices, render that statement in a way that allows "us" to "believe" "them," a translation that reduces their claims metaphorically, or symbolically or representationally in some way (Holbraad 2007), or to make our categories and concepts be the ones that have to change and shift, to make space for their claims within our world (see also discussions of belief in Chapter 7).

CRAIG: Ollie, I think we largely agree on this issue. As I noted, perspectivism is important because it allows the researcher to engage in new ways with difference and to partially suspend skepticism. I just worry about the assumed dualism in the literature between disregarding (i.e., the statement is a metaphor that wrongly represents reality) and adopting (what do I have to change about my understanding of the world to make their statement true?). I don't find that neat and tidy dualism very useful or accurate for the contexts in which I work.

OLLIE: This is why I think in archaeology, at the moment, there are two quite separate ontological projects that often get conflated (Alberti 2016a). Once more we need to start teasing out differences! The first is people who are interested in specific moments of ontological difference, precise encounters where radical alterity comes to the fore. The moment a body *is* a pot, the moment a jaguar *is* a shaman, the moment a rock *is* an ancestor (Wilkinson 2017a). The other is when we talk about ontology as a much more generalized sense of what the world *is*. I think people concerned with ontological difference get annoyed when people start talking about "the ontology of the Neolithic" or whatever, because for them ontology is about a critical methodological approach. Whereas for those who talk about "the ontology of the Neolithic, or Neolithic ontologies" or what have you, this is about trying to wrestle with the broader differences and similarities that exist between different historical worlds. The latter can sometimes be reduced to more straightforward cultural difference, becoming worldview-centered in your terms, but they don't have to, I would suggest. I don't think this is a case that one side is "right" about ontology and another is "wrong," but I think it can be a mistake to conflate them. This distinction is one I have thought about a lot, and I've learned a lot talking to people who take a different perspective to me on these issues like Ben Alberti and Darryl Wilkinson.

CRAIG: This is an excellent point. In Chapter 10, I concentrated most of my energy on the world-focused arguments rather than approaches concerned with singular instances of radical difference. I do wonder, however, with such approaches, what theory is at work before and after we encounter radical difference? Would it be okay to experiment with a relational ontology such as Peircean semiotics, feminist posthumanism, or new materialism? I feel that the literature isn't clear on this issue of what we do in the absence of radical difference. In those moments is it okay to explicitly rely on our metaontology? As already noted, I don't think we actually have a choice in the end.

OLLIE: In terms of the metaontology you work with, I think I agree with you, Craig, that it is impossible in the end to escape one's own standpoint – a point that feminist philosophers have of course been making for decades (e.g., Haraway 1988). However, just as Rachel describes, our own position can, indeed, must change; it is always shifting. For me, therefore, what I need a metaontology to do is to open me up to the world, to allow me to embrace that possibility for change, and to emphasize the relations of difference I wrote about in Chapter 2, as a productive force. The openness that comes from this philosophy, I hope, allows me to engage with other perspectives in a way that recognizes that the reality, or the truth, of the world will emerge relationally. In this sense, my commitment to Deleuzian philosophy, and the posthumanist feminism that has developed in part from readings of Deleuze, is an ethical one.

Conclusion

CRAIG: In this chapter, we explored different ways of categorizing theory, how our work is shaped by the disciplinary structure of academia, how collaboration factors into this, and how some of us think through notions of ontology and metaontology. With the discussion of categories, we emphasized a pragmatic standpoint, asking what these new categories *do* for us, for archaeology, and for the wider world. For instance, for me, my categories of ontological approach (Chapter 10) helped me to triangulate the broader forces at play behind different ontological arguments, such as relativism, realism, and the dualisms between scholar/world or western/Indigenous. With the discussion of disciplinarity and collaboration, we focused on the importance of difference as a productive and ever-changing force in our work, including in the very pages of this book. Finally, with the discussion of metaontologies, we laid bare some subtle distinctions, both between authors and between us and key thinkers in these areas. In the next chapter, we move on to review how our dialogues have helped develop our understanding of the critical terms that this book has investigated and we explore a series of questions that remain unresolved.

12

CONCLUSION

Continuing dialogues

Introduction

In the last 11 chapters, we have debated a range of critical topics in contemporary archaeological theory. From the status of relations, via the critical purchase provided by Indigenous thought, to the role of human experience, power, and the complexity of ontology, we have considered and debated a variety of viewpoints and perspectives. The aim of the book is to create new types of space in which to explicity reflect upon what we see as the key issues facing our discipline. This involved moving back and forth between abstract philosophies to concrete politics; this is as it should be. Archaeology is a discipline that studies the past, but that has impact and affect upon the present and future: it is always political.

In this concluding chapter, we summarize the major themes and discussion points of the book: relations, ontology, posthumanism, and Indigenous paradigms. We also debate a series of critical questions that arose from writing the book. We return to a dialogic format to do this because we do not necessarily all agree on each point, nor are we seeking closure to these debates. We see this book as a beginning rather than an end. By closing with questions, we aim to provoke further debate rather than offer a finished statement or a false sense of harmonious opinions. One of the key things that emerged through our dialogues is that the questions we ask and the answers we propose are situational, located, and contextual: they are also always changing. Programmatic approaches to archaeological theory often appear to suggest that there is one view, one way of working, one way of thinking that should be applied universally. In dialogue, we have found that the theories we need and the tools we use are rooted in the political and ethical contexts in which we work. We return to these points in dialogue later, after reviewing the book's four themes.

Relations

Relations have been a key theme in archaeology for the last 25 years, from the emergence of phenomenology (Thomas 1996) to questions about personhood (Brück 2006; Chapman 2000; Fowler 2004) and from the development of symmetrical archaeology (Witmore 2007) to recent concerns with new materialism (Conneller 2011). Relations emerged as a way to move away from fixity within the literature. Archaeologists' understanding of relations and how they work is not static and, in some cases, not all that clearly defined. In Chapter 2, Ollie explored three different ways that relations have been employed in archaeology: as epistemology (that is, the way past people understand the world); as methodology (that is, archaeological approaches that use relational network theory to model past societies); and as metaphysics (that is, a metaontological position that the world *is* relational). He then proposed an approach to relations, rooted in the thinking of Gilles Deleuze, which treated them as variously affective, intensive, extensive, and differential. In other chapters, we have explored the development of relational approaches in archaeology through the adoption of phenomenological approaches (Chapter 6) and the emergence of Actor-Network Theory (ANT) (Chapters 6 and 7). We have considered how different relational approaches work (Chapter 3), contrasting in particular ANT and new materialism (Chapter 7), and discussed the complex similarities and differences between Deleuzian inspired and Indigenous approaches to relations (Chapters 3 and 5). Other approaches to relations have included the development of an Indigenous relational framework (Chapter 4), a relational approach to power (Chapter 8), and a critique of Marxist dialectics (Chapter 9). Finally, in Chapter 11, we noted how and why Ollie and Craig characterized relational approaches in different ways for different purposes (Chapters 2 and 10).

In each of these cases, we stressed how relational approaches offer a means of moving beyond fixed categories and essences. Whether discussing typologies, objects, or moments of song, relations open us up to the world, and emphasize the ongoing interconnectedness of all existence. Focusing on relations allows us to disrupt traditional Western conceptions of the world: who is powerful or agentic, who or what counts as a body? This fundamental disruption challenges the centrality of the human in our narratives, as we will see later. It has also caused some worry amongst archaeologists. If agency, affect, and power emerge relationally, then how do we hold individual humans to account for their actions (Malm 2018; Ribeiro 2016)? Surely, so the critics claim, these approaches mean we dilute culpability to such an extent that we can no longer engage in the pursuit of social justice (Barrett 2016; Hodder 2014; Van Dyke 2015). Needless to say, this is not the position held by any of us. The approach to relations developed by Indigenous thinkers like Vine Deloria Jr. (2003) and Kim Tallbear (2019), as well as those emerging from within the Western canon by thinkers like Rosi Braidotti (2013) and Deleuze (2004), demonstrate that nothing could be further from the case. Instead, relational thinking provides a more accurate description of our condition, emphasizes connections between research and the political world in which it emerges, and shows how to develop more sustainable and effective solutions to our problems. Here the Indigenous concept of being in *good* relation with the world is critical (Nikel and Fehr 2020; Tallbear 2019). By focusing on how we are enmeshed and engaged relationally with humans and non-humans alike, we can attend to the world around us anew. This attention offers the possibility for those of us coming from European and settler colonist contexts to rethink and reconsider how it is we work with the world around us.

This means we need to embrace the importance of difference, not similarity, as we discussed in Chapter 2. Difference is traditionally viewed as the distance between two things; thus, we ask about differences between two kinds of tool, two kinds of site, or two kinds of people. In this traditional model, difference is viewed as negative, and often measured against an ideal type. Instead, following Deleuze (2004), we propose a positive version of difference, where it is a productive force in the world, no longer do we ask: "what do women lack in comparison to men?"; instead, we ask: "how do differences in the world produce different forms of subjectivity, and what might the positive and productive consequence of those differences be?" No longer do we ask: "why do Indigenous groups lack an understanding of Western science?"; instead, we ask: "what might different ways of Indigenous thinking teach Western science about the world?" We must attend to the difference that relations make, the differences that relations reveal, and the differences that make relations possible. By moving away from essentialist and universalizing discourses of singular identity toward the celebration of difference, we can both understand the past in more productive ways and create the space for new dialogues in the present.

Ontology

Considering difference as a productive force in the world, rather than measuring distance from an ideal, creates space to consider alternative ontologies from the ones we might most readily operate within. Ontology has become an increasingly popular topic of debate over the last decade or so, a trend exemplified by Benjamin Alberti and Tamara Bray's (2009) special edition of *Cambridge Archaeological Journal*, which followed hot on the heels of the expansion of ontological discussions in anthropology (e.g., Henare et al. 2007). These discussions helped open up a wider range of considerations about what archaeology really is and how it relates to other traditions of thought. Considerations of ontology ask us to critically think about not only how we understand the world but also what the world actually *is*. Archaeology has a different perspective on this problem than many other disciplines – we seek to explore worlds that could have been radically different from our own, many of which might not have textual sources documenting their philosophies. How do we approach this form of radical difference, and how do we think about the ways ontologies change over time?

The main discussions of ontology in this book took place in Chapters 10 and 11. In Chapter 10, Craig considered how the concept of ontology has been utilized in archaeology and how it has allowed different kinds of archaeology to emerge. Craig identified four key approaches: worldview-centered approaches (which treats ontology as what exists *according to particular cultural perspectives*); relations-centered approaches (metaontologies that treat the world as fundamentally relational regardless of cultural perspectives on it); object-centered approaches (which adopt an object-oriented ontology (OOO) drawn from the work of Graham Harman); and worlds-centered approaches (which attempt to access alternative ontologies unencumbered by the baggage of Western philosophy or "common sense"). This comparison showed that there are fundamentally different archaeological projects that focus on ontology, sometimes using the term in critically different ways. As is the case with "relations," we mean different things when we invoke "ontology," and this is precisely why Ollie avoided using the latter term in Chapter 2. Craig asks us to consider our own metaontologies and how these shape our understandings and engagements with the pasts that we study and the presents that we work within. His argument is for a critical approach to how we think about what exists in the world from an archaeological vantage point. The issue of metaontology reoccurred in several chapters throughout the book as the authors wrestled with how to engage with ontological difference without reducing it to a simple synonym for culture. Lindsay considered the similarities and differences across Indigenous ontologies and the relationship between Indigenous ontologies and Indigenous cultural identity (Chapter 4). What happens when we translate and transport Indigenous ontologies beyond their cultural context? The authors considered whether applying Indigenous ontologies elsewhere might be a form of radical decolonization or whether it is yet another form of appropriation of Indigenous beliefs (Chapters 5 and 10). Elsewhere, the authors considered the potential for adopting a flat ontology to allow different worlds to coexist in parallel without hierarchy (Chapters 5 and 8) and how a flat ontology can be used to critique modern Western ways of knowing the world (Chapter 8).

The issue of metaontology came to the fore in Chapter 11. The authors discussed whether everyone has a metaontology or whether metaontologies only emerge following conscious reflection and encounter with alternative ontologies. Do metaontologies shift and change? A critical point of comparison raised by Lindsay is the luxurious position European and settler colonist archaeologists occupy vis-à-vis the question of metaontology when compared to Indigenous people living in settler colonist worlds, in which multiple ontologies are an inescapable reality of daily life and one critical to survival. This point drives home the fact that ontology is not just another archaeological buzz word, or an academic play thing, but a critical inflection point for the discipline. Thinking ontologically opens up explorations of radical difference and of worlds different to our own, whoever we might be. It allows us to take the experiences of a Christian in sixth-century CE Byzantium seriously, just as it allows us to foreground the reality of life for an Indigenous person in a settler colonist world and the experience of being a settler colonist in a settler colonist world.

Posthumanism

The most recent of our four terms to emerge in archaeology is posthumanism. Posthumanist thinking is diverse and covers a range of different approaches (Crellin and Harris in review). Often, in archaeology, it is used to embrace a host of approaches from symmetrical archaeology, to new materialism, to the kinds of world-centered approaches Craig discussed in Chapter 11. In this book, we chose to follow a definition of posthumanism drawn from the work of Braidotti (2013) and elaborated on by the philosopher Francesca Ferrando (2019). Ferrando outlines posthumanism (as discussed in Chapter 7) as having three core elements: post-humanism (the process of moving beyond the damaging and limiting thinking of humanism that privileges a certain kind of human and excludes the vast majority of the species); post-anthropocentrism (the process of moving beyond an anthropocentric approach where humans are always at the "ontological apex" (Bennett 2010:ix) and are given 50% of the ontological space in any analysis (Harman 2016b:31)); and post-dualism (where the world is no longer neatly divided into purified categories like nature and culture (Latour 1993) but instead we adopt a fundamentally relational approach).

Posthumanism is an umbrella term. As we outlined in the introduction, approaches that are often placed under the umbrella include *ahumanism* (MacCormack 2020) and *OOO* (Harman 2018). In archaeology, it is often used to embrace *agential realism*, most readily associated with Karen Barad (2007), *new materialism*, most readily associated with the work of Deleuze and Felix Guattari (2004) and readings of their work by Manuel DeLanda (2016), and *symmetrical archaeology* (Witmore 2007). We chose to exclude any discussion of *transhumanism*, the desire for a perfected human form through technology, because it remains an Enlightenment project, rooted in dualisms, but also because it is squarely anthropocentric. In Chapter 8, Rachel outlined a posthumanist approach as a way of moving beyond some of the most damaging aspects of Western thinking, in relation to both humans and non-humans. Humanist and anthropocentric approaches have always been central to archaeological theory and have therefore tended to unthinkingly replicate modern inequalities in our discussions of past worlds. Rachel also considered the deployment of the phrase post-anthropocentric (following Braidotti 2013; Ferrando 2019) in comparison to the term "non-anthropocentric" that has, to date, been more readily used in archaeology and has the unfortunate baggage of implying a world without humans (cf. Cipolla in review b).

In Chapter 7, the authors debated where these various approaches belong and went on to consider how the lumping together of thinkers causes problems within archaeology as the significant differences between them are often elided (we also returned to this in Chapter 11). We explored the relationship between phenomenology, a fundamentally human-centric philosophy, and posthumanism as a post-anthropocentric philosophy. We considered the relationship between posthumanist critiques and Indigenous paradigms (Chapter 5) and in the same chapter considered the relationship of posthumanism to questions of politics and ethics. As we saw with our previous discussion of relations, critics of posthumanism have claimed that it is a fundamentally apolitical project with little capacity for taking ethical positions: this book makes it clear that this is not a view shared by the authors or one that can be sustained for all branches of posthumanism. A critical point here is that the posthumanisms explored in this volume are fundamentally *feminist* (Chapter 8) rather than apolitical or ahuman.

Posthumanism emerges in this book as a political and ethical commitment to create different past worlds, to critique the world of the modern West, and to build new possible futures where all humans are granted equal humanity and where people are no longer seen as separate from, and elevated above, the rest of the non-human world. This is not about a loss of focus on humans but about an extension of our focus, and our care, for both the humans that have been traditionally excluded and non-human others. The emphasis on including those who were excluded from humanism's definition of the human and who are often forgotten in archaeological narratives is intended to create a more diverse archaeology both in the present and of the past.

Indigenous paradigms

Indigenous paradigms have intersected with, and challenged, each of the other central themes of the book. As we saw in Chapter 1, the term itself comes from the work of Shawn Wilson (2001) who identifies Indigenous paradigms as having ontological, epistemological, methodological, and axiological components (Wilson 2001:175). Within Wilson's framework, ontology refers to the intersecting relationship between how individuals see the world and a broader understanding of being. As we discussed in Chapter 7, there are many possible and often-conflicting worldviews that researchers may hold, but these conflicts do not necessarily limit an individual's ability to embrace or take on an ontology different from their own as a historical framework. While Craig's (Chapter 10) and Lindsay's (Chapter 4) research with northeastern and southwestern Indigenous North American communities draw attention to the distinct worldviews that exist across Indigenous Peoples, there are enough overlaps across Indigenous groups to distinguish a generalized Indigenous ontology from a generalized Western (i.e., European-American) one. Throughout the subsequent dialogue sections, the authors discussed some of the parallels that exist between Indigenous ontologies and the relational and agency-based approaches advocated for by scholars who have positioned themselves within a variety of theoretical turns over the past two decades (e.g., new materialism, symmetrical archaeology, and cultural particularism).

Throughout this book we also discuss matters of epistemology, which Wilson (2001) understands as the fluid ways of knowing, which are passed on from one generation to the next in different forms, including stories, dances, place names, and songs. In various ways, all of the authors touch upon how knowledge is transmitted across time and space: for example, Sophie's investigation of the embodied experience of music within the Byzantine church in Chapter 6 and the subsequent discussion of the relational effects and functions of performances in Pueblo contexts (Chapter 7). Several of us also brought up the need to challenge dominant forms of knowledge production and transmission: a position that resonates with and has implications for Indigenous paradigms. As Rachel points out in Chapter 8, archaeological studies of the European Bronze Age often impose modern understandings of inequality and gender onto the archaeological record in ways that suppress alternative social relationships or models. In an entirely different vein, the dialogues in Chapter 11 draw attention to the various ways that archaeologist often try to categorize knowledge (Chapter 10) and when these categories create helpful analytical frameworks and when they serve to silence specific types of knowledge.

Finally, methodology and associated questions of axiology are at the heart of many of the chapters in this volume. Each of the authors is seeking to develop a research approach that stretches beyond or combines in new ways currently codified theoretical models. Despite our differences, we all value the collaborative process, whether that be working directly with Indigenous peoples (Chapter 10) or talking to thinkers outside of our research areas or disciplines (Chapter 3). As discussed by both Lindsay (Chapter 4) and Rachel (Chapter 8), methodology is not divorced from ethics – what Wilson means by Axiology – and therefore archaeologists ought to think through how their approaches may reinforce problematic power imbalances. While each author engages with ontology, epistemology, methodology, and axiology in different ways, we all seem to agree on the importance of critically assessing the relationship between Indigenous knowledge, social theory, and archaeological praxis.

Critical questions

Emerging from the discussion of our four titular themes are a series of critical questions that also appear throughout our dialogues. In the following sections, we provide summaries and context for each of these questions, followed by short responses from each author. By doing so, we allow the reader to see where we agree and disagree and, more importantly, where our different contexts and perspectives lead us to emphasize certain ways of thinking, or answers, over others. The focus here is on the political and ethical dimensions of our work, as well as what counts as archaeology. Nonetheless, each has inevitable implications for how we do archaeology as well.

Does theory have to translate? Or can we have local theory?

In Western Philosophy, it often seems as though the goal of theorists and philosophers is to create ideas that are applicable always and everywhere. Recently, with the elevation of Indigenous voices and critiques, archaeologists began asking new questions about turning Indigenous thinking into a form of alternative philosophy (see Chapter 5). Such a process would involve the removal of thinking from its original context and its translation elsewhere with potentially unknown and maybe even damaging consequences. Should the goal of theory be for it to be translatable? Or must it remain local? In fact, *should* it only be local?

RACHEL: At conferences, I often find that there is an expectation in some parts of the audience that I want everyone to adopt the same philosophy and way of thinking as me. I honestly think that we gain more when we aim not for homogenization of thinking but for productive discussion about our differences: the aim is not to make everyone think the same thing. Theory for me is local – the philosophies we need to decolonize thinking in the UK and Europe are not the same ones Indigenous communities in the Americas need.

OLLIE: I would say the aim of theory is to help me think about the world; therefore, it has to be fundamentally local, but that locality is my own perspective. I find the philosophy of Deleuze particularly useful because of the way it opens up new understandings of difference and through that allows me to reconceptualize past worlds and future possibilities. It helps me write about the past in a way that is critical of how it is presented in the here and now (cf. Deleuze 2006b:107).

CRAIG: It is crucial that we recognize the differing origin points, stories, and experiences from which specific theories come; we can try to avoid translating theories from one context to another, but we don't have complete control of this choice. I feel that I've been transformed by certain theories in ways that I can't shake off or mute; although I'm constantly mixing concepts from different locales (e.g., those of twentieth-century French philosophers, those of eighteenth-century Indigenous activists), the key is to remain as explicit as possible about my privileged place in the world and the origins of these different concepts.

LINDSAY: Almost all applications of social theory, whether they come from Indigenous peoples or elsewhere require translation. Indeed, most of what we call Indigenous philosophy within the academy is written by a small group of Native (often Annishnaabe) scholars, for example Gerald Vizenor and Leanne Simpson, and reflects their collective histories and worldviews. So when I apply, for example, Annishnaabe concepts to Southwestern Indigenous communities, I am already engaging in a form of trans-local translation. What is critical, I think, is that we reflect not only on which theories offer the best explanatory frameworks for our case studies but the impact of using those theories on the local communities that exist outside of the academic context.

SOPHIE: I would argue that theory is always both local and translated. The act of writing something down or communicating it at all is arguably an act of translation (cf. Latour 1999:58–9), but it is how explicitly we frame that translation and how careful we are with how we locate its relevance that make it useful or harmful in our local application of theory.

Are our ethics and politics always local?

If our theories need to embrace context and location, then is the same true for our ethics and politics? The long-standing aim of humanism and Enlightenment philosophy has been a call for a transcendent ethics, one committed first and foremost to the universal human, who shared in an inalienable set of rights. Yet both the history of Indigenous experience and the philosophy of posthumanism suggest that who or what counts as human is never as clear as the defenders of humanism would have us believe. Indeed, without a sense of location, how can we begin to define who counts as Indigenous, or when the concept of Indigeneity is important politically and when it might be dangerous?

LINDSAY: I think that our ethics and politics are always informed by our personal and collective experiences and are therefore profoundly local. The impulse to develop transcendent ethical practices, while in some ways appealing, rarely ends up producing genuinely "universal" frameworks. Instead, universalist aspirations more often end up echoing dominant perspectives and prerogatives. So for me, moving away from this universalizing impulse is a critical step toward making archaeology more reflective of and responsive to the particular politics and histories of the places it occurs and the peoples it studies.

SOPHIE: I agree with Lindsay that ethics and politics are profoundly local. I would take the rallying cry of second-wave feminism that "the personal is political" and flip it so that the political is also personal. By starting with acknowledging the situated conditions of both ourselves and the pasts we study, I think we work toward greater precision in understanding the past.

RACHEL: I think our ethics and politics are always local. As we write Chapter 12, the UK is in Covid-19 lockdown. On any "normal" day, I would feel deeply skeptical about being forced to stay at home by the government, but today it makes sense and is the ethically positive thing to do. Returning to archaeology, I think we can see the need for different ethics and politics when we reflect on power. In my own context, I want to deconstruct the damaging model of power that dominates in the West and show alternative ways of understanding power: my location and privilege make that the right decision. But for Indigenous groups, engaging with the settler colonist government, it probably does little good, in the short term, for them to dispute what exactly power is and how it works, when the force of that power is creating genuine inequality and racism.

CRAIG: For many of the reasons laid out by my co-authors here, I don't think we should strive toward a transcendent and universal ethics that applies to all times and places. But, to be clear, I don't think that this stance is the same as "anything goes," hyperrelativism. I feel that ethics must attend to local, material circumstances.

OLLIE: The question of who counts as Indigenous is one that immediately points me toward the need for local ethics and politics that are immanent to the questions we are posing and the problems we face, and not transcendent to them. Contrast, for example, the important Indigenous relationships with a site like Chaco Canyon in New Mexico, with claims that Neolithic sites in Britain belong to the "indigenous" people of those islands. The first is a tool for decolonizing, for resisting, for articulating power and connection in the face of prejudice, racism, and oppression. The latter, in the British context, *is itself a tool of prejudice, racism, and oppression.* Claims to a universal and ahistorical ethics and politics can never reconcile this tension, and so handover what should be the tool of the subaltern to those least in need of it.

What does decolonizing involve?

Decolonizing has recently become a buzz word in universities in North America, the UK, and elsewhere. In the UK context, where the history of colonialism is frequently suppressed, children learn little about the British colonial past at school, and the general public largely see themselves as divorced from the imperial legacy (despite the colonial wealth the country is built upon); decolonizing in universities has focused on the representation of scholars from diverse backgrounds. In North America, this takes a variety of different forms ranging from diversifying universities to challenging Eurocentric assumptions. It has also entailed calls to change the current power dynamics of the discipline to more concrete actions around the repatriation of lands, ancestors, and heritage. Eve Tuck and K. Wayne Yang (2012) offer an important and critical take on these diverse forms of decolonization in their article, "Decolonization Is Not a Metaphor." For them, diversifying reading lists, hiring new "diverse" faculty, or challenging Eurocentric and colonial assumptions are useful things to do, but these activities should *not* be conflated with decolonization. This is because, as the title of the article states, decolonization is not a metaphor. In short, they are concerned that many practices now labeled "decolonial" are actually just business as usual with little connection to real change in academic disciplines or in the broader world; this critique evokes the pragmatic question: *What difference does it make?* For Tuck and Yang, if it doesn't directly connect with tangible change and improvement of Indigenous lives, it isn't decolonization. This begs the question: What does *decolonization* mean for archaeology and for the authors of this book? Can the process ever be complete, and how does editing your reading list or abandoning terms such as "prehistory" fit within these efforts if at all?

SOPHIE: I think there are a couple of key misunderstandings of decolonization that are prevalent within the UK Academy. First, that decolonization is a process that can be completed, and, second, that broadening out the range of topics taught and studied from a Western cannon is axiomatically a decolonial move. It has been some time, to put it mildly, since Edward Said wrote Orientalism (1978), but we don't seem to have learnt the lesson that simply studying something is no guarantee that you are doing it ethically or with an eye to power relations. We must move beyond the lip-service paid to decolonization, but I don't think we need to throw the term away. Higher Education as it currently exists is fundamentally rooted in an imperial politics of knowledge, but we can strive to counteract this. For example, as a medievalist, it is essential that I pay attention to how white nationalists in the present are using false concepts of medieval Europe to try to legitimize their agenda. Everything I write and say in public has to work to counteract that narrative, starting with teaching the medieval world in a connected way that decenters Europe.

CRAIG: Archaeologists must guard against decolonization reverting back to business as usual. According to Marina La Salle and Richard Hutchings (2018:14), decolonization means the *end* of archaeology; for what it's worth, I disagree. For me, decolonization doesn't necessitate the end of archaeology because archaeologists *can* remake their discipline, and I think that they are in the process of doing so. Following thinkers like Tuck and Yang (2012), "decolonization" should be used sparingly and when it is used, it must remain anchored to transformations in power and authority and it should maintain means of assessing its success *or lack thereof* in these projects. In contrast to Tuck and Yang, I think diversifying reading lists and university faculties and rethinking archaeology's Eurocentric defaults are potential acts of decolonization as long as these activities articulate with the broader efforts to change the discipline.

LINDSAY: For me, decolonizing requires a radical and systemic shift in the social, economic, and political balance of power in order to create a more equitable distribution of resources and life opportunities across different communities. While I think there have been great strides made toward the incorporation of historically marginalized ethnicities, genders, and narratives into the disciplines of archaeology and anthropology, little change has occurred around structural issues like racism, harassment, and monetary flows. While I believe that we must continuously strive to achieve incremental change, I agree with Craig that the decolonization process will never fully be realized. Instead, it may be more helpful for us to think about "Indigenizing" social theory and archaeological praxis. As conceived by Daniel Wildcat (2006:419), Indigenizing requires us to reexamine and adopt the unique practices and perspectives of the people and places where our archaeological work takes place. This is a profoundly local move that is particularly powerful in the North American context, because it centers Indigenous traditions and politics that have often been erased or silenced.

RACHEL: Decolonizing is not easy: but I think that is the point. At the University of Leicester, we have made the predictable first steps – renamed modules, adjusted reading lists, and are working toward reducing the awarding gap between our BAME (Black, Asian and Minority Ethnic) and white students. It is important to realize that these things are not enough: decolonizing is an ongoing process. This past year Ollie and I have brought Indigenous paradigms into conversation with posthumanism in our teaching of the Neolithic and Bronze Age of Britain for third-year undergraduate students. We did this predominantly through the *All My Relations* (Wilbur and Keene) podcast. For our students, learning about the world of blood quantum, DNA testing, and reservations has clearly been incredibly eye-opening, making them reflect differently on their own world at home and their own past. It has made me reflect on my own shortcomings and forced me to think really carefully about my own privilege and what I can use that unearned privilege to achieve.

OLLIE: For me, decolonizing involves a continual process of learning and reflecting, of listening to and dwelling upon different ways of engaging with the world. One thing to keep in mind here, however, is that this also required us to recognize that our lives are full of contradiction and tensions. Just as it's possible to care deeply about the climate crisis, but ride in an airplane, it's possible, probably inevitable, that there will be tensions in the process of decolonizing our work. Whilst it is important and essential to keep working away at that, to challenge ourselves to do better, demanding perfection from the outset is simply a way of preventing the important process of change from ever getting going.

How do we share the load of challenging privilege?

Challenging privilege is an underlying theme in this book. It seems that we each share the goal of using our past for politically and ethically positive purposes in the present. Thinking about our own context and locatedness, as we did when we met in Syracuse and when we wrote Chapter 1, should cause us to reflect on our own privilege. As we wrote the dialogues of this book, it felt at times like Craig, and in particular Lindsay, were taking the load of teaching the rest of us about Indigenous paradigms and the rest of us worried that they were carrying too much weight. This is an area that we see debated often in feminist practice and activism: Why does the burden of challenging privilege often fall so unevenly? How do we share this task amongst us more equitably whilst also acknowledging the important experience and expertise of those who are hurt the most by inequitable systems?

RACHEL: Ideally, it should be our own responsibility to challenge our privilege and then to do the work of educating ourselves about the experiences of others and about the structural systems that cause oppression. In reality, that does not always happen. Our feminist and activist work should aim to be teamwork, work where we do not always have to carry the ball or run the whole marathon, work where we support each other and pick up the load when it gets heavy: a team can go further for longer than an individual. When we do challenge the privilege of others, we should aim to do so in a way that produces space for growth: tone is important. We need to use the opportunities that we are given to teach (Chapter 9) and use our teaching to highlight and disrupt privilege. Finally, we all have to learn to listen more, and to really hear what other people are saying.

CRAIG: I agree with Rachel that this has to be a communal effort. We must use the privilege that we have to make space for the less privileged. Returning to the previous question about decolonization, for example, it shouldn't be acceptable to hire one Indigenous colleague in a North American Anthropology Department and then begin celebrating the end of colonialism. That is just the start and the process will only find success when those who have privilege open their minds, begin sacrificing more of their power, and start taking more risks to open up new spaces and opportunities for underrepresented groups. Admittedly, for me, this is a work in progress.

OLLIE: I am very fortunate to work with, and write books with, people who challenge my privilege every day, and I don't take their work for granted. Part of my own work is the continuing and discomforting experience of reflecting on that challenge, working to form alliances, and supporting colleagues who don't have the same levels of privilege that I do. I think there is a tightrope to be walked in my case in terms of how you amplify the voices doing the work, support the work that is happening, but not in a way that means that your already loud voice (in my case that's both figurative and actual) comes to dominate. Learning to keep quiet is part of the work too.

SOPHIE: I largely agree with what has already been said. Privilege is a slippery thing. There were periods of time during writing this book that were a real struggle for me. I was precariously employed on short-term fractional academic contracts alongside working in catering and as a childminder while sleeping on a friend's couch for quite a lot of it, not a particularly unusual situation for an adjunct to be in. But just because 2018–2019 was a difficult year for me does not mean that I ceased to be privileged. Having privilege does not mean that you don't struggle, it just means that factors like the color of your skin, your heritage, and your gender identity have not made those struggles harder.

LINDSAY: I think that the reason why acts of privilege checking fall so unevenly is in part because of how uncomfortable this task can be. It requires the checker (often a historically disenfranchised person) to boldly confront dominant societal norms that can have negative repercussions for them. It also requires the checkee to become uncomfortable with their positionality and to work to change it. Overall, this is a profoundly humbling, embarrassing, and scary process for all parties. In order to redistribute this burden, I think having allies is critical. People in positions of normative power must not wait for the stereotypical "angry brown girl" to check them, but instead engage in self-reflection about their positionality and make the effort to seek out alternative ideas and uncomfortable conversations. They must also be willing to support marginalized groups or individuals when they speak truth to power.

How do we use the term "western"?

Western is a term that we have used throughout this book, most frequently in opposition to non-western or Indigenous. Our use of the term has been relatively uncritical, and it is a term that we have neither defined nor problematized. Yet it is a complex term with a complex history. What is western (just like what is Indigenous) is multiple and varied. How do we use the term? Should we capitalize it? How do we define it? What purpose does it serve in our narratives and theory?

RACHEL: In my work I tend to use the term Western to capture what we might see as the hegemonic and mainstream Euro-American view of the world. In theoretical discussions, I often use it as a shorthand for thinking rooted in dualisms, anthropocentrism, and humanism; or thinking that focuses on ownership, property, and the production of wealth. Western thinking is all too often deeply damaging. On the other hand, it is not something I can divorce myself from: the thinkers I use to critique these ideas, posthumanists like Braidotti or Ferrando, are also westerners and, of course, I too am a westerner.

OLLIE: Building on that, one of the critical things I think we can recognize is that there are within the western tradition ideas that are dominant and others that are quieter, more minor in key. One reason to celebrate and explore the minor is that it shifts the central difference from opposing western and Indigenous across a central chasm, where one lacks what the other offers, to exploring, once again, how difference is emergent and productive. Once you have a western tradition that celebrates its multiplicity, there is room for many other perspectives and many other forms of diversity.

SOPHIE: It is useful to be able to use "Western" as a sort of shorthand for canonical philosophical traditions from the Enlightenment onward, and I use the term very much as Rachel sets out previously. Using it in this way, and placing it in opposition to non-western and Indigenous categories, potentially reifies these divisions, while subsuming diverse perspectives within it ignores the specific context of ways of thinking – both of which are colonial moves. There is no easy way out of this, but writing with specificity is my goal here.

CRAIG: I primarily use the term "Western" to refer to specific intellectual traditions (i.e., how the Enlightenment instilled certain patterned modes of seeing and being in the world) and how these traditions manifested themselves in the settler colonies of North America and in the discipline of archaeology. I don't think of all western male scholars as Vitruvian men, but I am aware of the structural inequalities that stem from such tacit beliefs (as highlighted in Rachel's chapter). This means that these normative patterns remain dominant and therefore in need of critical scrutiny.

LINDSAY: I use the term "Western" in a very similar way to Craig. What I mean by Western is the particular ways of relating to and thinking about the world that emerged across Europe after the fifteenth century. From my perspective, the idea of the West was formed through the imperialistic enterprises of European states and their interface with various Indigenous peoples. In sum, Western has a spatial logic that refers to the ideas and behaviors of people in Europe, the UK, and now the United States and it also has a particular ideological bent derived from rationalism, Christianity, and capitalism. While I agree with Ollie that there are a range of traditions that fall under this umbrella, I would refer to things like posthumanism as lower-case "western" rather Western with a capital "W."

Metaontology – how do our views compare?

Throughout the book, we discussed our varied views and definitions of metaontology, particularly in Chapters 5, 10, and 11. As emphasized, this term is crucial for discussions of – and engagements with – radical alterity, collaboration, and the colonialist roots of our discipline. In particular, there seem to be some disagreements between the authors over (1) how each of us defines the status of the *meta-* in this term, and (2) whether a single person – usually the archaeologist in this case – can have more than one metaontology. Where does each of us stand on these issues?

CRAIG: Some invoke the term metaontology to refer to what might be crudely labeled "cross-cultural" comparison, while others use it to discuss how some archaeologists and academics – usually those with less privilege – are forced to work in multiple worlds (i.e., navigating the tenure system while protecting traditional knowledge within home communities; cf. Deloria 1997; Smith 2012). I use the term in a general way, defining it as the broadest scale at which any one person speculates on the nature of the world. For me, reserving the term for cross-cultural comparison possibly sets up a not-so-useful opposition based on normative expectations about difference; in other words, I remain open to people confronting radical difference in everyday life, not just when comparing what they see as culturally different. For me, any person has one metaontology because *it is the bridge* that allows them to navigate multiple worlds or ontologies, be they university systems or politics and tradition in home communities.

LINDSAY: I agree with Craig that the term "meta" in metaontology is self-referential, meaning that I am using the term to talk about an individual and that individual's framework for understanding the nature of reality and being. When I use the concept of metaontology, I am actually using it in a similar way to how I use the concept of worldview – one's personal ideas about how the world works that are drawn from a collective cultural reservoir and set of shared historical experiences. What follows from this definition is the question: "Can you have more than one worldview?" For me the answer is yes. One person can hold in their minds more than one way of understanding the world. These different intellectual frameworks are activated situationally rather than simultaneously. In this sense, I think we can talk about worldviews and metaontologies in the plural.

RACHEL: Everyone has their own ontology. For me, a metaontology is one that involves contact with some form of difference that allows us to reflect on our ontology, thereby seeing the shape of it more clearly as a result. Whilst I would argue that I have always had an ontology, my privilege means that I was not aware of the shape of it until I began to study at university and came across very different understandings of what exists in the world and how the world works. This process, of becoming aware of my ontology, is for me the emergence of a metaontology: realizing that very different worlds can exist.

OLLIE: If ontology is what actually exists, then metaontology is an act of reflection on what actually exists – it is an explicitly metaphysical process. On the one hand, we have our perspective on the world, and, on the other hand, a realization that other perspectives are possible – and equally real. When I'm thinking about Neolithic Britain, I know that the world operated in different ontological ways than the present. It was a world in which what materials could become, what bodies could do, and what architecture could create were different, radically different (Harris forthcoming). To explore that difference, I need a theoretical tool kit that allows for creative engagement with archaeological materials. If that difference is to emerge, those tools have to attend to ontological difference; that is, they will have to operate at a level that is metaontological.

SOPHIE: Metaontology is not something I had considered before engaging in these discussions, but I think I stand with Ollie and Rachel in framing metaontology as the level of analysis that allows us to think about the differences between ontologies. Otherwise, as Ollie points out in Chapter 11, what stops metaontology from being ontology?

Transformation of archaeology – what counts as archaeology?

There have been many ways in which archaeology has been defined, and today archaeological theory seems to be pulling the discipline in new directions. We have seen the growth of contemporary archaeology, focusing not just on the past but on the present world around us. We have seen symmetrical archaeologists like Bjørnar Olsen (2012:11) ask us to, "sacrifice the imperatives of historical narratives." Where does this leave archaeologists trying to explain historical change? Equally in a world with pressing concerns, politically, environmentally, socially and so on, can archaeology continue to exist as a means of understanding the past?

OLLIE: I am someone who has written about a lot of different periods from the very deep past, via my favorite period the Neolithic right up to the present and future, so for me I don't really have an issue with archaeologists dealing with a host of different times and places; contemporary archaeology is no less (or more) archaeology than studying the Bronze Age. What makes something archaeological for me is that it involves a creative act of assembling a particular past. That past can be immediate – it can be to all intents and purposes contemporary, or even a past located in the distant future (Dawney et al. 2017) – but it is still the past: a temporality we relate to in specific ways. Arranging these pasts into a form of historical narrative is one of the things archaeologists can do, but it is not the only thing. What makes our discipline specific is the process by which we gather and assemble the different potential materials that surround us and make them into a past that addresses one concern or another. As our needs change, we can assemble these pasts differently, and use them to answer new and pressing questions. This means archaeology remains relevant, and remains archaeology, even as we ask new questions and ask old questions in new ways.

CRAIG: Similar to Ollie, I see pasts – defined broadly – as crucial parts of archaeology. I do, however, remain skeptical of Olsen's statements concerning the imperatives of historical narratives, not because he seeks to avoid history, but rather because he presents his argument as a proposal for a sea change in archaeology. Perhaps this isn't Olsen's intent, but I don't want an archaeology that is homogeneous in its circumnavigation of history. I am, however, happy to have a host of colleagues approaching archaeology in a variety of different ways. As noted throughout this book, I see these differences as productive.

LINDSAY: I agree with Ollie and Craig that archaeology can and should be concerned with both the distant past and the more intimate present. As I've mentioned throughout this book, I think that one of the greatest attributes of archaeology is its ability to connect people across different time frames in ways that produce more complex and relevant narratives. To draw boundaries between what types of questions or periods archaeologists, ethnographers, or historians should engage in creates an unnecessarily simplistic intellectual atmosphere and engenders a piecemeal understanding of humanity and broader sociological processes. While I don't think that archaeology will ever be fully "decolonized," I do believe that it will continue to serve as an important tool for understanding the past as well as for making political claims in the present.

SOPHIE: I think that archaeologies can be multiple but at their core ask questions about the human condition through material remains. What we do within that remit should be informed by a politics of equity in the present.

RACHEL: For me all things are in process, they are not fixed, they do not have some internal kernel of truth or essence. Posthumanism teaches us that what humans are is always shifting and changing and that when we seek to fix a definition, it always acts to exclude and other. Archaeology as a concept, a discipline, a practice is no different: what archaeology is and what archaeology does is not fixed. Archaeology has been defined and redefined by different practitioners throughout its history. For me, it is about an ever-changing and ever affective relationship between the past and the present.

Conclusion

Books end. Dialogues need not. The aim of this book has been to explore the critical themes of relations, ontology, posthumanism, and Indigenous paradigms from differing perspectives. We have sought to bring into conversation emergent concerns with the politics of contemporary practice with the modes of power in the distant past, the possibilities for a phenomenology of song with the differential relations of a Viking boat burial. Our four themes, the multiple theories we have engaged with, and the five standpoints we take as authors are, of course, only a fraction of the differences that exist in archaeology. However, by taking a dialogic stance, we aim to have opened up our differences to explore uncertainties and discrepancies, to be honest about what we know, and what we do not. This means that this book does not amount to a singular statement on archaeological theory. All the authors have positions, some more closely aligned than others, but the aim of this book has not been to advocate for any one of them. Instead, what this book argues for is a fundamental openness: an openness to what it is we can do as archaeologists; to the opinions and perspectives of others; to the question of who counts as human and who gets listened to; to multiple ways of knowing the world; and a fundamental commitment to the multiplicity of that world. Such a position emphasizes self-doubt, the need to unsettle privilege, the constant reflection required by all of us, and the political nature of theory. All of the authors agree that there can be no turn to a safe and apolitical archaeology, that there can be no refuge in the idea that science, or anything else, can shield us from the realities of the impact of our positions and our arguments. We would also agree that talking, writing, reading, and listening take work, take time, but open up new vistas, new forms of thinking, and new forms of relation with each other and our work. It is only through an attention to voices other than our own that archaeology can make productive differences in the world as it exists and in the future for the people yet to come.

REFERENCES

Acebo, Nathan, and Desireé Martinez

2018 Towards an Analytic of Survivance in California Archaeology. *Society for California Archaeology Proceedings* 32:144–52.

Ahmed, Sara

2017 *Living a Feminist Life*. Duke University Press, Durham, NC.

Alberti, Benjamin

2014 Designing Body-Pots in the Formative La Candelaria Culture, Northwest Argentina. In *Making and Growing: Anthropological Studies of Organisms and Artefacts*, edited by Elizabeth Hallam and Tim Ingold, pp. 107–25. Ashgate, London.

2016a Archaeologies of Ontology. *Annual Review of Anthropology* 45:163–79.

2016b Archaeologies of Risk and Wonder. *Archaeological Dialogues* 23:138–45.

Alberti, Benjamin and Tamara L. Bray (editors)

2009 Special Section: Animating Archaeology: of Subjects, Objects and Alternative Ontologies. *Cambridge Archaeological Journal* 19:337–441.

Alberti, Benjamin, Severin Fowles, Martin Holbraad, Yvonne Marshall and Christopher L. Witmore

2011 'Worlds Otherwise': Archaeology, Anthropology, and Ontological Difference. *Current Anthropology* 52:896–912.

Alberti, Benjamin and Yvonne Marshall

2009 Animating Archaeology: Local Theories and Conceptually Open-Ended Methodologies. *Cambridge Archaeological Journal* 19:344–56.

Allard, Amélie

2018 Communities, Survivance, and Acts of 'Residence' in the Late Eighteenth-Century Fur Trade in Minnesota. *Midwest Archaeological Conference Occasional Papers* 2:67–86.

Allard, Amélie and Craig N. Cipolla

In press Failure and Colonialism in the North American Fur Trade: The View from Riverine Assemblages. *Historical Archaeology*, accepted 2019.

Allentoft, Morten E., Martin E. Sikora, Karl-Göran Sjögren, Simon Rasmussen, Morten Rasmussen et al.

2015 Population genomics of Bronze Age Eurasia. *Nature* 522:167–72.

Alt, Susan M.

2019 From Weeping Hills to Lost Caves. A Search for Vibrant Matter in Greater Cahokia. In *Ancient Urbanisms, New Materialisms*, edited by Timothy R. Pauketat and Susan M. Alt, pp. 19–39. Routledge, London.

Althusser, Louis

1977 *For Marx*. New Left Books, London.

Anagnostopoulos, Georgios

1994 *Aristotle on the Goals and Exactness of Ethics*. University of California Press, Berkeley, Los Angeles, and Oxford.

Appadurai, Arjun (editor)

1986 *The Social Life of Things: Commodities in Cultural Perspective*. Cambridge University Press, Cambridge.

Arentzen, Thomas

2017 Voices Interwoven: Refrains and Vocal Participation in the Kontakia. *Jahrbuch der Österreichischen Byzantinistik* 66:1–10.

Arnold, Bettina

2006 'Arierdämmerung': Race and Archaeology in Nazi Germany. *World Archaeology* 38:8–31.

Arola, Adam

2011 Native American Philosophy. In *The Oxford Handbook of World Philosophy*, edited by Jay L. Garfield and William Edelglass, pp. 562–74. University of Oxford Press, Oxford.

Atalay, Sonya

2006 Indigenous Archaeology as Decolonizing Practice. *American Indian Quarterly* 30:280–310.

2007 Global Application of Indigenous Archaeology: Community Based Participatory Research in Turkey. *Journal of the World Archaeological Congress* 3:249–70.

2008 Multivocality and Indigenous Archaeologies. In *Evaluating Multiple Narratives: Beyond Nationalist, Colonialist, and Imperialist Archaeologies*, edited by Junko Habu, Clare Fawcett and John M. Matsunaga, pp. 29–44. Springer, New York.

2010 'We Don't Talk about Çatalhöyük, We Live It': Sustainable Archaeological Practice Through Community-based Participatory Research. *World Archaeology* 42:418–29.

2012 *Community-Based Archaeology: Research with, by, and for Indigenous and Local Communities*. University of California Press, Berkeley.

Atalay, Sonya and Christine A. Hastorf

2006 Food, Meals, and Daily Activities: Food Habitus at Neolithic Çatalhöyük. *American Antiquity* 72:283–319.

Bailey, Kenneth D.

1994 *Typologies and Taxonomies*. Sage, London.

Bains, Paul

2006 *The Primacy of Semiosis: An Ontology of Relations*. University of Toronto Press, London.

Balter, Michael

2017a Ancient DNA Yields Unprecedented Insights into Mysterious Chaco Civilization. *Scientific American*. 22nd February 2017.

2017b The Ethical Battle Over Ancient DNA. In *SAPIENS*. Wenner-Gren Foundation.

Banfield, Emily

2018 *Tales from The Ontological Tern: An Examination of the Role and Meaning of Faunal Remains in the Neolithic Long Barrows of Wiltshire*. Unpublished PhD Thesis, University of Leicester.

Barad, Karen

2003 Posthumanist Performativity: Toward and Understanding of How Matter Comes to Matter. *Signs: Journal of Women in Culture and Society* 28:801–31.

2007 *Meeting the Universe Halfway: Quantum Physics and the Entanglement of Matter and Meaning.* Duke University Press, Durham, NC.

Barrett, John C.

2014 The Material Constitution of Humanness. *Archaeological Dialogues* 21:65–74.

2016 The New Antiquarianism? *Antiquity* 90:1681–6.

Baun, Jane

2007 *Tales from Another Byzantium: Celestial Journey and Local Community in the Medieval Greek Apocrypha.* Cambridge University Press, Cambridge.

Beck, Anna Severine

2018 Revisiting the Trelleborg House: A Discussion of House Types and Assemblages. *Norwegian Archaeological Review* 51:142–61.

Bennett, Jane

1994 The Force of Things: Steps Toward an Ecology of Matter. *Political Theory* 32:347–72.

2010 *Vibrant Matter: A Political Ecology of Things.* Duke University Press, London.

Bertelsen, Bjørn Enge and Synnøve Bendixsen

2016 Recalibrating Alterity, Difference, Ontology: Anthropological Engagements with Human and Non-Human Worlds. In *Critical Anthropological Engagements in Human Alterity and Difference*, edited by Bjørn Enge Bertelsen and Synnøve Bendixsen, pp. 1–40. Palgrave Macmillan, Cham.

Bessire, Lucas and David Bond

2014 Ontological Anthropology and the Deferral of Critique. *American Ethnologist* 41:440–56.

Betts, Matthew W., Susan E. Blair and David W. Black

2012 Perspectivism, Mortuary Symbolism, and Human-Shark Relationships on the Maritime Peninsula. *American Antiquity* 77:621–45.

Bhaskar, Roy

2008 *A Realist Theory of Science.* Routledge, London.

Bickle, Penny

2020 Thinking Gender Differently: New Approaches to Identity Difference in the Central European Neolithic. *Cambridge Archaeological Journal* 30:201–18.

Binford, Lewis

1962 Archaeology as Anthropology. *American Antiquity* 28:217–25.

Bird David, Nurit

2018 Persons or Relatives? Animistic Scales of Practice and Imagination. In *Rethinking Relations and Animism*, edited by Miguel Astor-Aguilera and Graham Harvey, pp. 25–34. Routledge, London.

Bogost, Ian

2012 *Alien Phenomenology, or What It's Like to Be a Thing.* University of Minnesota Press, Minneapolis.

Booth, Tom

2018 Exploring Your Inner Hades: DNA as Mortuary Archaeology. *Online Journal in Public Archaeology* 3:221–48.

2019 A Stranger in a Strange Land: A Perspective on Archaeological Responses to the Palaeogenetic Revolution from an Archaeologist Working Amongst Palaeogeneticists. *World Archaeology* 51:506–601.

Boozer, Anna Lucile

2014 The Tyranny of Typologies: Evidential Reasoning in Romano-Egyptian Domestic Archaeology. In *Material Evidence: Learning from Archaeological Practice*, edited by Robert Chapman and Alison Wylie, pp. 92–109. Routledge, London.

Bourdieu, Pierre

1977 *Outline of a Theory of Practice*. Translated by Richard Nice. Cambridge University Press, Cambridge.

Bowden, Sean, Simone Bignall and Paul Patton (editors)

2014 *Deleuze and Pragmatism*. Routledge, London.

Brace, Selina, Yoan Diekmann, Thomas J. Booth, Zuzana Faltyskova, Nadin Rohland et al.

2019 Population Replacement in Early Neolithic Britain. *Nature Ecology and Evolution* 3:765–71.

Braidotti, Rosi

2011a *Nomadic Subjects: Embodiment and Sexual Difference in Contemporary Feminist Theory*. Columbia University Press, New York.

2011b *Nomadic Theory: The Portable Rosi Braidotti*. Columbia University Press, New York, NY.

2013 *The Posthuman*. Polity, London.

2019a Affirmative Ethics and Generative Life. *Deleuze and Guattari Studies* 13:463–81.

2019b A Theoretical Framework for the Critical Posthumanities. *Theory, Culture and Society* 36:31–61.

2019c *Posthuman Knowledge*. Polity Press, Cambridge.

Brascoupé, Simon

1992 Indigenous Perspectives on International Development. *Akwe:kon* 9:6–17.

Brittain, Marcus and Oliver Harris

2010 Enchaining Arguments and Fragmenting Assumptions: Reconsidering the Fragmentation Debate in Archaeology. *World Archaeology* 42:581–94.

Brophy, Kenny

2018 The Brexit Hypothesis and Prehistory. *Antiquity* 92:1650–8.

Brown, Leslie and Susan Strega (editors)

2005 *Research as Resistance: Critical, Indigenous, & Anti-Oppressive Approaches*. Canadian Scholars' Press, Toronto, Ontario.

Brown, Linda A. and K. Emery

2008 Negotiations with the Animate Forest: Hunting Shrines in the Guatemalan Highlands. *Journal of Archaeological Method and Theory* 15:300–37.

Brown, Linda A. and William H. Walker

2008 Prologue: Archaeology, Animism and Non-Human Agents. *Journal of Archaeological Method and Theory* 15:297–9.

Brück, Joanna

2005a Experiencing the Past? The Development of a Phenomenological Archaeology in British Prehistory. *Archaeological Dialogues* 12:45–72.

2005b Homing Instincts: Grounded Identities and Dividual Selves in the British Bronze Age. In *The Archaeology of Plural and Changing Identities: Beyond Identification*, edited by Eleanor Casella and Chris Fowler, pp. 135–60. Routledge, London.

2006 Death, Exchange and Reproduction in the British Bronze Age. *European Journal of Archaeology* 9:73–101.

2009 Women, Death and Social Change in the British Bronze Age. *Norwegian Archaeological Review* 42:1–23.

2017 Gender and Personhood in the European Bronze Age. *European Journal of Archaeology* 20:37–40.

2019 *Personifying Prehistory: Relational Ontologies in Bronze Age Britain and Ireland*. Oxford University Press, Oxford.

Brück, Joanna and David Fontijn

2013 The Myth of the Chief: Prestige Goods, Power and Personhood in the European Bronze Age. In *The Oxford Handbook of the European Bronze Age*, edited by Harry Fokkens and Anthony Harding, pp. 197–215. Oxford University Press, Oxford.

Brughmans, Tom

2010 Connecting the Dots: Towards Archaeological Network Analysis. *Oxford Journal of Archaeology* 29:277–303.

2013 Thinking Through Networks: A Review of Formal Network Methods in Archaeology. *Journal of Archaeological Method and Theory* 20:623–62.

Buchli, Victor

2015 *An Archaeology of the Immaterial*. Routledge, London.

Burton, Bryan

1993 *Moving Within the Circle: Contemporary Native American Music and Dance*. World Music Press, Danbury.

Callicout, J. Baird

1989 *In Defense of the Land Ethic: Essays in Environmental Philosophy*. State University of New York Press, Albany.

Caraher, William

2019 Slow Archaeology, Punk Archaeology, and the 'Archaeology of Care'. *European Journal of Archaeology* 22:372–85.

Carlin, Neil

2018 *The Beaker Phenomenon? Understanding the Character and Context of Social Practices in Ireland 2500–2000 BC*. Sidestone Press, Leiden.

Certeau, Michel de

1984 *The Practice of Everyday Life*. University of California Press, Berkeley.

Chapman, John

2000 *Fragmentation in Archaeology: People, Places and Broken Objects in the Prehistory of South-Eastern Europe*. Routledge, London.

Cipolla, Craig N.

2013a *Becoming Brothertown: Native American Ethnogenesis and Endurance in the Modern World*. University of Arizona Press, Tucson, AZ.

2013b Native American Historical Archaeology and the Trope of Authenticity. *Historical Archaeology* 47:12–22.

2017a Postcolonial Archaeology in the Age of Things. In *Foreign Objects: Rethinking Indigenous Consumption in American Archaeology*, edited by Craig N. Cipolla, pp. 222–9. University of Arizona Press, Tucson.

2017b *Remaking Archaeology: Decolonizing Indigenous-Colonial Histories*. Wenner-Gren Foundation for Anthropological Research, Post PhD Grant, Grant 9401, Grant on file, Anthropology Department, Department of Art and Culture, Royal Ontario Museum, Toronto.

2018 Earth Flows and Lively Stone. What Difference Does 'Vibrant' Matter Make? *Archaeological Dialogues* 25:49–70.

2019 Taming the Ontological Wolves: Learning from Iroquoian Effigy Objects. *American Anthropologist* 121:613–27.

in review a Theorizing Indigenous-Colonial Interactions in the Americas. In *Handbook of the Archaeology of Indigenous-Colonial Interaction in the Americas*, edited by Sara Gonzalez and Lee Panich. Routledge, New York.

in review b Beyond Symmetry: The Breadth and Depth of Posthuman Archaeologies. *Cambridge Archaeological Journal.*

Cipolla, Craig N. and Amélie Allard

2019 Recognizing River Power: Watery Views of Ontario's Fur Trade. *Journal of Archaeological Method and Theory* 26:1084–105.

Cipolla, Craig N. and James Quinn

2016 Field School Archaeology the Mohegan Way: Reflections on Twenty Years of Community-Based Research and Teaching. *Journal of Community Archaeology and Heritage* 3:118–34.

Cipolla, Craig N., James Quinn and Jay Levy

2019 Theory in Collaborative Indigenous Archaeology: Insights from Mohegan. *American Antiquity* 84:127–42.

Clough, Patricia Ticineto

2009 The New Empiricism: Affect and Sociological Method. *European Journal of Social Theory* 12:43–61.

Collar, Anna, Fiona Coward, Tom Brughmans and Barbara J. Mills

2015 Networks in Archaeology: Phenomena, Abstraction, Representation. *Journal of Archaeological Method and Theory* 22:1–32.

Colwell-Chanthaphonh, Chip and T. J. Ferguson

2004 Virtue Ethics and the Practice of History. *Journal of Social Archaeology* 4:5–27.

Conneller, Chantal

2004 Becoming Deer. Corporeal Transformations at Star Carr. *Archaeological Dialogues* 11:37–56.

2011 *An Archaeology of Materials: Substantial Transformations in Early Prehistoric Europe.* Routledge, London.

Coole, Diana and Samantha Frost (editors)

2010 *New Materialisms: Ontology, Agency and Politics.* Duke University Press, Durham, NC.

Cordova, Viola F.

2007 *How It Is: The Native American Philosophy of V.F. Cordova.* University of Arizona Press, Tucson.

Cormack, Robin

2018 *Byzantine Art.* Oxford University Press, Oxford.

Course, Magnus

2010 Of Words and Fog. Linguistic Relativity and Amerindian Ontology. *Anthropological Theory* 10:247–63.

Creese, John

2017a Art as Kinship: Signs of Life in the Eastern Woodlands. *Cambridge Archaeological Journal* 27:643–54.

2017b Beyond Representation: Indigenous Economies of Affect in the Northeast Woodlands. In *Foreign Objects: Rethinking Indigenous Consumption in American Archaeology,* edited by Craig N. Cipolla, pp. 59–79. University of Arizona Press, Tucson.

Crellin, Rachel J.

2017 Changing Assemblages: Vibrant Matter in Burial Assemblages. *Cambridge Archaeological Journal* 27:111–25.

2020 *Change and Archaeology.* Routledge, London.

Crellin, Rachel J. and Oliver J.T. Harris

2020 Beyond Binaries: Interrogating Ancient DNA. *Archaeological Dialogues* 27:37–56.

in review What Difference Does Posthumanism Make? *Cambridge Archaeological Journal.*

Crossland, Zoë

2018 Forensic Afterlives. *Signs and Society* 6:622–44.

Crossland, Zoë and Alexander Bauer

2017 Im/Materialities: Things and Signs. *Semiotic Review* 4, https://semioticreview.com/ojs/index.php/sr/article/view/9. Date accessed: 3/30/2020.

Cummings, Vicki and Alasdair Whittle

2004 *Places of Special Virtue. Megaliths in the Neolithic Landscapes of Wales.* Oxbow, Oxford.

Davis, Heather and Zoe Todd

2017 On the Importance of a Date, or Decolonizing the Anthropocene. *Acme: An International Journal for Critical Geographies* 16:761–80.

Dawdy, Shannon Lee

2009 Millennial Archaeology. Locating the Discipline in the Age of Insecurity. *Archaeological Dialogues* 16:131–42.

Dawney, Leila, Tim Flohr Sørenson and Oliver J.T. Harris

2017 Future World: Anticipatory Archaeology, Materially Affective Capacities and the Late Human Legacy. *Journal of Contemporary Archaeology* 4:107–29.

De Beauvoir, Simone

1997 *The Second Sex.* Vintage Classics, London.

Deetz, James

1996 *In Small Things Forgotten.* Anchor Books/Doubleday, New York.

DeLanda, Manuel

1997 *A Thousand Years of Nonlinear History.* Zone Books, New York.

2002 *Intensive Science and Virtual Philosophy.* Continuum, London.

2006 *A New Philosophy of Society: Assemblage Theory and Social Complexity.* Continuum, London.

2016 *Assemblage Theory.* Edinburgh University Press, Edinburgh.

DeLanda, Manuel and Graham Harman

2017 *The Rise of Realism.* Polity, London.

Deleuze, Gilles

1988 *Spinoza: Practical Philosophy.* City Lights Books, San Francisco.

1990 *Expressionism in Philosophy: Spinoza.* Zone Books, Brooklyn, NY.

1991a *Empiricism and Subjectivity: An Essay on Hume's Theory of Human Nature.* Columbia University Press, New York, NY.

1991b *Bergsonism.* Zone Books, London.

2004 *Difference and Repetition.* Bloomsbury, London.

2006a *Foucault.* Bloomsbury, London.

2006b *Nietzsche and Philosophy.* Columbia University Press, New York.

2007 *Two Regimes of Madness, Revised Edition: Texts and Interviews 1975–1995.* Semiotext(e), South Pasadena, CA.

2015 *Logic of Sense.* Bloomsbury, London.

Deleuze, Gilles and Félix Guattari

1994 *What Is Philosophy?* Verso, London.

2004 *A Thousand Plateaus: Capitalism and Schizophrenia.* Continuum, London.

2013 *Anti-Oedipus.* Bloomsbury, London.

Deleuze, Gilles and Claire Parnet

2002 *Dialogues II.* Columbia University Press, New York, NY.

Deloria, Barbara, Kristen Foehner and Sam Scinta (editors)

1999 *Spirit & Reason: The Vine Deloria, Jr., Reader.* Fulcrum Publishing, Golden.

Deloria, Jr. Vine

1972 *Some Thoughts. Akwesasne Notes.* Cornwall Island Reserve, Rosseveltown.

1992 Relativity, Relatedness and Reality. *Winds of Change* 7:34–40.

1997 *Red Earth, White Lies: Native Americans and the Myth of Scientific Fact.* Fulcrum, Golden, CO.

2003 *God Is Red.* Fulcrum Publishing, Golden, CO.

2012 *The Metaphysics of Modern Existence.* Fulcrum Publishing, Golden, CO.

2014 *Custer Died for Your Sins: An Indian Manifesto.* University of Oklahoma Pres, Noman, OK.

Denzin, Norman K., Yvonna S. Lincoln and Linda Tuhiwai Smith (editors)

2008 *Handbook of Critical and Indigenous Methodologies.* Sage Publications, Los Angeles.

Descola, Philippe

2013 *Beyond Nature and Culture.* Translated by Janet Lloyd. The University of Chicago Press, Chicago.

Dion, Susan D.

2009 *Braiding Histories: Learning from Aboriginal Peoples' Experiences and Perspectives.* University of British Columbia Press, Vancouver.

Dixon, Hayley

2019 Neo-Nazis at the National Trust: Far-Right Groups are Trying to Take Back Ancient Sites. *The Telegraph.* 9th August 2019, www.telegraph.co.uk/news/2019/08/09/neo-nazis-national-trust-far-right-groups-trying-takeback-ancient/

Domańska, Ewa

2006 The Return to Things. *Archaeologia Polona* 44:171–85.

Draşovean, Florin, Wolfram Schier, Alex Bayliss, Bisserka Gaydarska and Alasdair Whittle

2017. The Lives of Houses: Duration, Context and History at Neolithic Uivar, Romania. *European Journal of Archaeology* 20:636–62.

du Boulay, Juliet

1974 *Portrait of a Greek Mountain Village.* Clarendon Press, Oxford.

Dubowchik, Rosemary

2002 Singing with the Angels: Foundation Documents as Evidence for Musical Life in Monasteries of the Byzantine Empire. *Dumbarton Oaks Papers* 56:277–96.

Ebersbach, Renate, Thomas Doppler, Daniella Hofmann and Alasdair Whittle

2017 No Time Out: Scaling Material Diversity and Change in the Alpine Foreland Neolithic. *Journal of Anthropological Archaeology* 45:1–14.

Edgeworth, Matt

2011 *Fluid Pasts: Archaeology of Flow.* Bloomsbury, London.

Ferrando, Francesca

2019 *Posthumanist Philosophy.* Bloomsbury, London.

Ferrera, Maria J.

2016 The Transformative Impact of Cultural Portals on the Ethnic Identity Development of Second-Generation Filipino-American Emerging Adults. *Journal of Ethnic & Cultural Diversity in Social Work* 26:236–53.

Fixico, Donald L.

2003 *The American Indian Mind in a Linear World: American Indian Studies and Traditional Knowledge.* Routledge, New York and London.

Flannery, Kent V.

1982 The Golden Marshalltown: A Parable for the Archaeology of the 1980s. *American Anthropologist* 84:265–78.

Fleming, Andrew

2006 Post-Processual Landscape Archaeology: A Critique. *Cambridge Archaeological Journal* 16:267–80.

Fontijn, David

2005 Giving Up Weapons. In *Warfare, Violence and Slavery in Prehistory*, edited by Mike Parker Pearson and Nick Thorpe, pp. 145–54. Archaeopress, Oxford.

Fontijn, David and Harry Fokkens

2007 The Emergence of Early Iron Age 'Chieftains' Graves'. In *The Earlier Iron Age in Britain and the Near Continent*, edited by Colin Haselgrove and Rachel Pope, pp. 354–73. Oxbow Books, Oxford.

Ford, James A.

1954 Comment on A.C. Spaulding, 'Statistical Techniques for the Discovery of Artifact Types'. *American Antiquity* 19:390–1.

Foucault, M.

1978 *The History of Sexuality*. Vintage Books, New York.

1979 *Discipline and Punish: The Birth of the Prison*. Vintage Books, New York

1980 *Power/Knowledge: Selected Interview and Other Writings 1972–1977*. Pantheon Books, New York.

2002 *The Order of Things*. Routledge, London.

Fowler, Chris

2000 The Individual, the Subject, and Archaeological Interpretation. Reading Luce Irigaray and Judith Butler. In *Philosophy and Archaeological Practice: Perspectives for the 21st Century*, edited by Cornelius Holtorf and Hakan Karlsson, pp. 107–33. Bricoleur Press, Götborg.

2001 Personhood and Social Relations in the British Neolithic with a Case Study from the Isle of Man. *Journal of Material Culture* 6:137–63.

2004 *The Archaeology of Personhood: An Anthropological Approach*. Routledge, London.

2008 Fractal Bodies in the Past and Present. In *Past Bodies: Body-Centred Research in Archaeology*, edited by Dušan Borić and John E. Robb, pp. 47–57. Oxbow, Oxford.

2013 *The Emergent Past: A Relational Realist Archaeology of Early Bronze Age Mortuary Practices*. Oxford University Press, Oxford.

2016 Relational Personhood Revisited. *Cambridge Archaeological Journal* 26:397–412.

2017 Relational Typologies, Assemblage Theory and Early Bronze Age Burials. *Cambridge Archaeological Journal* 27:95–109.

Fowler, Chris and Oliver J.T. Harris

2015 Enduring Relations: Exploring a Paradox of New Materialism. *Journal of Material Culture* 20:127–48.

Fowles, Severin

2013 *An Archaeology of Doings: Secularism and the Study of Pueblo Religion*. School for Advanced Research, Santa Fe.

2016 The Perfect Subject (Postcolonial Object Studies). *Journal of Material Culture* 21:9–27.

Fredengren, Christina

2013 Posthumanism, the Transcorporeal and Biomolecular Archaeology. *Current Swedish Archaeology* 21:53–71.

Frieman, Catherine and Daniela Hofmann

2019 Present Pasts in the Archaeology of Genetics, Identity, and Migration in Europe: A Critical Essay. *World Archaeology* 51:528–45.

Frisbie, Charlotte J. (editor)

1980 *Southwestern Indian Ritual Drama*. University of New Mexico Press, Albuquerque.

Froystad, Katinka

2016 Alter-Politics Reconsidered: From Different Worlds to Osmotic Worlding. In *Critical Anthropological Engagements in Human Alterity and Difference*, edited by

Bjørn Enge Bertelsen and Synnøve Bendixsen, pp. 229–52. Palgrave Macmillan, Cham.

FT

2018 *Response to a Question on Relations, or, That Relations Are External to Their Terms*, www.patreon.com/fucktheory/posts.

Furholt, Martin

2018 Massive Migrations? The Impact of Recent aDNA Studies on Our View of Third Millennium Europe. *European Journal of Archaeology* 21:159–78.

Gallivan, Martin D.

2016 *The Powhatan Landscape: An Archaeological History of the Algonquian Chesapeake*. Society and Ecology in Island and Coastal Archaeology. University of Florida Press, Gainesville.

Garcia-Rovira, Irene

2015 What About Us? On Archaeological Objects or the Objects of Archaeology. *Current Swedish Archaeology* 23:85–108.

Garroutte, Eva-Marie

2003 *Real Indians: Identity and the Survival of Native America*. University of California Press, Berkeley.

Gell, Alfred

1998 *Art and Agency: An Anthropological Theory*. Clarendon Press, Oxford.

Gellner, Ernest

1995 *Anthropology and Politics: Revolutions in the Sacred Grove*. Blackwell, Oxford.

Gero, J. and M. Conkey (editors)

1991 *Engendering archaeology*. Blackwell, Oxford.

Gerstel, Sharron, Chris Kyriakakis, Konstantinos Raptis, Spyridon Antonopoulos and James Donahue

2018 Soundscapes of Byzantium: The Acheiropoietos Basilica and the Cathedral of Hagia Sophia in Thesaloniki. *Hesperia: The Journal of the American School of Classical Studies at Athens* 87:177–213.

Giddens, Anthony

1984 *The Constitution of Society: Outline of a Theory of Structuration*. University of California Press, Berkeley.

Gill, Jerry H.

2002 *Native American Worldviews: An Introduction*. Humanity Press, New York.

Gillespie, Susan D.

2001 Personhood, Agency, and Mortuary Ritual: A Case Study From the Ancient Maya. *Journal of Anthropological Archaeology* 20:73–112.

Gonzalez, Sara, Ian Kretzler and Brice Edwards

2018 Imagining Indigenous and Archaeological Futures: Building Capacity with the Confederated Tribes of Grande Ronde. *Archaeologies* 14:85–114.

Gosden, Chris

1994 *Social Being and Time*. Blackwell, Oxford.

2004 *Archaeology and Colonialism: Culture Contact from 5000 BC to the Present*. Cambridge University Press, Cambridge.

Gosden, Chris, Colin Renfrew and Elizabeth De Marrais (editors)

2004 *Rethinking Materiality: The Engagement of Mind with the Material World*. McDonald Institute for Archaeological Research, Cambridge.

Grinde, Donald A., Jr.

1995 Historical Narratives of Nationhood and the Semiotic Construction of Social Identity: A Native American Perspective. In *Issues in Native American Cultural Identity*, edited by Michael K. Green, pp. 201–22. Peter Lang, New York.

Grosz, Elizabeth

1994 *Volatile Bodies: Towards a Corporeal Feminism.* Indiana University Press, Bloomington, IN.

Haak, Wolfgang, Iosif Lazaridis, Nick Patterson, Nadin Rohland, Swapan Mallick, et al.

2015 Massive Migration from the Steppe Was a Source for Indo-European Languages in Europe. *Nature* 522:207–11.

Hage, Ghassan

2012 Critical Anthropological Thought and the Radical Political Imaginary. *Critique of Anthropology* 32:308–85.

2015 *Alter-Politics: Critical Anthropology and the Radical Imagination.* Melbourne University, Melbourne.

Hakenbeck, Suzanne E.

2019 Genetics, Archaeology and the Far Right: An Unholy Trinity. *World Archaeology* 51:517–27.

Hallowell, A. Irving

1960 Ojibwa Ontology, Behavior, and World View. In *Primitive Views of the World: Essays from Culture in History,* edited by Stanley Diamond, pp. 49–82. Columbia University Press, New York.

Hamilakis, Yannis

2013 *Archaeology and the Senses: Human Experience, Memory and Affect.* Cambridge University Press, Cambridge.

2017 Sensorial Assemblages: Affect, Memory and Temporality in Assemblage Thinking. *Cambridge Archaeological Journal* 27:169–82.

Haraway, Donna

1988 Situated Knowledges: The Science Question in Feminism and the Privilege of Partial Perspective. *Feminist Studies* 14:575–99.

2016 *Staying with the Trouble: Making Kin in the Chthulucene.* Duke University Press, Durham, NC.

Harding, Anthony

2018 Bronze Age Encounters: Violent or Peaceful? In *Warfare in Bronze Age Society,* edited by Christian Horn and Kristian Kristiansen, pp. 16–22. Cambridge University Press, Cambridge.

Harman, Graham

2009 *Prince of Networks: Bruno Latour and Metaphysics.* Re.Press, Melbourne.

2011 *The Quadruple Object.* Zero Books, Winchester.

2016a *Immaterialism.* Polity, Cambridge.

2016b On Behalf of Form: The View From Archaeology and Architecture. In *Elements of Architecture: Assembling Archaeology, Atmosphere and the Performance of Building Spaces,* edited by Mikkel Bille and Tim Flohr Sørensen, pp. 30–46. Routledge, London.

2018 *Object-Oriented Ontology: A New Theory of Everything.* Pelican, London.

Harris, Oliver J.T.

2014 Revealing Our Vibrant Past: Science, Materiality and the Neolithic. In *Early Farmers: The View from Archaeology and Science,* edited by Alasdair Whittle and Penny Bickle, pp. 327–45. Proceedings of the British Academy, Oxford.

2016a Affective Architecture in Ardnamurchan: Assemblages at Three Scales. In *Elements of Architecture: Assembling Archaeology, Atmosphere and the Performance of Building Space,* edited by Mikkel Bille and Tim Flohr Sørensen, pp. 195–212. Routledge, London.

2016b Becoming Post-Human: Identity and the Ontological Turn. In *Creating Material Worlds: Theorising Identity in Archaeology,* edited by Elizabeth Pierce, Anthony Russell, Adrián Maldonado and Louisa Cambell, pp. 17–37. Oxbow, Oxford.

2017 Assemblage and Scale in Archaeology. *Cambridge Archaeological Journal* 27:127–39.
2018a More Than Representation: Multiscalar Assemblages and the Deleuzian Challenge to Archaeology. *History of the Human Sciences* 31:83–104.
2018b Towards Virtual Typologies. *Norwegian Archaeological Review* 51:162–5.
2019 Commentary: The City and the City. In *New Materialisms Ancient Urbanisms*, edited by Susan M. Alt and Timothy R. Pauketat, pp. 245–59. Routledge, London.
Forthcoming *Assembling Past Worlds: Materials, Bodies and Architecture in Neolithic Britain*. Routledge, London.

Harris, Oliver J.T. and Craig N. Cipolla
2017 *Archaeological Theory in the New Millennium: Introducing Current Perspectives*. Routledge, London.

Harris, Oliver J.T., Hannah L. Cobb, Colleen E. Batey, Janet Montgomery, Julia Beaumont, Héléna Gray, Paul Murtagh and Phil Richardson
2017 Assembling Places and Persons: A Tenth-Century Viking Boat Burial from Swordle Bay on the Ardnamurchan Peninsula, Western Scotland. *Antiquity* 91:191–206.

Harris, Oliver J.T. and Rachel J. Crellin
2018 Assembling New Ontologies from Old Materials: Towards Multiplicity. In *Rethinking Relations and Animism: Personhood and Materiality*, edited by Miguel Astor-Aguilera and Graham Harvey, pp. 55–74. Routledge, London.

Harris, Oliver J.T. and John Robb
2012 Multiple Ontologies and the Problem of the Body in History. *American Anthropologist* 114:668–79.

Harrison-Buck, Eleanor and Julia A. Hendon (editors)
2018a *Relational Identities and Other-Than-Human Agency in Archaeology*. University Press of Colorado, Luisville, CO.

Harrison-Buck, Eleanor and Julia A. Hendon
2018b An Introduction to Relational Personhood and Other-Than-Human Agency in Archaeology. In *Relational Identities and Other-Than-Human Agency in Archaeology*, edited by Eleanor Harrison-Buck and Julia A. Hendon, pp. 3–28. University Press of Colorado, Louisville, CO.

Harvey, Susan A.
2006 *Scenting Salvation: Ancient Christianity and the Olfactory Imagination*. University of California Press, Berkley CA.

Havelka, Miloš
2016 'A-Politics', 'Anti-politics', 'Non-political Politics' and 'Sub-politics' as Threats and Challenges. *Social Studies* 1:9–22.

Hawkes, Jacquetta
1968 The Proper Study of Mankind. *Antiquity* 42:255–62.

Hegmon, Michelle
2003 Setting Theoretical Egos Aside: Issues and Theory in North American Archaeology. *American Antiquity* 68:213–43.

Heidegger, Martin
1962 *Being and Time*. Blackwell, Oxford.
1971 *Poetry, Language, Thought*. Harper and Row, New York.

Henare, Amiria, Martin Holbraad and Sari Wastell (editors)
2007 *Thinking Through Things: Theorising Artefacts Ethnographically*. Routledge, London.

Henderson, James Sa'ke'j Youngblood
2000 Challenges of Respecting Indigenous World Views in Eurocentric education. In *Voice of the Drum: Indigenous Education and Culture*, edited by Roger Neil, pp. 59–80. Kingfisher Publication, Brandon, Manitoba.

Heth, Charlotte (editor)
1992 *Native American Dance: Ceremonies and Social Traditions*. National Museum of the American Indian, Smithsonian Institution, Washington, DC.
Heyd, Volker
2017 Kossinna's Smile. *Antiquity* 91:348–59.
Heywood, Paolo
2012 Anthropology and What There Is: Reflections on 'Ontology'. *Cambridge Journal of Anthropology* 30:143–51.
Hill, Erica
2018 Personhood and Agency in Eskimo Interactions with the Other-Than-Human. In *Relational Identities and Other-Than-Human Agency in Archaeology*, edited by Eleanor Harrison-Buck and Julia A. Hendon, pp. 29–50. University Press of Colorado, Louisville, CO.
Hill, Norbert S.
1994 *Words of Power: Voices from Indian America*. Fulcrum Publishing, Golden.
Hodder, Ian
1982 Theoretical Archaeology: A Reactionary View. In *Structural and Symbolic Archaeology*, edited by Ian Hodder, pp. 1–16. Cambridge University Press, Cambridge.
1986 *Reading the Past*. Cambridge University Press, Cambridge.
2012 *Entangled: An Archaeology of the Relationships Between Humans and Things*. Wiley-Blackwell, Oxford.
2014 The Asymmetries of Symmetrical Archaeology. *Journal of Contemporary Archaeology* 1:228–30.
2016 *Studies in Human-Thing Entanglement*, Online publication www.ian-hodder.com/books/studies-human-thing-entanglement.
Hodder, Ian (editor)
1982 *Symbolic and Structural Archaeology*. Cambridge University Press, Cambridge.
Hodder, Ian and Gavin Lucas
2017 The Symmetries and Asymmetries of Human-Thing Relations. A Dialogue. *Archaeological Dialogues* 24:119–37.
Hodder, Ian and Angus Mol
2016 Network Analysis and Entanglement. *Journal of Archaeological Method and Theory* 23:1066–94.
Hodder, Ian and Robert W. Preucel
1996 *Contemporary Archaeology in Theory: A Reader*. Blackwell, Oxford.
Hofmann, Daniela
2015 What Have Genetics Ever Done for Us? The Implications of aDNA Data for Interpreting Identity in Early Neolithic Central Europe. *European Journal of Archaeology* 18:454–76.
Holbraad, Martin
2007 The Power of Powder: Multiplicity and Motion in the Divinatory Cosmology of Cuban Ifá (or Mana, Again). In *Thinking Through Things: Theorising Artefacts Ethnographically*, edited by Amiria Henare, Martin Holbraad and Sari Wastell, pp. 189–225. Routledge, London.
2009 Ontology, Ethnography, Archaeology: An Afterword on the Ontography of Things. *Cambridge Archaeological Journal* 19:431–41.
Holbraad, Martin and Morten Axel Pederson
2017 *The Ontological Turn: An Anthropological Exposition*. Cambridge University Press, Cambridge.

Horn, Christian

2011 Deliberate Destruction of Halberds. In *Bronze Age Warfare: Manufacture and Use of Weaponry*, edited by Marion Ucklemann and Marianne Mödlinger, pp. 53–65. Archaeopress, Oxford.

2018 Warfare vs Exchange? Thoughts on an Integrative Approach. In *Warfare in Bronze Age Society*, edited by Christian Horn and Kristian Kristiansen, pp. 47–60. Cambridge University Press, Cambridge.

Horn, Christian and Kristian Kristiansen

2018 Introducing Bronze Age Warfare. In *Warfare in Bronze Age Society*, edited by Christian Horn and Kristian Kristiansen, pp. 1–15. Cambridge University Press, Cambridge.

Horning, Audrey

2014 Challenging Colonial Equations? The Gaelic Experience in Early Modern Ireland. In *Rethinking Colonialism Through Archaeology*, edited by Neal Ferris, Rodney Harrison and Michael V. Wilcox, pp. 293–314. Oxford University Press, Oxford.

Horsburgh, K. Anne

2018 David Reich's Who We Are and How We Got Here: Ancient DNA and the New Science of the Human Past. *Current Anthropology* 59:656–7.

Howey, Meghan

2018 Dead Kettles and Indigenous Afterworlds in Early Colonial Encounters in the Maritimes. In *Relational Identities and Other-Than-Human Agency in Archaeology*, edited by Eleanor Harrison-Buck and Julia A. Hendon, pp. 51–71. University Press of Colorado, Louisville, CO.

Husserl, Edmond

1970 *Logical Investigations*. Routledge, London.

Ingold, Tim

2000 *Perceptions of the Environment: Essays in Livelihood, Dwelling and Skill*. Routledge, London.

2007 Materials Against Materiality. *Archaeological Dialogues* 14:1–16.

2008 When ANT meets SPIDER: Social Theory for Arthropods. In *Material Agency: Towards a Non-Anthropocentric Approach*, edited by Carl Knappett and Louis Malafouris, pp. 209–15. Springer, New York.

2011 *Being Alive: Essays in Movement, Knowledge and Description*. Routledge, London.

2013 *Making: Anthropology, Archaeology, Art and Architecture*. Routledge, London.

Jantzen, Detlef, Ute Brinker, Jörg Orschiedt, Jan Heinemeier, Jürgen Piek, et al.

2011 A Bronze Age Battlefield? Weapons and Trauma in the Tollense Valley, Northeastern Germany. *Antiquity* 85:417–33.

Jeffery, Peter

2018 Aural architecture in Jerusalem, Rome, Constantinople, and Alexandria. In *Aural Architecture in Byzantium: Music, Acoustics and Ritual*, edited by Bissera Pentcheva, pp. 32–55. Routledge, London.

Jervis, Ben

2014 *Pottery and Social Life in Medieval England: Towards a Relational Approach*. Oxbow, Oxford.

2018 *Assemblage Thought and Archaeology*. Routledge, London.

Johnson, Matthew

1996 *An Archaeology of Capitalism*. Blackwell, Cambridge.

Jones, Andrew Meirion

2001 *Archaeological Theory and Scientific Practice*. Cambridge University Press, Cambridge.

2005 Lives in Fragments? Personhood in the European Neolithic. *Journal of Social Archaeology* 5:193–224.

2012 *Prehistoric Materialities: Becoming Material in Prehistoric Britain and Ireland.* Oxford University Press, Oxford.

2018a The Archaeology of Art: Practice, Intra-action and Affect. In *The Archaeology of Art: Materials, Practices, Affects*, edited by Andrew Meirion Jones and Andrew Cochrane, pp. 19–30. Routledge, London.

2018b Art in the Making. In *The Archaeology of Art: Materials, Practices, Affects*, edited by Andrew Meirion Jones and Andrew Cochrane, pp. 183–92. Routledge, London.

Jones, Andrew Meirion and Yannis Hamilakis

2017 Archaeology and Assemblage. *Cambridge Archaeological Journal* 27:77–84.

Joyce, Rosemary

2002 *The Languages of Archaeology.* Wiley-Blackwell, Oxford.

Kant, Immanuel

1964 *Groundwork of the Metaphysic of Morals.* Translated by H. J. Paton. Harper & Row, New York.

Keane, Webb

2013 Ontologies, Anthropologists, and Ethical Life. *Hau* 3:186–91.

Kennet, Douglas J., Stephen Plog, Richard J. George, Brendan J. Culleton, Adam S. Watson, Pontus Skoglund, Nadin Rohland, Swampan Mallick, Kristin Stewardson, Logan Kistler, Steven A. LeBlanc, Peter M. Whiteley, David Reich and George H. Perry

2017 Archaeogenomic Evidence Reveals Prehistoric Matrilineal Dynasty. *Nature Communications* 8(14115).

Keogh, Rebecca and Joel Pearson

2018 The Blind Mind: No Sensory Visual Imagery in Aphantasia. *Cortex* 105:53–60.

Knappett, Carl

2005 *Thinking Through Material Culture: An Interdisciplinary Perspective.* University of Pennsylvania Press, Philadelphia, PA.

2011 *An Archaeology of Interaction: Network Perspectives on Material Culture and Society.* Oxford University Press, Oxford.

2012 Meaning in Miniature: Semiotic Networks in Material Culture. In *Excavating the Mind: Cross-Sections Through Culture, Cognition and Materiality*, edited by Niels N. Johannsen, Mads Jessen and Helle J. Jensen, pp. 87–109. Aarhus University Press, Aarhus.

Knappett, Carl and Lambros Malafouris

2008 *Material Agency Towards a Non-Anthropocentric Approach.* Springer, New York.

Kohn, Eduardo

2013 *How Forests Think.* University of California Press, Berkeley.

2015 Anthropology of Ontologies. *Annual Review of Anthropology* 44:311–27.

Krell, David F.

1977 *Heidegger: Basic Writings.* Routledge, London.

Kristiansen, Kristian

1998 *Europe Before History.* Cambridge University Press, Cambridge.

1999 The Emergence of Warrior Aristocracies in Later European Prehistory and Their Long-Term History. In *Ancient Warfare: Archaeological Perspectives*, edited by John Carman and Anthony Harding, pp. 175–89. The History Press, Stroud.

2018 Warfare and the Political Economy: Europe 1500–1100BC. In *Warfare in Bronze Age Society*, edited by Christian Horn and Kristian Kristiansen, pp. 23–46. Cambridge University Press, Cambridge.

Kristiansen, Kristian and Thomas Larsson
2005 *The Rise of Bronze Age Society: Travels, Transmissions and Transformations*. Cambridge University Press, Cambridge.
Kuhn, Thomas S.
1962 *The Structure of Scientific Revolutions*. University of Chicago Press, Chicago.
Kymlicka, Will
1989 *Liberalism, Community, and Culture*. Oxford University Press, Oxford.
LaDuke, Winona
1983 From the Natural to Synthetic and Back Again. In *Marxism and Native Americans*, edited by Ward Churchill, pp i–iix. South End Press, Boston.
Laluk, Nicholas C.
2017 The Indivisibility of Land and Mind: Indigenous Knowledge and Collaborative Archaeology Within Apache Contexts. *Journal of Social Archaeology* 17:92–112.
La Salle, Marina and Richard M. Hutchings
2018 'What Could Be More Reasonable?' Collaboration in Colonial Contexts. In *The Oxford Handbook of Public Heritage Theory and Practice*, edited by Angela M. Labrador and Neil Asher Silberman, pp. 223–38. Oxford University Press, Oxford.
Latour, Bruno
1988 *Science in Action: How to Follow Scientists and Engineers through Society*. Harvard University Press, Cambridge, MA.
1993 *We Have Never Been Modern*. Harvard University Press, Cambridge, MA.
1999 *Pandora's Hope: Essays on the Reality of Science Studies*. Harvard University Press, Cambridge, MA.
2004 *Politics of Nature: How to Bring the Sciences into Democracy*. Harvard University Press, Cambridge, MA.
2005a *Reassembling the Social: An Introduction to Actor Network Theory*. Oxford University Press, Oxford.
2005b From Realpolitik to Dingpolitik. In *Making Things Public: Atmospheres of Democracy*, edited by Bruno Latour and Peter Weibel, pp 4–31. MIT Press, Cambridge, MA.
2018 *Down to Earth: Politics in the New Climatic Regime*. Polity, London.
Latour, Bruno and Peter Weibel
2002 *Iconoclash: Beyond the Image Wars in Science Religion and Art*. MIT Press, Cambridge, MA.
Lavelle, Daniel
2019 Aphantasia: Why a Disney Animator Draws a Blank on His Own Creations *Guardian* 10th April: London.
Leone, Mark P.
1988 The Georgian Order as the Order of Merchant Capitalism in Annapolis, Maryland. In *The Recovery of Meaning: Historical Archaeology in the Eastern United States*, edited by Mark P. Leone and Parker B. Potter Jr., pp. 235–61. Smithsonian Institution Press, Washington, DC.
Lewis, Michael and Tanja Staehler
2010 *Phenomenology: An Introduction*. Bloomsbury, London.
Liebmann, Matthew
2012 The Rest Is History: Devaluing the Recent Past in the History of the Pueblo Southwest. In *Decolonizing Indigenous Histories: Exploring Prehistoric/Historic Transitions in Archaeology*, edited by Maxine Oland, Siobhan H. Hart and Liam Frink, pp. 19–44. University of Arizona Press, Tucson.
Liebmann, Matthew and Uzma Z. Rizvi (editors)
2008 *Archaeology and the Postcolonial Critique*. AltaMira Press, Lanham.

Lightfoot, Kent G.

1995 Culture Contact Studies: Redefining the Relationship Between Prehistoric and Historical Archaeology. *American Antiquity* 60:199–217.

Lingas, Alexander

1996 *Sunday Matins in the Byzantine Cathedral Rite: Music and Liturgy.* Unpublished PhD Thesis, University of British Columbia.

2006 Medieval Byzantine Chant and the Sound of Orthodoxy. In *Byzantine Orthodoxies*, edited by Andrew Louth and Augustine Cassiday, pp. 131–50. Ashgate, Aldershot.

2013 From Earth to Heaven: The Changing Musical Soundscape of Byzantine Liturgy. In *Experiencing Byzantium*, edited by Claire Nesbit and Mark Jackson, pp. 311–58. Ashgate, Aldershot.

Linke, Uli

2012 Reimagining Alterities: The Formation of Identities Through Memory, History, and Place. *Review of Anthropology* 41(3):188–212.

Lipson, Mark, Anna Szécsényi-Nagy, Swapan Mallick, Annamária Pósa, Balázs Stégmár et al.

2017 Parallel Palaeogenomic Transects Reveal Complex Genetic History of Early European Farmers. *Nature* 551:368–72.

Little, Barbara J.

2007 *Historical Archaeology: Why the Past Matters.* Routledge, London.

Little, Barbara J. and Paul A. Shackel (editors)

2007 *Archaeology as a Tool of Civic Engagement.* AltaMira, Walnut Creek, CA.

Locke, John

1821 *Two Treatises of Government.* Whitmore and Fenn, London

Lorde, Audre

1983 The Master's Tools Will Never Dismantle the Master's House. In *This Bridge Called My Back: Writings by Radical Women of Color*, edited by Cherrie Moraga and Gloria Anzaldú, pp. 94–101. Kitchen Table Press, New York.

Lucas, Gavin

2005 *The Archaeology of Time.* Routledge, London.

2012 *Understanding the Archaeological Record.* Cambridge University Press, Cambridge.

Lydon, Jane and Uzma Z. Rizvi (editors)

2010 *Handbook of Postcolonial Archaeology.* Left Coast Press, Walnut Creek.

MacCormack, Patricia

2012 *Posthuman Ethics: Embodiment and Cultural Theory.* Routledge, New York.

2020 *The Ahuman Manifesto: Activism for the End of the Anthropocene.* Bloomsbury, New York.

MacCormack, Patricia (editor)

2014 *The Animal Catalyst: Toward Ahuman Theory.* Bloomsbury, New York.

Malm, Andreas

2018 *The Progress of This Storm: Nature and Society in a Warming World.* Verso, London.

Marshall, Yvonne

2008 Archaeological Possibilities for Feminist Theories of Transition and Transformation. *Feminist Theory* 9:25–45.

Marshall, Yvonne and Benjamin Alberti

2014 A Matter of Difference: Karen Barad, Ontology and Archaeological Bodies. *Cambridge Archaeological Journal* 24:19–36.

Marx, Karl

1990 *Capital.* Penguin, New York.

Massumi, Brian

2002 *Parables for the Virtual: Movement, Affect, Sensation.* Duke University Press, London.

2015 *The Politics of Affect.* Polity, London.

Martinez, Desiree

2012 A Land of Many Archaeologists: Archaeology with Native Californians. In *California: Contemporary Issues in Archaeology,* edited by Terry L. Jones and Jennifer E. Perry, pp. 355–68. Left Coast Press, Walnut Creek.

Mathieson, Iain, Iosif Lazaridis, Nadin Rohland, Swapan Mallick, Nick Patterson, et al.

2015 Genome-Wide Patterns of Selection in 230 Ancient Eurasians. *Nature* 528: 499–503.

Mathieson, Iain, Songül Alpaslan-Roodenberg, Cosimo Posth, Anna Szécsényi-Nagy, Nadin Rohland, et al.

2018 The Genomic History of Southeastern Europe. *Nature* 555:197–203.

Matthews, Christopher

2010 *The Archaeology of American Capitalism.* University Press of Florida, Gainesville.

McClain, Joseph

2018 President Signs Legislation Granting Federal Recognition to Six Virginia Tribes. In *William & Mary News.* William & Mary University, Williamsburg, www.wm.edu/news/stories/2018/william-mary-celebrates-movement-toward-federal-recognition-for-six-local-tribes.php. Date accessed: 5/5/2020.

McGhee, Robert

2008 Aboriginalism and the Problems of Indigenous Archaeology. *American Antiquity* 73:579–97.

McGuire, Randall H.

1992 *A Marxist Archaeology.* University of Arizona Press, Tucson.

2006 Marxism and Capitalism in Historical Archaeology. In *The Cambridge Companion to Historical Archaeology,* edited by Dan Hicks and Mary C. Beaudry, pp. 123–42. Cambridge University Press, Cambridge.

McKie, Robin

2017 Did Dutch Hordes Kill Off the Early Britons Who Started Stonehenge. *Guardian.* 20th May 2017, www.theguardian.com/uk-news/2017/may/20/dutch-invaders-stonehenge-ancient-britons

McNiven, Ian J.

2016 Theoretical Challenges of Indigenous Archaeology: Setting and Agenda. *American Antiquity* 81:27–41.

McPherson, Dennis H. and J. Douglas Rabb

2011 *Indian from the Inside: Native American Philosophy and Cultural Renewal.* McFarland & Company, Jefferson.

Meller, Harald

2017 Armies in the Early Bronze Age? An Alternative Interpretation of Únětice Culture Axe Hoards. *Antiquity* 91:1529–45.

Meskell, Lynn and Robert W. Preucel (editors)

2004 *A Companion to Social Archaeology.* Blackwell, Malden.

Meyer, Leroy and Tony Ramirez

1996 Wakinyan Hotan, the Thunder Beings Call Out: The Inscrutability of Lakota/Dakota Metaphysics. In *From Our Eyes: Learning from Indigenous Peoples,* edited by Sylvia O'Meara and Douglas West, pp. 89–105. Garamond Press, Toronto.

Miller, Daniel (editor)

2005 *Materiality.* Duke University Press, Durham, NC.

Miller, Daniel and Christopher Tilley
1984 Ideology, Power and Prehistory: An Introduction. In *Ideology, Power and Prehistory*, edited by Daniel Miller and Christopher Tilley, pp. 1–15. Cambridge University Press, Cambridge.

Miller, Jay
1983 Numic Religion: An Overview of Power in the Great Basin of Native North America. *Anthropos* 78:337–54.

Mills, Barbara J.
2017 Social Network Analysis in Archaeology. *Annual Review of Anthropology* 46:379–97.

Mitchell, W.J.T.
2005 *What Do Pictures Want? The Lives and Loves of Images*. University of Chicago Press, Chicago.

Morar, Nicolae, Thomas Nail and Daniel W. Smith
2014 Introduction: Foucault Special Issue: Foucault and Deleuze. *Foucault Studies* 17:4–10.

Mörtz, Tobias
2018 Violence and Ritual in Late Bronze Age Britain: Weapon Depositions and Their Interpretation. In *Warfare in Bronze Age Society*, edited by Christian Horn and Kristian Kristiansen, pp. 168–97. Cambridge University Press, Cambridge.

Mrozowski, Stephen A.
1999 Colonization and the Commodification of Nature. *International Journal of Historical Archaeology* 3:153–66.

Nadasdy, Paul
2007 The Gift in the Animal: The Ontology of Hunting and Human-Animal Sociality. *American Ethnologist* 34:25–43.

Nesbitt, Claire
2012 Shaping the Sacred: Light and the Experience of Worship in Middle Byzantine Churches. *Byzantine and Modern Greek Studies* 36:139–60.

Nicholas, George
1997 Education and Empowerment: Archaeology with, for and by the Shuswap Nation, British Colombia. In *At a Crossroads: Archaeology and First Peoples in Canada*, edited by George P. Nicholas and Thomas Andrews, pp. 85–104. Archaeology Press, Barnaby BC.

Nikel, Sarah and Amanda Fehr (editors)
2020 *In Good Relation: History, Gender, and Kinship in Indigenous Feminisms*. University of Manitoba Press, Winnipeg.

Olalde, Iñigo, Selina Brace, Morten Allentoft, Ian Armit, Kristian Kristiansen, et al.
2018 The Beaker Phenomenon and the Genomic Transformation of Northwest Europe. *Nature* 555:190–6.

Olsen, Bjørnar
2003 Material Culture After Text: Remembering Things. *Norwegian Archaeological Review* 36:87–104.
2007 Keeping Things at Arms Length: A Genealogy of Symmetry. *World Archaeology* 39:579–88.
2010 *In Defense of Things: Archaeology and the Ontology of Objects*. Altamira Press, Plymouth.
2012 After Interpretation: Remembering Archaeology. *Current Swedish Archaeology* 20:11–34.

Olsen, Bjørnar and Þóra Pétursdóttir
2014 *Ruin Memories: Materialities, Aesthetics and the Archaeology of the Recent Past*. Routledge, London.

Olsen, Bjørnar, Michael Shanks, Timothy Webmoor and Christopher L. Witmore
2012 *Archaeology: The Discipline of Things.* University of California Press, Berkeley, CA.
Olsen, Bjørnar and Christopher L. Witmore
2015 Archaeology, Symmetry and the Ontology of Things. A Response to Critics. *Archaeological Dialogues* 22:187–97.
Pagan-Jimenez, Jaime R.
2004 Is All Archaeology at Present a Postcolonial One?: Constructive Answers from an Eccentric Point of View. *Journal of Social Archaeology* 4:200–13.
Panich, Lee M.
2013 Archaeologies of Persistence: Reconsidering the Legacies of Colonialism in Native North America. *American Antiquity* 78:105–22.
Panich, Lee M. and Tsim D. Schneider
2014 *Indigenous Landscapes and Spanish Missions: New Perspectives from Archaeology.* University of Arizona Press, Tucson.
2019 Categorical Denial: Evaluating Post-1492 Indigenous Erasure in the Paper Trail of American Archaeology. *American Antiquity* 84:651–68.
Parker Pearson, Mike
1984 Economic and Ideological Change: Cyclical Growth in the Pre-state Societies of Jutland. In *Ideology, Power and Prehistory*, edited by Daniel Miller and Christopher Tilley, pp. 69–92. Cambridge University Press, Cambridge.
1999 *The Archaeology of Death and Burial.* Sutton Publishing, Stroud.
Parker Pearson, Mike and Ramilisonina
1998 Stonehenge for the Ancestors: The Stones Pass on the Message. *Antiquity* 72:308–26.
Pauketat, Timothy R.
2007 *Chiefdoms and Other Archaeological Delusions.* Altamira Press, Walnut Creek, CA.
2012 *An Archaeology of the Cosmos: Rethinking Agency and Religion in Ancient America.* Routledge, London.
Pauketat, Timothy R. and Susan M. Alt
2018 Water and Shells in Bodies and Pots: Mississippian Rhizome, Cahokian Poiesis. In *Relational Identities and Other-Than-Human Agency in Archaeology*, edited by Eleanor Harrison-Buck and Julia A. Hendon. University Press of Colorado, Louisville, CO.
Pentcheva, Bissera V.
2006 The Performative Icon. *The Art Bulletin* 88:631–55.
2010 *The Sensual Icon: Space, Ritual and the Senses in Byzantium.* Pennsylvania State Press, Pennsylvania.
2011 Hagia Sophia and Multisensory Aesthetics. *Gesta* 50:93–111.
2014 Performing the Sacred in Byzantium: Image, Breath and Sound. *Performance Research* 19:120–8.
2017 *Hagia Sophia: Sound, Space, and Spirit in Byzantium.* Pennsylvania State University Press, University Park, PA.
Pentcheva, Bissera V. (editor)
2018 *Aural Architecture in Byzantium: Music, Acoustics and Ritual.* Routledge, London.
Pétursdóttir, Þóra
2012 Small Things Forgotten Now Included, Or What Else Do Things Deserve? *International Journal of Historical Archaeology* 16:577–603.
Pétursdóttir, Þóra and Bjørnar Olsen
2018 Theory Adrift: The Matter of Archaeological Theorizing. *Journal of Social Archaeology* 18:97 117.

Pitman, Derek and Roger Doonan
2018 Beyond the Grave: Crafting Identities in the Middle Bronze Age Southern Trans Urals. In *Warfare in Bronze Age Society*, edited by Christian Horn and Kristian Kristiansen, pp. 119–35. Cambridge University Press, Cambridge.
Polacca, Lyman
2016 Interview with Lindsay M. Montgomery and Chip Colwell. Denver Museum of Nature and Science Archives, Denver.
Povinelli, Elizabeth A.
1995 Do Rocks Listen? The Cultural Politics of Apprehending Australian Aboriginal Labor. *American Anthropologist* 97:505–18.
Preucel, Robert W.
2006 *Archaeological Semiotics*. Wiley-Blackwell, Oxford.
2012 Of God Stones and Dance Plazas: The Material Mediation of Historical Consciousness. In *Excavating the Mind: Cross-Sections Through Culture, Cognition and Materiality*, edited by Neils N. Johannsen, Mads Jessen and Helle J. Jensen, pp. 111–32. Aarhus University Press, Aarhus.
Preucel, Robert W. and Stephen A. Mrozowski (editors)
2010 *Contemporary Archaeology in Theory: The New Pragmatism*. Wiley-Blackwell, Malden, MA.
Puar, Jasbir K.
2012 'I Would Rather Be a Cyborg than a Goddess': Becoming-Intersectional in Assemblage Theory. *Philosophia* 2:50–66.
Raasted, Jorgen
1986 Byzantine Liturgical Music and Its Meaning for the Byzantine Worshiper. In *Church and People in Byzantium*, edited by Rosemary Morris, pp. 49–58. University of Birmingham Press, Birmingham.
Rabinow, Paul (editor)
1984 *The Foucault Reader*. Pantheon Books, New York.
Reich, David
2018 *Who We Are and How We Got Here: Ancient DNA and the New Science of the Human Past*. Pantheon, London.
Reyes-Foster, Beatriz M.
2016 Latour's AIME, Indigenous Critique, and Ontological Turns in a Mexican Psychiatric Hospital: Approaching Registers of Visibility in Three Conceptual Turns. *Anthropological Quarterly* 89:1175–200.
Ribeiro, Artur
2016 Against Object Agency: A Counterreaction to Sørenson's 'Hammers and Nails'. *Archaeological Dialogues* 23:229–35.
Richardson, Laura-Jane and Tom Booth
2017 Response to 'Brexit, Archaeology and Heritage: Reflections and Agendas'. *Papers from the Institute of Archaeology* 27, p.Art. 25. http://doi.org/10.5334/pia-545.
Robb, John E.
2010 Beyond Agency. *World Archaeology* 42:493–520.
Robb, John E. and Oliver J.T. Harris
2013 *The Body in History: Europe from the Paleolithic to the Future*. Cambridge University Press, Cambridge.
2018 Becoming Gendered in European Prehistory: Was Neolithic Gender Fundamentally Different. *American Antiquity* 83:128–47.
Sahlins, Marshall and Elman Service
1960 *Evolution and Culture*. University of Michigan Press, Ann Arbor.

Said, Edward
1978 *Orientalism*. Penguin, London.
Scheiber, Laura L. and Mark D. Mitchell (editors)
2010 *Across a Great Divide: Continuity and Change in Native North American Societies, 1400–1900*. University of Arizona Press, Tucson.
Schmidt, Peter R. and Stephen A. Mrozowski
2013 The Death of Prehistory: Reforming the Past, Looking to the Future. In *Death of Prehistory*, edited by Peter R. Schmidt and Stephen A. Mrozowski, pp. 1–25. Oxford University Press, Oxford.
Scully, Vincent
1975 *Pueblo: Mountain, Village, Dance*. Viking Press, New York.
Secretariat of the Permanent Forum on Indigenous Peoples
2004. The Concept of Indigenous Peoples. In *Workshop on Data Collection and Disaggregation for Indigenous Peoples*. United Nations, New York.
Seigworth, Gregory J. and Melissa Gregg
2010 An Inventory of Shimmers. In *The Affect Theory Reader*, edited by Melissa Gregg and Gregory J. Seigworth, pp. 1–25. Duke University Press, Durham.
Shanks, Michael
2007 Symmetrical Archaeology. *World Archaeology* 39:589–96.
Shanks, Michael and Christopher Tilley
1982 Ideology, Symbolic Power and Ritual Communication: A Reinterpretation of Neolithic Mortuary Practices. In *Symbolic and Structural Archaeology*, edited by Ian Hodder, pp. 129–54. Cambridge University Press, Cambridge.
Shepherd, Nick
2017 Naming the Indigenous. In *Archaeologies of Us and Them: Debating History, Heritage and Indigeneity*, edited by Charlotte Hillerdal, Anna Karlstrom and Carl-Gösta Ojala, pp. 33–7. Routledge, London and New York.
Silliman, Stephen W.
2009 Change and Continuity, Practice and Memory: Native American Persistence in Colonial New England. *American Antiquity* 74:211–30.
2010 Crossing, Bridging, and Transgressing Divides in the Study of Native North America. In *Across a Great Divide: Continuity and Change in Native North American Societies, 1400–1900*, edited by Laura L. Scheiber and Mark D. Mitchell, pp. 258–76. University of Arizona Press, Tucson.
2014 Archaeologies of Indigenous Survivance and Residence: Navigating Colonial and Scholarly Dualities. In *Rethinking Colonial Pasts Through Archaeology*, edited by Neal Ferris, Rodney Harrison and Michael V. Wilcox, pp. 57–75. Oxford University Press, Oxford.
Simard, Suzanne
2009 The Foundational Role of Mycorrhizal Networks in Self-Organization of Interior Douglas-Fir Forests. *Forest Ecology and Management* 258:95–107.
Smith, Laurajane
2004 *Archaeological Theory and the Politics of Cultural Heritage*. Routledge, London.
Smith, Linda Tuhiwai
2012 *Decolonizing Methodologies: Research and Indigenous Peoples*, Second Edition. Zed Books, London.
Spaulding, Albert C.
1953 Statistical Techniques for the Discovery of Artefact Types. *American Antiquity* 18:305–13.
1954 Reply to Ford. *American Antiquity* 19:391–3.

Spinoza, Baruch

1996 *Ethics.* Penguin, London.

Spivak, Gayatri Chakravorty

1988 Can the Subaltern Speak? In *Marxism and the Interpretation of Culture,* edited by Cary Nelson and Lawrence Grossberg, pp. 271–313, University of Illinois Press, Urbana, IL.

Stevenson, J.T.

1992 Aboriginal Land Rights in Northern Canada. In *Contemporary Moral Issues,* edited by Wesley Cragg, pp. 297–311. McGraw-Hill Ryerson, Toronto.

Strathern, Marilyn

1988 *The Gender of the Gift: Problems with Women and Problems with Society in Melanesia.* Cambridge University Press, Cambridge.

1992 *After Nature: English Kinship in the Late 20th Century.* Cambridge University Press, Cambridge.

Sweet, Jill D.

1983 Ritual and Theatre in Tewa Ceremonial Performances. *Ethnomusicology* 27: 253–69.

1992 The Beauty, Humor, and Power of Tewa Pueblo Dance. In *Native American Dance: Ceremonies and Social Traditions.* National Museum of the American Indian, Smithsonian Institution, Washington, DC.

Taber, John

1983 *Transformative Philosophy: A Study of Sankara, Fichte, and Heidegger.* University of Hawaii Press, Honolulu.

Tafoya, Terry

1987 *Circles and Cedar: Native American Epistemology and Clinical Issues.* Paper presented at the Native American Studies Conference, Sault Sainte Marie, Michigan.

Taft, Robert F.

1992 *The Byzantine Rite: A Short History.* Liturgical Press, Collegeville Mi.

TallBear, Kim

2013 *Native American DNA: Tribal Belonging and the False Promise of Genetic Science.* University of Minnesota Press, Minneapolis.

2014 Standing With and Speaking as Faith: A Feminist-Indigenous Approach to Inquiry. *Journal of Research Practice* 10:Article N17, http://jrp.icaap.org/index.php/jrp/article/view/405/371.

2019 Caretaking Relations, Not American Dreaming. *Kalfou: A Journal of Comparative and Relational Ethnic Studies* 6. https://doi.org/10.15367/kf.v6i1.228.

Tedlock, Barbara and Dennis Tedlock

1992 *Teaching from the American Earth: Indian Religion and Philosophy.* Liveright Press, New York.

Thomas, Julian

1996 *Time, Culture and Identity: An Interpretive Archaeology.* Routledge, London.

2002 Taking Power Seriously. In *The Dynamics of Power,* edited by Maria O'Donovan, pp. 35–50. Southern Illinois University Press, Carbondale, IL.

2004 *Archaeology and modernity.* Routledge, London.

2015 The Future of Archaeological Theory. *Antiquity* 89:1287–96.

Thrift, Nigel

2008 *Non-Representational Theory: Space, Politics, Affect.* Routledge, London.

Tilley, Christopher

1994 *A Phenomenology of Landscape: Places, Paths and Monuments.* Berg, Oxford.

2004 *The Materiality of Stone: Explorations in Landscape Phenomenology 1.* Berg, Oxford.

Tillyard, Henry J.W.
1935 *Handbook of the Middle Byzantine Musical Notation*. Levin & Munksgaard, Copenhagen.
Todd, Zoe
2014 Fish Pluralities: Human-Animal Relations and Sites of Engagement in Paulatuuq, Arctic Canada. *Érudes Inuit Studies* 38:217–38.
2016 An Indigenous Feminist's Take on the Ontological Turn: 'Ontology' is Just Another Word for Colonialism. *Journal of Historical Sociology* 29:4–22.
Tomkins, Sylvan S.
1982 Affect Theory. In *Emotion in the Human Face*, edited by Paul Ekman, Wallace V. Friesen and Phoebe Ellsworth pp. 353–95. Cambridge University Press, Cambridge.
Trigger, Bruce
1970 Aims in Prehistoric Archaeology. *Antiquity* 44:26–37.
2006 *A History of Archaeological Thought: Second Edition*. Cambridge University Press, Cambridge.
Troelsgård, Christian
2018 Byzantine Chant Notation: Written Documents in an Aural Tradition. In *Aural Architecture in Byzantium: Music, Acoustics and Ritual*, edited by Bissera Pentcheva, pp. 82–113. Routledge, London.
Trouillot, Michel-Rolph
2003 *Global Transformations: Anthropology and the Modern World*. Palgrave MacMillan, New York.
Tsing, Anna Lowenhaupt
2015 *The Mushroom at the End of the World: On the Possibility of Life in Capitalist Ruins*. Princeton University Press, Princeton.
Tuck, Eve and K. Wayne Yang
2012 Decolonization Is Not a Metaphor. *Decolonization: Indigeneity, Education & Society* 1:1–40.
Turner, Daniel
2006 *This Is Not a Peace Pipe: Towards a Critical Indigenous Philosophy*. University of Toronto Press, Toronto.
Vander Linden, Mark
2016 Population History in Third-Millennium-BC Europe: Assessing the Contribution of Genetics. *World Archaeology* 48:714–28.
Vandkilde, Helle
2018 Body Aesthetics, Fraternity and Warfare in the Long European Bronze Age: Postscriptum. In *Warfare in Bronze Age Society*, edited by Christian Horn and Kristian Kristiansen, pp. 229–43. Cambridge University Press, Cambridge.
Van Dyke, Ruth
2015 Materiality in Practice: An Introduction. In *Practicing Materiality*, edited by R. Van Dyke, pp. 3–32. University of Arizona Press, Tucson, AZ.
Van Oyen, Astrid
2015 Actor-Network Theory's Take on Archaeological Types: Becoming, Material Agency and Historical Explanation. *Cambridge Archaeological Journal* 25: 63–78.
2016 Historicizing Material Agency: From Relations to Relational Constellations. *Journal of Archaeological Method and Theory* 23:354–78.
Vellodi, Kamini
2014 Diagrammatic Thought: Two Forms of Constructivism in C.S. Peirce and Gilles Deleuze. *Parrhesia* 19:79–95.

Venkatesan, Soumhya
2010 Ontology Is Just Another Word for Culture. *Critique of Anthropology* 30:152–200.
Viveiros de Castro, Eduardo
1992 *From the Enemy's Point of View: Humanity and Divinity in an Amazonian Society*. University of Chicago Press, Chicago, IL.
1998 Cosmological Deixis and Amerindian Perspectivism. *Journal of the Royal Anthropological Institute* 4:469–88.
2003 *Anthropology (AND) Science*, https://sites.google.com/a/abaetenet.net/nansi/abaetextos/anthropology-and-science-e-viveiros-de-castro. Date accessed: 15/8/2018.
2004 Exchanging Perspectives: The Transformation of Objects into Subjects in Amerindian Cosmologies. *Common Knowledge* 10:463–84.
2007 The Crystal Forest: Notes on the Ontology of Amazonian Spirits. *Inner Asia* 9:153–72.
2010 Intensive Filiation and Demonic Alliance. In *Deleuzian Intersections: Science, Technology, Anthropology*, edited by Casper B. Jensen and Kjetil Rödje, pp. 219–54. Berghahn, Oxford.
2012 Cosmological Perspectivism in Amazonia and Elsewhere. *HAU: Masterclass Series* 1:45–168.
2013 The Relative Native. *Hau: Journal of Ethnographic Theory* 3:473–502.
2014 *Cannibal Metaphysics*. Univocal Publishing, Minneapolis.
2015a *The Relative Native: Essays on Indigenous Conceptual Worlds*. Hau Books, Chicago.
2015b Who Is Afraid of the Ontological Wolf? Some Comments on an Ongoing Anthropological Debate. *Cambridge Journal of Anthropology* 33:2–17.
Vizenor, Gerald
1999 *Manifest Manners: Narratives on Postindian Survivance*. University of Nebraska Press, Lincoln.
2008 *Survivance: Narratives of Native Presence*. University of Nebraska Press, Lincoln.
von Scheve, Christian
2018 A Social Relational Account of Affect. *European Journal of Social Theory* 21:39–59.
Watkins, Joseph
2000 *Indigenous Archaeology: American Indian Values and Scientific Practice*. AltaMira, Walnut Creek.
Watts, Christoper
2008 On Mediation and Material Agency in the Peircean Semeiotic. In *Material Agency: Towards a Non-Anthropocentric Approach*, edited by Carl Knappett and Lambros Malafouris, pp. 187–207. Springer, New York, NY.
2013a Relational Archaeologies: Roots and Routes. In *Relational Archaeologies: Humans, Animals, Things*, edited by Christopher Watts, pp. 1–20. Routledge, London.
2013b *Relational Archaeologies: Humans, Animals, Things*. Routledge, London.
Waziyatawin, Angela Wilson and Michael Yellow Bird (editors)
2005 *For Indigenous Eyes Only: A Decolonizing Handbook*. School for Advanced Research, Santa Fe.
Weber, David J.
2005 *Bárbaros: Spaniards and Their Savages in the Age of Enlightenment*. Yale University Press, New Haven.
Webmoor, Timothy
2007 What About 'One More Turn after the Social' in Archaeological Reasoning? Taking Things Seriously. *World Archaeology* 39:563–78.
Webmoor, Timothy and Christopher L. Witmore
2008 Things Are Us! A Commentary on Human/Things Relations Under the Banner of a 'Social Archaeology'. *Norwegian Archaeological Review* 41:1–18.

Weismantel, Mary
2015 Seeing Like an Archaeologist: Viveiros de Castro at Chavín de Huantar. *Journal of Social Archaeology* 15:139–59.
Wellesz, Egon
1961 *A History of Byzantine Music and Hymnography. Revised and Enlarged.* Clarendon Press, London.
Welton, Donn
1999 *The Essential Husserl: Basic Writings in Transcendental Phenomenology.* Indiana University Press, Bloomington IN.
White, Leslie
1943 Energy and the Evolution of Culture. *American Anthropologist* 45:335–56.
Whitridge, Peter
2004a Whales, Harpoons, and Other Actors: Actor-Network Theory and Hunter-Gatherer Archaeology. In *Hunters and Gatherers in Theory and Archaeology*, edited by George M. Crothers, pp. 445–74. Center for Archaeological Investigations, Southern Illinois University, Carbondale, IL.
2004b Landscapes, Houses, Bodies, Things: 'Place' and the Archaeology of Inuit Imaginaries. *Journal of Archaeological Method and Theory* 11:213–50.
Whitt, Lauri Anne
1995 Indigenous peoples and the Cultural Politics of Knowledge. In *Issues in Native American Cultural Identity*, edited by Michael K. Green, pp. 223–72. Peter Lang, New York.
Wilcox, Michael
2009 *The Pueblo Revolt and the Mythology of Conquest: An Indigenous Archaeology of Contact.* University of California Press, Berkeley.
2010 Marketing Conquest and the Vanishing Indian: An Indigenous Response to Jared Diamond's Archaeology of the American Southwest. *Journal of Social Archaeology* 10:92–117.
Wildcat, Daniel R.
2006 Indigenizing the Future: Why We Must Think Spatially in the Twenty-first Century. *American Studies* 46:417–40.
Wilkinson, Darryl
2013 The Emperor's New Body: Personhood, Ontology and the Inka Sovereign. *Cambridge Archaeological Journal* 23:417–32.
2017a Is There Such a Thing as Animism? *Journal of the American Academy of Religion* 85:289–311.
2017b *Uncertain Allies? The Place of Indigenous Metaphysics in Posthumanist Thought.* Paper Presented at The Theoretical Archaeology Group Conference, Cardiff, December 2017.
Williams, Howard
2014 Memory through Monuments: Movement and Temporality in Skamby's Boat Graves. In *Med Hjärta Och Hjärna: En Vänbok Till Professor Elisabeth Arwill-Nordbladh*, edited by Henrik Alexandersson, Alexander Andreeff and Annika Bünz, pp. 397–413. University of Gothenburg, Gothenburg.
Wilson, Shawn
2001 What Is Indigenous Research Methodology? *Canadian Journal of Native Education* 25:175–9.
2008 *Research Is Ceremony: Indigenous Research Methods.* Fernwood Publishing, Halifax, Nova Scotia, Canada & Winnipeg, Manitoba, Canada.
Wiseman, Joseph J.
N.d. *Judicial Toolkit on Indian Law: An Overview of Key Federal Indian Law Cases.* California Judicial Branch, https://www.courts.ca.gov/documents/Key-Federal-Indian-Law-Cases.pdf

Witmore, Christopher L.
2006 Vision, Media, Noise and the Percolation of Time: Symmetrical Approaches to the Mediation of the Material World. *Journal of Material Culture* 11:267–92.
2007 Symmetrical Archaeology: Excerpts of a Manifesto. *World Archaeology* 39:546–62.
2014 Archaeology and the New Materialisms. *Journal of Contemporary Archaeology* 1:203–24.

Wohlleben Peter
2016 *The Hidden Life of Trees: What They Feel, How They Communicate – Discoveries From a Secret World.* Greystone Books, Vancouver.

Wybrew, Hugh
1990 *The Orthodox Liturgy: The Development of the Eucharistic Liturgy in the Byzantine Rite.* St Vladimir's Seminary Press, New York, NY.

Wylie, Alison
1997 Good Science, Bad Science, Or Science as Usual? Feminist Critiques of Science. In *Women in Human Evolution*, edited by Lori D. Hager, pp. 29–54. Routledge, New York.

Zedeño, María Nieves
2008 Bundled Worlds: The Roles and Interactions of Complex Objects from the North American Plains. *Journal of Archaeological Method and Theory* 14:362–78.
2009 Animating by Association: Index Objects and Relational Taxonomies. *Cambridge Archaeological Journal* 19:407–17.
2013 Methodological and Analytical Challenges in Relational Archaeologies: A View from the Hunting Ground. In *Relational Archaeologies: Humans, Animals, Things*, edited by Christopher Watts, pp. 117–34. Routledge, London.

INDEX